# A Better World Is Possible

# A Better World Is Possible

*An Exploration of*
*Western and Eastern Utopian Visions*

## Ambrose Mong

*Foreword by*
Mark DeStephano

James Clarke & Co

**James Clarke & Co**
P.O. Box 60
Cambridge
CB1 2NT
United Kingdom


www.jamesclarke.co
publishing@jamesclarke.co


ISBN: 978 0 227 17692 4


*British Library Cataloguing in Publication Data*
A record is available from the British Library


First published by James Clarke & Co, 2018

For Denis Chang,
CBE, QC, SC, LLD (Hon.), JP

# Table of Contents

# Foreword

If a perfect society is unattainable, why even try to attain one? If Jesus – God Himself – could not bring peace to the human race, what can human beings possibly do to achieve it? In *A Better World Is Possible: An Exploration of Western and Eastern Utopian Visions*, Dr Ambrose Mong deviates somewhat from his usual realm of academic inquiry to consider one of the most abstract and enticing subjects imaginable: the possibility that human beings could actually construct a utopia on earth. If it is admitted that those same human beings are individually and communally flawed and inherently selfish, why would one even waste time entertaining such a fantasy? This book demonstrates that, despite the apparent futility of the subject, many of the greatest minds in history have devoted considerable time – and ink – to creating imaginary worlds that they believed could serve as a template for the construction of an actual earthly paradise. But who, precisely, would waste so much effort on so useless a venture? As Dr Mong admirably shows, such concerns were very much the focus of various celebrated philosophers and theologians, Western and Eastern, who judged that the world could, with dedication and work, become an earthly wonderland.

Despite appearances, the current inquiry is not an abstract meditation but very much based in reality. What gave rise to Dr Mong's fascinating study was a hyperbolic comment made after a visit by Theodore Sorensen, an advisor to President John F. Kennedy, to Singapore's Prime Minister Lee Kuan Yew: "I now feel my life is complete; I have been to Utopia." Of course, anyone who is not a native or has not visited Singapore would surely ask, "And how did this happen? Who was responsible?" In the minds of many, and in the opinion of Dr Mong himself, the person who worked this modern-day miracle was none other than Lee himself. Widely admired as one of the most enlightened, virtuous, and effective leaders of the twentieth century, Lee (reg.1954-2011) embodied many of the qualities and implemented many of the policies proposed by various utopian thinkers down through the ages. The selection of such thinkers arrayed by Dr Mong is impressive: Thomas More, Ignacio Ellacuría, Confucius, Mo Tzu, Kang Youwei, Pierre Teilhard de Chardin, and Francis Fukuyama. Not bound by the parameters of one age, one geographical location, one social class, one philosophical system, or one faith, these thinkers witnessed strife and suffering but strove to look beyond the woes of their age. They sought to envisage a time and a place in which the causes of the turmoil experienced in their time would be eliminated through the use of intellect and the voluntary acceptance of the will to do good for all people.

Beginning with a consideration of what constitutes utopian thinking, Dr Mong segues into a discussion of what a "civilization of poverty" – a civilization of compassion – offers humanity, as opposed to the oft-asserted benefits of capitalism, which has been embraced by most of the nations of the world. As is evident, most of the world's population has not benefitted from the capitalist system, and yet most governments continue to proffer the hope that eventually its benefits will trickle down to all people. Based as it is on the premise that consumer culture will necessarily improve the standard of living of the world's population – a false hope, Dr Mong argues – capitalism bears a heavy price tag and is actually doing far more harm than good. But what elements are lacking such that capitalism, especially as it has been articulated in the West, has not delivered on its promises? Dr Mong answers the question concisely: capitalism values money but not the human person. But, while capitalism is currently the reigning form of utopianism that has captured the world's imagination, other forms of utopian thought have not been lacking.

One of the most fascinating aspects of Dr Mong's work is his sensitivity to cultural and religious differences. Rich in comparative analysis, this book reminds us that the search for a model of how to construct an earthly paradise is universal. And, whether the quest for utopia be undertaken from a philosophical, economic, political, or religious perspective, one element remains the same in all of them: the need to place the good of the human person at the center of the model. Any system that fails to promote the commonweal is destined to failure. Thus, in a very real way, the search for utopia may be viewed as a quest for the commonweal, a truth that has been apparent to great thinkers in both the West and the East.

If such utopian models are available to humanity, then, returning to our original question, why does so much of the world's population continue to suffer? Dr Mong answers this query by allowing utopian thinkers to speak for themselves. As we find in the work of each of them, the good have been thwarted by the arbitrary social and intellectual norms that we human beings have constructed to protect our own interests, to the detriment of the common good. As Dr Mong shows so powerfully, careful analysis of the work of utopian thinkers makes obvious the many human flaws that increase human suffering. As we note what they urge, working backwards, so to speak, we deduce the many ways in which we human beings prefer to seek our own good to the exclusion of others. We invent philosophical arguments, political systems, racial categories, and even theologies, somehow imagining that the exclusion of some people will lead to utopia. Nothing could be further from the truth.

As a former Chairman of the Board of the United States Catholic China Bureau and a "Scholar of the People's Republic of China," I have often been asked to speak about China and the Chinese people. A very common question posed to me is: "Whither China? What do the Chinese Communists want?" Although baldly phrased, the meaning of the question is clear. In fact, the question seems to me to be a version of what utopian thinkers have always asked. The answer to the question is equally clear. The "Chinese Communists" want what all human beings want: to be loved, honored, and cared for, to have the opportunity to use our talents, to live comfortably and free from fear and coercion, to feel needed, and to live in peace with ourselves and others. If the answer to this human quest is so simple, why have we not attained earthly utopia? Dr Mong demonstrates that past utopian associations with philosophical and theological systems have largely been discarded in favor of secular states based on liberal democracy. In the mind of Francis Fukuyama, for example, liberal democracy is the hope of humankind rather than Christianity because it seeks utopia in this world, and not in a future kingdom of heaven. Dr Mong, or, as it might be more appropriate to recognize here, Father Mong, reminds us that Fukuyama has "missed out on realized eschatology." Roman Catholic theology, which obviously resides in the Roman Catholic Church, was given the mission to preach the saving Gospel of Jesus Christ for all peoples. Dr Mong, following the thought of Jacques Dupuis, argues that true utopianism may be found in this attainable reality in which, "In spite of differences, members of different religious traditions are co-members of the reign of God in history, journeying together towards the fullness of God's kingdom."

Dr Mong has written a comprehensive, balanced, highly informative, and enjoyable work that makes complicated material understandable for us all. What is more, thanks to Dr Mong's wonderful explanation of the many ways that we can strive to realize utopia here and now, they are even more accessible for us to put into practice.

Mark DeStephano, Ph.D.
Saint Peter's University
Jersey City,
New Jersey, U.S.A.

# Preface

After his first visit to Singapore, Theodore Sorensen, adviser to and speech-writer for John F. Kennedy, was reported to have told Lee Kuan Yew, "I now feel my life is complete; I have been to Utopia."[1] Lee, of course, never claimed to have created a utopia even though he actually transformed a Third World backwater with no natural resources into a First World nation. Within a generation, Lee transformed Singapore into one of the most prosperous and advanced nations in the world with his unique blend of Confucianism and Western-style capitalism. Further, the example of Singapore provided Deng Xiaoping, former paramount leader of China, with a blueprint for establishing a harmonious society of which even Confucius would have approved.

Few Asian leaders have achieved the status accorded to Lee and fewer still have had the influence over world leaders that he wielded in his lifetime. He turned Singapore into an oasis of peace and prosperity within a region troubled by widespread political and economic turmoil. A visionary and a pragmatist, keenly aware of Singapore's limitations, he sought to educate the population and to take advantage of the country's strategic geographical location. Riding on the wave of globalization, Lee transformed Singapore's economy and, in the process, turned the country into a world-class financial, commercial and transportation centre. Indeed, Singapore's port and airport are still renowned for their efficiency and outstanding service today.

---

1. Tom Plate, http://www.scmp.com/comment/insight-opinion/article/2098993/.

Like a father to the nation he created, Lee guided the country as "Minister Mentor" after he had stepped down as Prime Minister in 1990. Moreover, he believed that the family was the true building block of society, rather than the individual. He had great faith in familial values and he deplored the selfish individualism so prevalent in Western societies.[1] Lee made the national interest his overriding concern and pursued it selflessly. The Prime Minister's Office in Singapore is vested with much power which Lee used for the common good.

In *Datong shu* or *"The Book of Great Unity,"* Kang Youwei (1858-1927) calls for the abolition of the institution of family in his blueprint for a utopian project. Kang acknowledges that it is easier to love one's children than to obey one's parents. He also believes that the more people in the family, the more conflicts there will be and that this is one of the basic causes of human suffering. Further, Kang argues that the institution of the family goes against the common good because people tend to give priority to taking care of their own kind. The family is a necessary institution in times of disorder, but it becomes an obstacle in our effort to establish a utopia where there is equality, peace and harmony.

This current work is a study of utopian visions from both Western and Eastern traditions. The writings of Ignacio Ellacuría and other liberation theologians inspired me to explore the utopian idea that, in the midst of suffering, pain and breakdown, a better world is not only possible but necessary.

Thomas More's portrait on the wall of Denis Chang's Chambers led me to delve deeper into More's thought. I am grateful to Lai Pan-chiu and Lauren Pfister for introducing me to *Datong shu* by Kang Youwei. Special thanks go to Patrick Tierney F.S.C., Columba Cleary O.P., Vivian Lee, Patrick Colgan S.C.C., Scott Steinkerchner O.P., Francis Chin and Kim Tansley for proofreading and editorial assistance.

Thanks also to the following people who have supported me in my writing endeavors all these years: Peter Phan, Abraham Shek, Rosalind Wong, Waris Santoso, Philip Lee, Reginaldus Amleni, Emmanuel Dispo, Esther Chu, Charles Chu, Cloris Lim, William Chan, Venny Lai, Hilia Chan, Kim Tansley, Kenzie Lau, Adelaide Wong, Josephine Chan, Teresa Au, Teresa Choi, Tommy Lam, Emily Law, Teoh Chin Chin, Garrison Qian, Leo Tan, George Tan, Vivencio Atutubo, Gemma Yim and Henrietta Cheung. This work is also written in memory of Brother Emmanuel, F.S.G. (1933-2017), a French-Canadian missionary, who dedicated his whole life to the education of young people in Singapore. He was determined to show under-privileged youth that a better future was possible.

---

1. Manish Gyawali, "Lee Kuan Yew's Enduring Legacy," http://thediplomat.com/2015/04/lee-kuan-yews-enduring-legacy/.

Last, but not least, I am very grateful to the publishing team at James Clarke & Co., especially Bethany Churchard, Angharad Thomas, Debora Nicosia, Dorothy Luckhurst and Adrian Brink, for bringing this modest work to print. Any errors that remain are, of course, my own.

Ambrose Mong
Hong Kong
Feast of St. Dominic
8 August 2018

# Introduction

*But the poor person does not exist as an inescapable fact of destiny.*

Gustavo Gutiérrez,
*A Theology of Liberation* (1973)

This volume is a sequel to my book, *A Tale of Two Theologians* (Cambridge: James Clarke & Co., 2017). *A Tale of Two Theologians* focusses on the writings of Gustavo Gutiérrez and Michael Amaladoss as they construct a theology relevant to Third World economies afflicted by exploitation and oppression. Disowning the life of jet-setting intellectuals, these two theologians are known for their pastoral work with the poor and the marginalized. They declare a different world is not only possible but necessary.

The quest for a better society has its origin in utopian political projects such as Plato's *Republic* (c.381BC) and Marx's vision of the proletariat in *The Communist Manifesto* (1848). Baptizing this utopian tradition, as it were, Gutiérrez and Amaladoss attempt to build the kingdom of God on earth by improving civil institutions so that all people can lead lives with adequate basic necessities.

The search for a better world has always existed throughout our history, partly because, as Jesus said, the poor are always with us (Mark 14:7). The ancient Greeks envisaged an ideal society in the *polis* or city-state, while the Romans dreamed of an idyllic past in Virgil's Arcadia. The book of Genesis in the Old Testament describes a utopian Eden managed by Adam and Eve. In modern times, we imagine a society where technology offers all kinds of conveniences and creature comforts, from smart phones to driverless cars. Utopias as conceived by the ancients accepted the fact that resources were limited and human wants unlimited. Thus, their "ideal society" was one that stressed simplicity and restricted luxurious consumption. In contrast, modern-styled utopias are places of abundance. Furthermore, inequality was acceptable in ancient utopias, such as in Plato's *Republic*, but in modern utopias, the emphasis is on equality.[1]

This work seeks to provide a selection of utopian writings representing Western tradition, Thomas More, Ignacio Ellacuría, Teilhard de Chardin, and representing Eastern tradition, Confucius, Mo Tzu and Kang Youwei. Despite coming from different cultures and eras, these writers, not surprisingly, have much in common in their quest for a better world, especially in their emphasis on compassion for humanity, social justice and peace. Instead of labelling utopias as "Western" and "non-Western," Jacqueline Dutton prefers to use the term "intercultural imaginaries," which she feels is more appropriate for the study of several traditions that seek to build a better world.[2] These intercultural imaginaries, steeped in their own local traditions and worldviews, pre-dated More's *Utopia*. Social dreaming or the desire for a better life is essentially a universal concept.

Utopian studies appear to have gone out of fashion among scholars since the publication of Francis Fukuyama's *The End of History and the Last Man* (1992) and the barrage of criticism it attracted over the idea of liberal democracy as the final destination in the evolution of human society. Are we then losing hope that a better world is possible when we have experienced a loss of faith in globalization and universalist notions such as human compassion, peace, justice and democratic equality? It has become clear in the last decades that a classless global society in which people of all nations can enjoy the same opportunities, such as access to decent housing, healthcare, and education, cannot be achieved easily.

1. The American and French Revolutions championed the principle of egalitarianism: Gregory Claeys, *Searching for Utopia: The History of an Idea* (New York: Thames & Hudson, 2011), 13. Facebook, a social media website, plans to make the world a better place. Chief executive Mark Zuckerberg wants to use his social network to "build communities" and to "bring the world closer together." In terms of social structure, Zuckerberg believes Facebook is "probably one of the larger institutions that can help empower people to build communities." One of his recent interests is to make the world a less divisive place: *South China Morning Post*, Monday, 2 July 2017, C8.

2. Jacqueline Dutton, "'Non-western' Utopian Traditions," in Gregory Claeys, *The Cambridge Companion to Utopian Literature* (Cambridge: Cambridge University Press, 2010), 224.

There were two significant attempts made in the twentieth century to create a classless society: on one hand, the Marxist proletarian revolution resulting in the abolition of private property and entrepreneurship; on the other, the welfare state proposed by western intellectuals to ensure equality of opportunity for our children and modelled on the Scandinavian countries. Many thinkers and politicians now have little faith in these two so-called utopian scenarios.[1]

It is not philosophical speculation, but rather historical narrative that can help us to envisage a better future, according to Richard Rorty. Specifically, we need to tell a story about what has happened and what we hope may happen in the near future. Written more than five hundred years ago, Thomas More's *Utopia* is surprisingly popular to this day and is included in the reading list of humanities studies because it tells a thought-provoking story with multivalent meanings. Hence, this present work starts with More's *Utopia* and a focus on his impassioned plea for social justice. More's discussion on the plight of the poor, the issues of private property, religious tolerance and his criticism of Western society is cleverly woven into an engaging story.

The stories that people tell regarding their country or the birth of an ideal society constitute their community as nation. In other words, "nation is narration."[2] Philosophers in their discourse, however, tend to start with notions like "truth," "identity," "self," and "subject." Such an attempt seems to lead to the conclusion that they have lost hope and are unable to construct any narrative of progress that could become a reality in the future. "A turn away from narration and utopian dreams toward philosophy seems to me a gesture of despair."[3]

Globalization is supposed to increase the wealth of nations by removing trade and communication barriers. Unfortunately, because of the lack of national control of laws, money accumulated by global trade is either stashed away by super-rich multinationals (for tax avoidance purposes) or taken over by criminal organisations. This situation only widens the gap between the corporate rich and the working poor (and not between developed and developing nations, as was once commonly believed). The absence of a global polity means that the rich can do what

---

1. Richard Rorty, *Philosophy and Social Hope* (Harmondsworth, Middlesex: Penguin Books, 1999), 230-31.
2. Stefan Berger, Linas Eriksonas, and Andrew Mycock, "Introduction: Narrating the Nation: Historiography and Other Genres," in *Narrating the Nation: Representations in History, Media and the Arts* (New York: Berghahn Books, 2011), 1-16, http://www.jstor.org/stable/j.ctt9qdcbq.5.
3. Rorty, *Philosophy and Social Hope*, 232.

they choose to increase their wealth and influence even more. In the end, says Rorty, there are only two socially influential groups: "the super-rich and the intellectuals."[1] The latter group attempts to study the harm done by the former through international talking shops which are generally viewed as harmless and impotent. These jet-setting intellectuals need to take on a more activist role in helping to mold the social and economic policies of political leaders, ultimately to create a more just and equitable world.

More importantly, without the support of men and women who struggled, fought, and died for a just and equitable world, the idea of utopia would remain no more than vapour-ware, confined only to intellectual discussion, without practical, economic benefits. As a historical programme, utopia refers to the heroic efforts of people to establish a qualitatively different society with a new set of social relations – utopia is meant to be dynamic and revolutionary. In the tradition of Thomas More, utopian thought is a driving force in history because of its subversive nature.[2]

Fátima Vieira holds that "utopias are by essence dynamic . . . born out of a given set of circumstances, their scope not limited to a criticism of the present; indeed, utopias put forward projective ideas that are to be adopted by future audiences, which may cause real change."[3] Thus, utopia has two aspects: a denunciation of the existing order and the annunciation of a new world to come. The intolerable situation borne by the poor and marginalized needs to be denounced and the hope for a better future needs to be announced to prevent despair and cynicism. These two aspects of utopia, denunciation and annunciation, must be carried out in *praxis* – in concrete historical situations.[4] In other words, they must go beyond purely verbal level – they call for specific political actions.

Possessing a utopian consciousness and hope implies an attempt to establish a better world or a vastly improved state of life but it does not mean searching for a perfect life. It is based on the belief that a different world is possible. More's *Utopia*, for example, provides an account of a vastly improved society; however, human nature is not perfect as crime still exists. With good management and government, we can have a better

1.  Rorty, *Philosophy and Social Hope*, 233.
2.  Gustavo Gutiérrez, *A Theology of Liberation*, translated and edited by Sister Caridad Inda and John Eagleson (Maryknoll, NY: Orbis Books, 1973), 232.
3.  Fátima Vieira, "The Concept of Utopia," in Claeys, *The Cambridge Companion to Utopian Literature*, 8.
4.  Gutiérrez, *A Theology of Liberation*, 233.

world. "Perfection," is fundamentally a theological concept although it is related to utopianism in some ways. A perfect life is an ideal not attainable here on earth for mere mortals. Utopian communities were built in the past and may be realisable in the near and distant future with all their imperfections and limitations.

## Outline and Sequence of the Work

Chapter one explores Thomas More's *Utopia* (1516) highlighting his concern for the poor and his criticism of European society at that time. This chapter calls our attention to More's indictment of his own native land and his pleas for social justice. More presents the Utopians as non-Christians who are nevertheless open to Gospel values. A religiously pluralistic nation, Utopia's commonwealth is meant to be a challenge to More's so-called Christian contemporaries.

The present economic and political systems in the Third World have failed to provide everyone with adequate food, shelter, and healthcare, let alone education. Therefore, there exists an urgent need to find an alternative way of government. Chapter two examines the writings of the Jesuit martyr, Ignacio Ellacuría (1930-89) and others, regarding their vision of a different world, a "civilization of poverty," that upholds the centrality of compassion. Critical of the institutional Church, Ellacuría's emphasis on the messianic aspect of Christianity involves the liberation of the whole person and the transformation of society into a more humane one.

Associated with utopian ideas, assisted by technology, globalization boasts of removing economic and social barriers, uniting the world as one global village, promoting mutual understanding and a constructive interchange of ideas. Unfortunately, globalization has in fact led to the widening of the gap between the rich and the poor nations. Dominated by multinational companies and driven by the relentless pursuit of profit that threatens to destroy the environment, globalization is in reality a form of cultural imperialism, *Americanization* to be specific. Chapter three studies the Church's social teaching that attempts to promote the humanization of the market and the protection of local cultures against the onslaught of globalization that claims to be universal.

Related to life in the *polis* or city-state and influenced by Christianity, Western utopias look towards the future and the world to come. Eastern utopias, on the other hand, are identified with agrarian life and the Golden Age in primitive times as evident, for example, in the Peach Blossom arcadia of Tao Yuanming. In the tradition of Thomas More,

Western utopia means "no place," whereas Chinese utopia generally refers to "a better place." Chapter four explores an alternative vision of utopia with a focus on the humanistic and social-relationship teachings of Confucius (551-479BC) and concludes with the economic success story of Singapore that adopts certain pragmatic aspects of Confucianism as its ideology.

Chapter five focusses on the utopian vision and teachings of Mo Tzu (470-391BC), whose thought – known as Mohism – was at one time a challenge to Confucianism. Mo Tzu stresses the universality of love that resembles Christianity. His ideal world is one that emphasises simplicity and frugality because he believes we can only live luxuriously and extravagantly at the expense of others. Not keen on creating an egalitarian society, Mo Tzu's interest is in meritocracy. In this chapter we examine his vision of an ideal society in his discourses on "Honouring the Worthy," "Identifying with One's Superior," "Universal Love," "Against Offensive Warfare," and "The Will of Heaven."

Considered the first political utopian writer in China, Kang Youwei (1858-1927) was a leader of the Hundred-Day Reform Movement of 1898. He sought to introduce Western ideas that could co-exist with conservative Chinese traditions. Chapter six examines Kang's best work, *Datong shu (The Book of Great Unity)*, where he lays out a blueprint to construct a better world with principles drawn from Confucianism, Buddhism and Daoism. Written with utopian consciousness, Kang aims to unite not only his long-suffering nation, but the world at large, by abolishing social, political and economic boundaries, and institutions that are deemed harmful to humanity.

Teilhard de Chardin's understanding of a united humanity was linked to his experience in Asia where he envisages the possible unity of diverse faiths such as Christianity, Buddhism and Daoism. A model of utopian hope, he perceives religious beliefs in terms of the energy that fused people's faith and ability to forge a better life. A Christian and a supporter of Darwin's Theory of Evolution at the same time, Teilhard believed in the convergence of all things, including religions, in the kingdom of God at the end of time. In chapter seven, we examine Teilhard's understanding of the convergence of religions culminating in the Christ, "the Alpha and Omega." Finally, this work concludes with a critique of Francis Fukuyama's *The End of History and the Last Man* by holding that the end of history had arrived in the person of Jesus Christ.

# 1
# Utopia

*A map of the world that does not include Utopia is not worth even glancing at, for it leaves out the country at which Humanity is always landing. And when Humanity lands there, it looks out, and, seeing a better country, sets sail. Progress is the realisation of Utopias.*

Oscar Wilde[1]

A society without a utopian spirit would lack the collective will to change for the better. The belief in utopia – an ideal society where humans thrive in peace, prosperity and security – has been one of the driving forces of change in history. The earliest recorded event of such social change or revolution is the overthrow of the Shang Dynasty in China in 1046BC. The rebel leaders' justification was that the Shang king was cruel, corrupt and had lost the "mandate" of heaven.[2] Revolutions have continued unto modern times,[3] espousing similar ideological goals. Such goals as

---

1. Oscar Wilde, "The Soul of Man Under Socialism," in *De Profundis and Other Writings*, with an introduction by Hesketh Pearson (Harmondsworth: Penguin Books, 1973), 34.
2. The Mandate of Heaven or *Tian-ming*, is superficially similar to the European Divine Right of Kings. Its utopian principle, promulgated by the Duke of Zhou, is simple: the king must always strive to build a just society for his people; when he stops doing so, someone else has the divine right to take over. See Kallie Szczepanski, "What is the Mandate of Heaven?" https://www.thoughtco.com/the-mandate-of-heaven-195113.
3. Examples in modern times include the Glorious Revolution in England in 1688, the American Revolution of 1765-83, the French Revolution of 1789-99, the

promulgated by the revolutionary leaders were framed in the utopian ideals of establishing a new society or nation-state where individuals or communities live their lives under humane and equitable conditions and serve a common goal of economic prosperity, military security and shared religious worship.

People of many societies and in different ages have attempted to translate their dreams of a more just society into political and economic policies for the perceived common good. But utopian theory is unique in its fundamental conviction that social and political conditions can be developed in such a way as to transform society radically into one where none will lack basic necessities; where people can enjoy enduring peace, harmony among neighbours and personal fulfillment under an agreed set of principles and practices. In other words, there will be no barrier to the earthly progress to perfection of humankind. Utopian leaders, writers and thinkers, from the Duke of Zhou (the brain behind the forces that overthrew the ruling Shang Dynasty establishment in the eleventh century BC) to the European Enlightenment figures and, more recently, to socialist visionaries such as Vladimir Lenin and Mao Zedong, were individuals who proclaimed their conviction in happiness for the greatest number and made conscious efforts to promulgate it, in their published works, speeches, and political activities. They were convinced that progress was not only desirable, but possible; thus, they displayed remarkable determination in their efforts to realise their dreams of impacting change.

Utopian theory has provided inspiration for equally ambitious social and political reforms which have either been carried out or which have been regarded as feasible. Not just a theoretical concept, utopia has a hold on reality as well. Its value lies not in its relation to the present but towards the future: "Just as the hidden God, who will always remain hidden, provokes us to try to uncover the veil, to discover perfect truth and perfect morality, so utopia's 'nowhereness' incites the search for it."[1] Here utopia is associated with divine revelation.

In this chapter, we explore Thomas More's *Utopia* (1516) with a focus on the plight of the poor, the debate on the possession of private property, the issue of religious tolerance, and his indictment of contemporary European society. Furthermore, we interpret More's masterpiece as an impassioned plea for social justice. More's *Utopia* attempts to show that a better world is possible, although he does not expect to see it in his

---

Taiping Revolution of 1850-64 and the Bolshevik Revolution of 1917, all in the name of heralding a new millenarian utopia.

1.  Krishnan Kumar, *Utopianism* (Milton Keynes: Open University Press, 1991), 3.

lifetime. R.W. Chambers remarks that in English, "utopian" signifies something "visionary" and "unpractical."[1] More's *Utopia* is five hundred years old and his ideas remain relevant; they continue to influence those who seek a better world.

The attempt to construct a utopia as a political project can have uncertain, undesirable consequences, and even the opposite effect – resulting in the authoritarian and despotic governments that exist in many countries dominated by totalitarian or military regimes. Nonetheless, utopian ideas are important for political and for societal progress. Without utopian conceptions, politics would be without vision and direction. Instead of hope, we would fall into complacency, or worse – despair. With utopia, we open up the possibility of a better world. Mindful of the many failed utopian enterprises in modern times, this chapter contends that it is not the realisation of our utopian dream that is important; rather, what is important is that we maintain the spirit of utopia. The very essence of utopianism is about desire and hope for a better world.

## Philosophy of Hope

Throughout history, people have entertained the hope that long-lasting solutions to our social, political and economic problems can be found. This may be achieved by starting all over again in a new world or by destroying the present world order. Their individual understanding of an ideal community may be different, inspired by religion or by economic and social principles; however, it is not the specific features of the commonwealth that are significant but rather, the determination to improve the *common* welfare of their fellow men and women.

Leszek Kolakowski holds that utopianism, which:

> emerged as an artificially concocted proper name, has acquired, in the last two centuries, a sense so extended that it refers not only to a literary genre, but to a way of thinking, to a mentality, to a philosophical attitude, and is being employed in depicting cultural phenomena going back into antiquity.[2]

---

1. R.W. Chambers, "The Rational Heathens," in William Nelson, ed., *Twentieth Century Interpretations of Utopia* (Englewood Cliffs, NJ: Prentice-Hall, 1968), 17.
2. Quoted in Lyman Tower Sargent, *Utopianism: A Very Short Introduction* (Oxford: Oxford University Press, 2010), 5.

A philosophy of hope, utopianism "is characterized by the transformation of generalized hope into a description of a non-existent society."[1] Although it describes an ideal society that is non-existent or possible only in the future, utopianism inspires people with the hope of building a better world.

Influenced by the Enlightenment, social critics of the flawed social structure believed that change and the improvement of humankind was part of human evolutionary process. Being optimistic, they believed "the tempo of progress depended merely on the use of reason to discover the laws of nature which regulated social affairs, that is, the relations of man to man."[2] These critics no longer accepted the unjust status quo where classes were set apart by distrust, poverty was considered a curse, and excess wealth was both flaunted and considered a blessing. Against liberal economists who were indifferent towards the sufferings of people, they refused to look upon workers as mere commodities of labor, subjected to market trends and business cycles. They did not seek to reform capitalism; they sought to abolish it. Therefore, one tends to associate utopian vision with modern socialism.

According to Gregory Claeys, to view liberalism as anti-utopian would be a mistake for a number of reasons. First, liberalism presents itself as utopian, promising economic prosperity based on the division of labor. Second, liberalism recognizes its own deficiencies and offers a compromise with socialism. Third, liberalism promises "an idealized democracy" as an alternative to monarchy and plutocracy. Nonetheless, it has often led to governance by a few wealthy people. Combined with globalization of the market, liberalism presents itself as utopian. Fourth, liberalism believes the good life includes the maximization of individual freedom; it promotes the relentless pursuit of wealth, and thus encourages selfishness and greed.[3]

## Biographical Sketch

Born on 7 February 1478 in London to a successful lawyer, the young Thomas More spent time in the household of John Morton, Archbishop of Canterbury. He studied at Oxford and qualified as a lawyer, although at one point he had considered pursuing religious life in the Franciscan Order. In 1517, More became one of King Henry VIII's most trusted advisers and civil servants. He acted as Henry's secretary, interpreter,

---

1. Sargent, *Utopianism: A Very Short Introduction*, 8.
2. Leo Loubere, *Utopian Socialism: Its History since 1800* (Cambridge, Massachusetts: Schenkman Publishing Company, 1974), 7.
3. Claeys, *Searching for Utopia*, 10-11.

speech writer, chief diplomat, adviser, and confidant. More became the Speaker of the House of Commons in 1523. During this time, he gained a reputation as a humanist scholar. As a close friend of Desiderius Erasmus of Rotterdam, a renowned Catholic thinker, More wrote treatises against Martin Luther and the Protestant Reformation. A passionate defender of Catholic orthodoxy, More also wrote against heresy, banned unorthodox books, and took on the responsibility to interrogate heretics.

More was made Lord Chancellor in 1529 (the equivalent of Prime Minister today) at which point in time King Henry was determined to divorce his wife, Catherine of Aragon. When Henry declared himself "Supreme Head of the Church in England," More resigned from the chancellorship. He was against Henry's divorce and separation of the Church in England from Rome. In 1534, More was arrested for refusing to swear the Oath of Succession (recognizing Anne Boleyn as Queen), refusing to repudiate the Pope, and for refusing to accept the annulment of Henry's marriage. Tried for treason at Westminster, on 6 July 1535 he was beheaded on Tower Hill. More ended his life "in the faith and for the faith of the Catholic Church, the king's good servant but God's first." Erasmus wrote that More's "soul was more pure than snow" and his "genius was such that England never had and never again will have its like." Declared a martyr, Thomas More was beatified by the Catholic Church in 1886, and canonized by Pius XI in 1935.[1]

## Thomas More's *Utopia*

Defined as "nowhere" or "no place," the term "Utopia" was coined by More in 1516. With its roots in the Hellenistic tradition, utopia is seen as essentially a Western concept in the sense that there is no utopian thought in other cultures that is secular.[2] There are Indian and Chinese Mahayana utopian thoughts; however, these are based on religious cosmologies.

---

1. Adapted from *History*, http://www.bbc.co.uk/history/historic_figures/more_sir_thomas.shtml, and *Sir Thomas More: Biography, Facts and Information*, https://englishhistory.net/tudor/citizens/sir-thomas-more/. For a detailed biography see Peter Ackroyd, *The Life of Thomas More* (London: Chatto & Windus, 1998), and Robert Bolt, *A Man for All Seasons* (London: Methuen, 1995).
2. Kumar, *Utopianism*, 33. Kumar argues that Asian and other non-western utopian traditions were influenced by Christianity. Sargent, however, maintains that utopian tradition existed outside the West before Thomas More's work. Following contact with the West, those in the East adapted it to suit their own special circumstances and Eastern utopian traditions are thus significantly different from More's *Utopia* in form and content. Sargent, *Utopianism*, 67.

In *Utopia*, More uses the device of imaginary conversations in Antwerp between Raphael Hythloday and a character with his own name. In these imaginary conversations, Hythloday describes More's actual visit to Flanders in 1515 and narrates his story in the presence of Peter Gilles, the Town Clerk of Antwerp. Hythloday presents the ideal life in Utopia while More listens intently. Paul Turner holds that Hythloday is in reality Thomas More's mouthpiece.[1] In other words, Hythloday's narrative embodies More's own views. In an age when criticism of the social and political system in England could easily result in far-reaching negative consequences, More needed to present his subversive story in humorous dialogue to disclaim responsibility.

## Plato: the *Republic* and *Laws*

Arguably, Plato laid the foundation for the utopian tradition when he distinguished between the material world and the ideal world. Plato affirmed that reality existed in the realm of ideas. Hence, in Western intellectual tradition, the material world is imperfect and thus human beings must aspire towards the ideal. Traditionally, the Church interpreted this aspiration as a repudiation of the material world in favour of the world to come. Modern utopian writers, however, seek to bring about heaven on earth, as it were, without denying Christian dualism. For example, Leo Loubere holds that "in a better earthly society men might even find it easier to save their souls and enter the higher paradise of God."[2] Edward Schillebeeckx goes so far as to say that there is no salvation outside the world – *extra mundum nulla salus*.[3] Experiences of pain and suffering are basic to our human existence and they form the basis for solidarity among people and commitment to create a better and more humane world.

Thomas More identified *Utopia* as the study of the "best state of a commonwealth" and placed his celebrated work within the ancient Greek tradition of conducting debate regarding the advantages and disadvantages of various political models. In fact, the original title is *Concerning the Best State of a Commonwealth and the New Island of Utopia*. Without doubt, More was indebted to Plato's *Republic* and *Laws*.

---

1. Thomas More, *Utopia*, translated with an introduction and notes by Paul Turner (London: Penguin Books, 2003), xiv.
2. Loubere, *Utopian Socialism*, 5.
3. This statement of Schillebeeckx is in contrast to the Church dogma, *extra ecclesiam nulla salus*, which means outside the Church there is no salvation. See Edward Schillebeeckx, *The Church: The Human Story of God* (New York: Crossroad, 1990), 5-15.

For example, in the *Republic*, we read about an ideal model of a just city governed by philosopher-kings. The city is the locus of utopian ideology.

Following the Egyptians, the Greek understanding of a happy human existence was "epitomized by life in the *polis*, or city-state."[1] Ancient understanding of the ideal life or the perfect commonwealth was thus perceived in terms of city life or the urban environment. Lewis Mumford claims that "the first utopia was the city itself." Thomas More easily adheres to this tradition because "the city had the advantage of mirroring the complexities of society within a frame that respected the human scale."[2]

Further, "the city belonged to the divine order and must obey its principles; but the discovery and application of these principles were the work of human reflection and human action."[3] Thus, constructed by humans, the city was an artefact, the product of rational thinking. Reason enables individuals to express their nature and helps them to correct their ways. With the help of rational planning, rational regulation and rational administration, the city has the potential to offer the good life to people. This includes the existence of social hierarchy and division of labor with topographical division of the city into various regions.

In Plato's *Laws*, we see the introduction of a code of constitutional, civil and criminal laws in the administration of a polity, regarded as a "second-best regime." The advantage of this "second-best regime" is that it could be implemented, unlike the ideal (best) society governed by a class of guardians or philosopher-kings. In *Laws*, Plato endorses the possession of private property and at the same time, he suggests various ways to curb greediness, selfishness and injustice.[4]

Further, in *Laws*, we witness Plato giving relatively important social roles to women and engaging in frank discussion regarding the sexual nature of marriage. These themes are also evident in More's *Utopia*. The most significant influence of Plato on More's work, however, lies in More's treatment of government: the Utopian regime is made up of magistrates, assemblies, and elections. The system of government recommended by Plato and More is one that exists between monarchy and democracy. In this political system, there is neither a single ruler with absolute control over his dominion nor is there a complete dependence on the population.

---

1. Claeys, *Searching for Utopia*, 7.
2. Lewis Mumford, "Utopia, the City and the Machine," in Frank E. Manuel, ed., *Utopias and Utopian Thought* (Boston: Beacon Press, 1966), 3.
3. Krishnan Kumar, *Utopianism*, 12.
4. Thomas More, *Utopia*, translated by Ralph Robynson, 1556, edited with an introduction by David Harris Sacks (Boston: Bedford/St Martin, 1999), 9.

More, however, did not create an island with features taken slavishly from both the *Republic* and *Laws*. He expanded the idea of common property and substituted the philosopher-kings with a system of councils and assemblies functioning under a judicial system. Thus, Utopia is not an ideal community ruled by wisdom, love and perfect knowledge, but a "law state." In other words, More's *Utopia* is "a 'first-best' society in its policies and a 'second-best' in its constitution and system of laws."[1] In writing *Utopia*, More appropriated the best of *The Republic* and *Laws* as well as Aristotle's thought.

## Aristotle: *Politics*

Accepting the right to own private property, More agreed with Aristotle who criticized Plato's proto-communism. In Aristotle's thinking, the possession of private property forms the basis of public and private morality. If everything is in common, no one will be held responsible for anything. This would result in poverty because no one takes care of the common good. Aristotle argues, "Everyone thinks chiefly of his own, hardly at all of the common interest; and only when he is himself concerned as an individual."[2]

Aristotle maintains that "property should be in a certain sense common, but, as a general rule, private; for, when everyone has a distinct interest, men will not complain of one another, and they will make more progress, because everyone will be attending to his own business".[3] Aristotle believes that, when human beings have their own private possessions, they have the opportunity to share them with others. Therefore, possessing private property allows people to develop the virtue of generosity: "there is the greatest pleasure in doing a kindness or service to friends or guests or companions, which can only be rendered when a man has private property."[4] In Plato's proto-communism, such "benevolent disposition" does not seem to exist. In More's *Utopia*, however, the concern for the impoverished laborers and farmers in England is one of the major themes.

---

1. Ibid., 11.
2. Aristotle, *Politics*, translated by Benjamin Jowett, Book II, Part III, http://classics.mit.edu/Aristotle/politics.2.two.html. Thomas More's *Utopia* defers from Plato's proto-communism: "It is the product of the social evils and incipient economic tendencies of the Renaissance." It is also based on concrete living experience. Karl Kautsky, "Utopian Socialism," in *Twentieth Century Interpretations of Utopia*, 14.
3. Aristotle, *Politics*, Book II, Part V.
4. Ibid.

## Plight of the Poor

In the *Republic*, Plato speaks of oligarchies that have "both the extreme wealth and utter poverty." The wealthy contribute nothing to society. Plato says, for example, a particular wealthy man seemed to be a member of the ruling body, however, in actual fact, "he was neither ruler nor subject, but just a spendthrift."[1] Plato stated that these wealthy people have a great train of idle servants who are without any skills to enable them to earn a living by trade. When their master dies, these good-for-nothing servants are left with no occupation and thus they turn to theft in order to survive.

Under a similar theory, Raphael Hythloday in Book I of More's *Utopia* criticises the many noblemen who live off the labor of others by constantly raising the rent of their tenants and thus bleeding them white. There are a great many noblemen who live idly "like drones on the labor of other people."[2]

Hythloday also comments on the social dislocation brought about by "enclosure" or the fencing of the open fields of the feudal system for sheep farming because of the increasing profitability of the wool trade. Critical of the wealthy, including the nobility, gentry, and even some abbots, who "have grown dissatisfied with the income that their predecessors got out of their estates. They're no longer content to lead lazy, comfortable lives, which do no good to society – they must actively do it harm, by enclosing all the land they can for pasture, and leaving none for cultivation."[3] Hythloday expands on his theme, explaining that this enclosing has led to the destruction of houses and whole towns, preserving the churches only for sheep barns. Thousands of farmers have been evicted with nowhere to go. Thus, many of the farmers, their family members and workers, became thieves, who were eventually hanged. Some became tramps and beggars, liable to be arrested as vagrants.

There was a great outcry against the greed of the wealthy in More's native England in the sixteenth century: arable land was taken over for sheep farming and many of the tenants were left with nothing for their livelihood.[4] Farmers found themselves out of work because there was

---

1. Plato, *Republic* (Auckland, NZ: The Floating Press, 2009) Book VIII, 554, and ProQuest ebrary.
2. More, *Utopia*, trans. Paul Turner, 23.
3. Thomas More, *Utopia*, trans. Paul Turner, 25. More was no outspoken critic of the Church, but, as a sincere, devout and traditional Catholic, he had to speak out against the corruption of the ecclesiastical authorities and some members of religious orders who lived off the fat of the land.
4. See G.R. Elton, *England under the Tudors* (London: Methuen & Co., 1974), 229-38.

no land left for cultivation. In modern times, we have observed how industrial development and technological innovations have enriched a few individuals and at the same time impoverished a large segment of the population. Like Plato, More, the author, is critical of oligopoly where wealth is concentrated in the hands of a few who control the price of commodities. England, which seemed to be fortunate in its abundance with all kinds of livestock, could be destroyed by the greed of a few. "Thus a few people have converted one of England's natural advantages into a national disaster."[1] What is scandalous is the fact that extreme poverty exists side by side with excessive luxury. As a champion of the rights of the oppressed, *Utopia* speaks out against the arrogance of the ruling class.

Critical of the legal system, Hythloday also comments on the reason why England is plagued with so many thieves and robbers, and on the stern measures taken against them by the law. The death penalty for theft is far too severe and unjust, he says that the way to stop people from stealing is to provide them with some kind of livelihood. This advice from Hythloday is still relevant today: "Stop the rich from cornering the markets and establishing monopolies."[2] He views social and political problems in depth and in perspective; he realises that the problem of theft cannot be solved merely by punishing thieves, because stealing is the result of poverty, which is the product of an unjust social system. Highlighting the problem of theft is the author's means of attacking the unjust social system in England and the greed of the nobility and people whose main concern was the accumulation of wealth.

## Question of Private Property

Against private property and capitalism, *Utopia* also discusses the shortcomings of a society where money is the measure of all things. It is not possible for a commonwealth to be just or prosperous if the good things in life are in the possession of very few people and the rest are utterly poor. Hythloday comments favourably on the Utopians who share things equally among themselves and where everyone lives in abundance. He understands why Plato refused to be the legislator of people who rejected laws that required them to share their goods equally. In *Laws*, Plato maintains that the best commonwealth would be the one that embraced what we would now refer to as communism: "The first

---

1. More, *Utopia*, trans. Paul Turner, 26.
2. Ibid., 27.

and highest form of the state and of the government and of the law is that in which there prevails most widely the ancient saying, that 'Friends have all things in common.'"[1] Plato believed that the success of public welfare lies in the equal allocation of resources. Such equality is difficult to achieve if private property exists.

A nation may have an abundance of goods, but if everyone grabs as much as he or she can, the outcome will be that a few individuals end up owning the whole lot and the rest of the people will be left in poverty. Hythloday says, "Wealth will tend to vary in inverse proportion to merit."[2] Thus, we end up with two categories of people, the rich who are greedy, unscrupulous and useless, and the poor, who are simple, unassuming, and whose work is more beneficial to society. It is no wonder that Jesus preaches to the crowd: "Blessed are you who are poor, for yours is the kingdom of God" (Luke 6:20).

Hythloday is convinced that unless private ownership of property is abolished, there can be no equitable distribution of goods nor can human beings conduct their business happily. As long as private property remains, "the vast majority of the human race, and the vastly superior part of it, will inevitably go on laboring under a burden of poverty, hardship, and worry."[3] Legislation can help to lessen the sufferings of the poor by limiting the amount of land a person can own, but as long as property and industry are privately owned, it is challenging to maintain a harmonious society.

Against a classless society, More maintains that people will not be entirely satisfied if all things are held in common. In the absence of a profit motive, people have no monetary incentive to work hard and dependence on others will make them lazy. More's objection to the abolition of private property and to the promotion of all things being held in common is derived from Aristotle's *Politics* (II):

> Property should be in a certain sense common, but, as a general rule, private; for, when everyone has a distinct interest, men will not complain of one another, and they will make more progress, because everyone will be attending to his own business. . . . It is clearly better that property should be private, but the use of it common; and the special business of the legislator is to create in men this benevolent disposition . . . how immeasurably greater is the pleasure, when a man feels a thing to be his own . . . there is

---

1. Plato, *Laws* (Tustin, CA: Xist Classics, 2016), chapter 12, 238, ProQuest ebrary.
2. Thomas More, *Utopia*, trans. Paul Turner, 44.
3. Ibid., 45.

the greatest pleasure in doing a kindness or service to friends or guests or companions, which can only be rendered when a man has private property.[1]

More is of the opinion that the commonwealth cannot be stable and prosperous without the possession of private property and the inequality that accompanies it. Raphael Hythloday, however, is convinced that if More had lived in Utopia, he would not be against communism. Besides practicing communism, Utopians are willing to learn and adopt the best ideas from Europe. Specifically, unlike the English, Utopians are not complacent and that is why they are so progressive, Hythloday points out to More. Utopia embodies the equality that More thinks impractical and yet, this commonwealth is happy, well-governed, with its great and venerable institutions. Logan and Adams hold that the context that the author, More, provided for his account of Utopia is "a dispute about the degree of compatibility of the moral and the expedient in political life, and, in particular, on the question of whether the ideal of equality is compatible with stability and prosperity."[2] This work can be viewed as an attempt to answer what is the best condition for a commonwealth.

## Dignity of Labor

In Book II of More's *Utopia*, Hythloday stresses the importance of agricultural work, as well as special trades in Utopia, where both men and women have to work. Utopians work six hours a day with free time for further education. Those not academically inclined may spend more time on a particular trade. Despite their relatively short working hours, there is no shortage of essential goods in Utopia because both men and women work. In other countries, Hythloday comments, there are many people who do little or no work at all. These people include priests, members of religious orders, aristocrats, ruffians and beggars.

In places where money is the only standard of value, there are bound to be unnecessary trades, which merely provide entertainment and the supply of luxury goods. Whereas in Utopia, Hythloday observes, because everybody is doing useful work, they can produce enough to meet their basic needs with shorter working days. There are workers to repair roads and do other communal works, and people have more time to cultivate their minds, which is the secret of a happy life. The main point is that people are encouraged to spend their time constructively.

1. Aristotle, *Politics*, Book II, Part V.
2. Thomas More, *Utopia*, edited by George M. Logan and Robert M. Adams (Cambridge: Cambridge University Press, 2002), xxiv.

This idea of performing useful and productive work to satisfy genuine human needs in a well-organized commonwealth comes from Plato's *Republic*. Applying a similar concept, wealth or money is discredited in Utopia. In fact, Utopians cannot understand why useless substances such as gold are considered more precious than human lives. Nor, can they understand why an ignorant person should be respected and obeyed just because he is wealthy. What puzzles Utopians is the foolish way some may worship a rich person because he is rich. Through education and reading, Utopians realise that it is senseless to worship wealth for wealth's sake.

## Ethical Theory

Utopians also believe that human happiness consists of having pleasure of a higher sort: "happiness is the *summum bonum* towards which we're naturally impelled by virtue – which in their definition means following one's natural impulse."[1] The Utopians regard the enjoyment of life – having pleasure – "as the natural object of all human efforts, and natural, as they define it, is synonymous with virtuous." Pleasure is defined as "any state or activity, physical or mental, which is naturally enjoyable."[2] Here Hythloday is critical of the wealthy who take perverse pleasure in showing off their power and status because they belong to the landed gentry. Other imprudent pleasures include accumulating wealth, such as gold, or gambling, hawking, and hunting for no practical reason. For the Utopians, these activities have nothing to do with real pleasures because they do not contribute to human wellbeing: they are the outcome of bad habits. On the other hand, good physical and mental health is regarded as true pleasure.

To enjoy ourselves "naturally" means that we do not hurt other people when we are having a good time or that such pleasure does not interfere with greater pleasures or cause negative effects.[3] Nature also ensures that all human beings can enjoy life as no one has the monopoly of her affections. Created and loved by God, Utopians believe that our souls are immortal. Like Christians, Utopians believe we shall be rewarded or punished in the next life depending on the way we conduct ourselves in the present one. If we are good to one another, we shall be rewarded in the next world, and *vice versa*.

More's *Utopia* thus examines the central question of ethical concern modelled on Aristotle's *Politics*: what constitutes the happy life for the individual? It explores the importance of communal goals necessary

---

1. Thomas More, *Utopia*, trans. Paul Turner, 72.
2. Ibid., 73.
3. Ibid., 74.

for achieving the happiness of its citizens. The foundation of Utopian teaching is moral philosophy – what constitutes a happy life. Granted that human beings are selfish by nature, Utopians, however, believe that only virtuous living can bring us the greatest happiness. A life of virtue includes enjoying contemplative leisure. Utopians also believe individual happiness is not compatible with special privileges granted to a few wealthy people. Happiness comes from leading a virtuous life and from the consciousness of a good life. In other words, Utopians favour "mental pleasures, which they consider of primary importance, and attribute mostly to good behaviour and a clear conscience."[1]

The idea of virtuous living comes from Cicero who holds that:

> if they [virtues] have been maintained at every period – if one has lived much as well as long – the harvest they produce is wonderful, not only because they never fail us even in our last days (though that in itself is supremely important), but also because the consciousness of a well-spent life and the recollection of many virtuous actions are exceedingly delightful.[2]

Although Utopians are not Christians, their idea of a good life mirrors the Gospel teaching. This brings us to the question of religious practice.

## Religious tolerance

Several religious systems exist in Utopia but most of the inhabitants believe in a single divine power that is external, infinite and beyond the comprehension of the human mind. This divine power is not "a physical substance" but "an active force" which they call "the Parent". Utopians do not recognize any form of the divine, but believe it is this divine force that is the source of everything, the "beginnings and ends, all growth, development and change."[3] All the different religions in Utopia acknowledge that there is one Supreme Being who is responsible for the creation and sustenance of the universe. They all call him "Mythras," a being identical with nature.[4]

Hythloday remarks that Utopians are gradually turning away from inferior creeds and embracing a more reasonable religion like the Christian faith. Perhaps this is due to divine inspiration or the fact that

---

1. Ibid., 78.
2. Cicero (106BC-43BC), *On Old Age*, III, The Harvard Classics, http://www.bartleby.com/9/2/1.html.
3. Thomas More, *Utopia*, trans. Paul Turner, 98.
4. Ibid., 99.

Christianity promotes a kind of communism that is part of its religious and cultural belief. For this reason, quite a number of Utopians are baptized as Christians and are anxious to receive all the sacraments of the Church.

Utopians do not discourage non-Christians from adopting the Christian faith because religious tolerance is one of the basic principles of their constitution. However, a person who criticises another's religion will be charged with disturbing the peace and sent into exile. Hythloday says that this has indeed happened to an over-zealous, newly baptized Christian who condemned the religious beliefs of others.

Utopians realise that constant quarrels regarding religion will make the nation weak and vulnerable to attacks from outside. They thus enact a law by which everyone is free to practice whatever religion they choose. They are also free to spread their faith provided they do it quietly, politely and rationally. Furthermore, they are not allowed to attack other religious beliefs or to use force or violence. Utopians understand that it is possible that God made different people believe in different religions so that He could be worshipped in diverse ways. Therefore, it is wrong to force others to embrace one's own religion. If there is only one true religion and the rest false, truth will eventually prevail of its own accord. Thus, differences in religious matters must be discussed calmly and rationally. If it is decided by force of arms, there is a fear that the worst kind of superstitions would persist because "the worst people are always the most obstinate."[1]

Even though the choice of creed is left to the individual in Utopia, the people are not allowed to believe in anything that is incompatible with human dignity. They must be convinced that the good are rewarded and the bad are punished. "Anyone who thinks differently has, in their view, forfeited his right to be classed as a human being, by degrading his immortal soul to the level of an animal body. Still less do they regard him as a Utopian citizen."[2] Such people clearly do not care much about the Utopian way of life and consequently are regarded as contemptible.

Utopians have a positive outlook towards death. They mourn for a sick person but never mourn for a death, unless a person is unwilling to face death. This would be regarded as a bad sign suggesting that the person in question is afraid of punishment and must be dragged into God's presence. They perform the deceased's funeral in sorrowful silence pleading for God's mercy and then bury his body. In contrast, when a person dies in a cheerful and positive disposition, no one mourns for him. Instead, they sing for joy at his funeral and lovingly commend his

1. Ibid., 101.
2. Ibid.

soul to God. In the spirit of reverence, they cremate his body, remember the person's good character and career, and encourage others to follow his example. The dead person is like a guardian angel who lives in their midst reminding them to be good.

## Indictment

*Utopia* is more than the narrative of an ideal society, it also serves as an indictment of the failings and inadequacies of England at that time. It had the aim of influencing the government and laws of England, as Erasmus wrote: "He published his *Utopia* for the purpose of showing, what are the things that occasion mischief in commonwealths; having the English Constitution especially in view."[1] The island of Utopia, in fact, resembles England and perhaps Thomas More had an idea how England could be, if it adopted the Utopian way of life.

England in the sixteenth century was a country where a few people lived luxuriously while thousands of people starved or were hanged for stealing food. To remedy this situation of gross injustice, More felt that a programme of austerity and a curtailment of individual liberty was needed. His writing aims to persuade Christians to do better than the Utopian pagans:

> The *Utopia* does not attempt a final solution of the problems of human society . . . but it contains an appeal addressed to all of us, which allows of no refusal, that we should try and do each one his share to mend our own selves and ease the burden of our fellow-men, to improve mankind and prepare for the life to come.[2]

More may say that *Utopia* does not attempt to solve the problems that human society faces, but he is certainly suggesting a blueprint.

The commonwealth of Utopia has its advantages and disadvantages. It is an egalitarian society where no one lacks basic necessities, such as food and housing. There is no opportunity for secret assembly and one must spend one's leisure time on state-sanctioned activities. Personal freedom is restricted in many ways. In fact, Utopia anticipates the welfare state of modern times and its restrictions remind us of countries with totalitarian regimes. Perhaps More wanted to show us that we cannot have a perfect society on earth; strong central authority is required if society is to function well with minimal conflict.

---

1. Kautsky, "Utopian Socialism," 14.
2. Quoted in Thomas More, *Utopia*, trans. Paul Turner, xvi.

In addition, More's *Utopia* contrasts the virtues of a pagan country with the vices of the Christian West. In contemporary Europe, for instance, there were despotic rulers, senseless wars, and general anarchy, whereas in Utopia, people enjoy peace and security, law and order. In Europe, freedom of conscience was suppressed but, in Utopia, there is respect for human dignity. Instead of the selfishness and greed of a few people in Europe, leading to the impoverishment of the rest of the population, in Utopia there is collaboration for the common good so there is plenty for all. Above all, Utopians prefer the pleasure of the mind while Europeans are bent on materialistic pursuits.[1]

In Utopia, everything is under public ownership and no one fears the lack of basic necessities as long as the state-owned storehouses are full. There are no beggars as everybody has a share of the country's goods. No one owns anything and yet all are rich – "for what greater wealth can there be than cheerfulness, peace of mind, and freedom from anxiety?"[2]

Compared with other countries, Utopia certainly has a superior system. Some countries reward only the nobility, goldsmiths and people who produce luxury goods, which are non-essentials. In contrast, laborers such as farm-hands, carpenters and coal-heavers are so poorly paid that they die poverty-stricken in their old age. "As if it weren't unjust enough already that the man who contributes most to society should get the least in return, they make it worse, and then arrange for injustice to be described as justice."[3]

Critical of the existing social system, Hythloday cannot help but think that there is a conspiracy of the wealthy to promote their interests under the guise of organizing society. They exploit laborers through all kinds of cunning practices, which they later enforce by law. "Thus, an unscrupulous minority is led by its insatiable greed to monopolize what would have been enough to supply the needs of the whole population."[4]

Hythloday maintains that Utopians are happier because money is abolished. This has also resulted in the disappearance of crime because the abolition of money leads to the abolition of criminal behavior, which frequent punishments are powerless to prevent. Without money, poverty vanishes.

---

1. H.W. Donner, "A Moral Fable," in Nelson, ed., *Twentieth Century Interpretations of Utopia*, 34.
2. Thomas More, *Utopia*, trans. Paul Turner, 110.
3. Ibid., 111.
4. Ibid.

Thomas More certainly was not satisfied with the society in which he lived, but he did not resign himself to the world as he found it. Even if he could not hope for the realization of his ideal society, he continued to hope that Utopian institutions would be established in Europe. More's satire represented his deepest longing: he wanted the educated elites to be running the society. This means that the literary educated were not to be thought of as a separate class, even though "they were an elite of the intellectually gifted and the morally most advanced."[1] Members were to be recruited from other groups such as the working class; More had wished for a class of scholars in England to resemble Plato's philosophers, an elite group who had overcome ambitions and passions. From this group of people, the highest officials of the state, such as priests, senators and even princes, would be chosen by election.

## Problem of pride

In *Utopia*, we discover that pride has prevented people from adopting the Utopian system. Pride leads people to be dissatisfied with what they have and to be satisfied only if they have more than others. Pride makes people gloat over another's misfortune. This sin is deeply embedded in human nature. But Hythloday is glad that at least one country on this planet has established a system that could be adopted universally – the Utopian way of life. This manner of living provides "not only the happiest basis for a civilized community, but also one which, in all human probability, will last forever."[2]

The Utopian way of living has eliminated the root cause of human ambition and pride that has led to conflicts in our society. When compared with the social, political and economic systems of contemporary England, the Utopian way was certainly closer to Christian values. All the more shameful for Europeans, More seems to imply, because the Utopians never had the advantage of hearing the Gospel.

Utopians are presented as non-Christians but open to the teaching of Christ. Following the virtuous principles of the ancients, they can be regarded as "anonymous Christians" and they represent a challenge to Thomas More's own corrupted England.

"Utopia is clearly meant to hold the mirror up to More's England."[3] It is an indictment of European cultural heritage in the light of the demands of the Gospel. Without the benefits of Christian revelation, Utopians

---

1. Gerhard Ritter, "*Utopia* and Power Politics," in Nelson, ed., *Twentieth Century Interpretations of Utopia*, 41.
2. Thomas More, *Utopia*, trans. Paul Turner, 112.
3. Kumar, *Utopianism*, 2.

using reason could achieve "the best state of the commonwealth." David Sacks holds that "perhaps reason could find ways to minimize the effects of sin in the world by channelling human pride away from its destructive paths."[1]

In More's *Utopia*, Hythloday believes crime could be eliminated by providing more work and by the abolition of private property. At the same time, he is aware that pride could distort our human judgment and resist the building of an ideal society:

> I've no doubt that either self-interest, or the authority of our Saviour Christ – Who was far too wise not to know what was best for us, and far too kind to recommend anything else – would have led the whole world to adopt the Utopian system long ago, if it weren't for that beastly root of all evil, pride.[2]

## A Better World Is Possible

Utopian ethics is a mixture of Stoicism and Epicureanism. Stoicism implies the ability to endure suffering and pain without complaint. The goal of this ethical doctrine is freedom from passion (suffering) through the pursuit of reason. In other words, one needs to be objective and unemotional to make clear judgment or decision.

The ethics of Epicureanism appears to be the opposite of Stoicism but the consequences are the same in the end: freedom from pain and suffering. Thomas More was struck by the "hedonic calculus" of Epicureanism. Epicurus's rule that, "in choosing among pleasures, one should always choose a greater pleasure over a lesser, and should reject any pleasure that will eventually result in pain."[3]

In attempting to resolve political conflicts, More thought this Epicurean principle might be applied. At the same time, More believed things could be made a little better and more bearable by convincing those in power. Hythloday says: "You must handle everything as tactfully as you can, and what you can't put right you must try to make as little wrong as possible."[4] In other words, even if the world is not perfect, you can make it less bad.

If achieving utopia in our present world seems impossible, at least there is a way to lessen political conflicts and ameliorate our current social conditions, which for some people, are almost unbearable. In the

1. Thomas More, *Utopia*, trans. Ralph Robynson, 1556, ed. David Harris Sacks, 19.
2. Thomas More, *Utopia*, trans. Paul Turner, 112.
3. Thomas More, *Utopia*, ed. George M. Logan and Robert M. Adams, xxviii.
4. Thomas More, *Utopia*, trans. Paul Turner, 42.

final paragraph of Book II of *Utopia*, More refrains from criticizing the Utopian way of life, "communism minus money," offering instead "polite remarks about the Utopian system."[1] More hopes that he and Hythloday can discuss the matter again soon. David Sacks comments that in *Utopia* More's actions "represent an implicit endorsement of the efficacy of rhetoric in making possible continued human sociability."[2] Debate is important because in debating we can reveal ambiguities, contradictions and practical limitations. In constructing his conversation in *Utopia*, Thomas More expresses his hope that social and political benefits can be realized through debate or rational discussion of fundamental questions regarding human rights, justice, and peace, issues that concern the welfare of the commonwealth.

Sacks maintains that:

> the social capacity to exchange views on a common basis changes a mere association of people into a commonwealth – a community with ongoing interests and enterprises and a need for mutual support among its members, the sort of place about which it is possible to ask whether it has attained the best state.[3]

In this regard, More and Hythloday both share the same view regarding the meaning and purpose of social and political life and both utilize their knowledge to realize their objectives. Trusting in human reason, they abhor the use of force and violence in the exercise of power.

## Social Justice

Written five hundred years ago, *Utopia* has themes that resonate today. For example, assistance for the terminally ill, the ordination of women as priests in the church, the role of women in war and the denunciation of hunting animals for "sport." The central theme is, of course, the issue of poverty and social justice: how to get rid of an unjust socio-economic system dominated by the rich and powerful. Thomas More challenges us to work for a more equitable society where social justice prevails and where economic power is to be placed in the hands of the population. Besides his literary accomplishment, More's genius in this work lies in his

---

1. Ibid., 113.
2. Thomas More, *Utopia*, trans. Ralph Robynson, 1556, ed. David Harris Sacks, 21.
3. Ibid., 23.

power to inspire serious thinking about social justice.[1] It is an important text in the history of social and political thought, a social commentary that is more relevant than ever.

In More's opinion, social justice means all members of society have equal opportunity to develop their talents and skills for the common good. Social justice occurs when there is an equitable distribution of goods and services, limited hours of work, and security from market manipulation by the rich and powerful. In such a society, people have no worries about making a living – there is work for all. Although More was not the first humanist scholar to identify the pursuit of wealth as a vice in political life, he was the first to see its corruptive influence as the main cause of social injustice. As an experienced lawyer and statesman, More was able to grasp the complex connection between the levers of economic, social, and political power.[2] In *Utopia*, More makes a passionate plea for social justice. After five hundred years, this clarion call to remedy gross inequalities of wealth and power is more urgent than ever.

## Dystopia

Unfortunately, the utopias we have witnessed in our own time have turned out to be "varieties of hell." Among the most well-known of such hells is one envisaged in Philip K. Dick's influential book, *Do Androids Dream of Electric Sheep?* (1968), which was adapted for the Blade Runner movies in 1982 and 2017.

Karl Popper holds that those who attempted to establish "heaven on earth" ended up making it a hell. This suggests that one person's utopia is another person's dystopia.[3] Utopianism is fraught with contradictions. More's utopian vision is ironic and ambiguous. Utopia means "no place" – it represents an ideal, giving our political programme a sense of direction and progress. Utopias are essentially "visions of what *should* be, even if

---

1.  Lawrence Wilde, *Thomas More's Utopia: Arguing for Social Justice* (London: Routledge, 2017), 3. For a comprehensive interpretation of *Utopia* as a plea for social justice, see J.H. Hexter, *More's Utopia: The Biography of an Idea* (New York: Harper Torchbook, 1965), Edward Surtz, *The Praise of Pleasure: Philosophy, Education and Communism in More's Utopia* (Cambridge, MA: Harvard University Press, 1957), and George M. Logan, *The Meaning of More's Utopia* (Princeton, NJ: Princeton University Press, 1983).
2.  Wilde, *Thomas More's Utopia*, 109.
3.  Edward Rothstein, "Utopia and its Discontents," in Edward Rothstein, Herbert Muschamp and Martin E. Marty, *Visions of Utopia* (Oxford: Oxford University Press, 2003), 4-5.

they show what *shouldn't* be. Utopias are visions we care about because they have implications for *this* world; they are attempts to say what this world could be and what should be worked for."[1]

Utopias are fine if they are merely visions, but once realized, they become repugnant. As such, utopia simply cannot exist and, if it did, it would be an unbearable place. For example, in the last century we have witnessed the atrocities and horrors of Nazi Germany, the Soviet dictatorship, the Cultural Revolution in China, and so on. These grew out of various utopian visions. This also suggests that utopianism leads not to freedom but to tyranny and collective enslavement. This is the case because we need a strong central authority to construct and enforce the harmonious society that we think is ideal. At the same time, we value liberty and freedom; however, happiness and harmony come with the high price of obedience. The duty to obey central authority is fundamental for any supposed utopian society to succeed. Edward Rothstein maintains that, "The more perfect the utopia, the more stringent must be the controls. We are left with, yes, Big Brother. And utopia becomes totalitarianism with a barely human face."[2]

Regarding the attempt to produce a perfect human society, Leszek Kolakowski writes: "The strictures boil down to this: first, a universal fraternity is unconceivable; second, any attempt to implement it is bound to produce a highly despotic society which, to simulate the impossible perfection, will stifle the expression of conflict, and thus destroy the life of culture, by a totalitarian coercion."[3] Kolakowski continues:

> A feasible utopian world must presuppose that people have lost their creativity and freedom, that the variety of human life forms and thus personal life has been destroyed, and that all of mankind has achieved the perfect satisfaction of needs and accepted a perpetual deadly stagnation as its normal condition.[4]

Such a world would signify stagnation of our society, and an end to progress and enrichment in our lives.

---

1. Ibid., 3.
2. Ibid., 7.
3. Leszek Kolakowski, "The Death of Utopia Reconsidered," in Brewster Kingman and Sterling M. McMurrin, eds., *The Tanner Lectures on Human Values* (Salt Lake City: University of Utah Press, 1983), 237, *eBook Collection (EBSCOhost)*, EBSCO*host* (accessed 24 March 2017).
4. Ibid., 238.

Karl Popper deliberates that utopianism is dangerous and self-defeating because it leads to violence. Utopias are unsuccessful projects, according to Popper, because it is impossible to determine ends in a scientific way. Utopians conceive what an ideal society should be and then formulate all political actions to that end – this inevitably leads to conflicts and violence because they tolerate no dissent. Popper argues that the utopians must always win, must defeat and crush their opponents, who do not profess their own utopian faith.[1] Popper views utopians as religious zealots bent upon achieving their political goals at all costs, ever ready to annihilate "heretical" views. Not open to opinion of others, they use violence to suppress criticism and to destroy all opponents. In other words, "they become gods."[2]

Popper believes people are attracted to utopianism because they fail to realise that we really cannot create a heaven on earth. Instead of attempting to establish utopia, Popper believes society should follow a work-in-progress model whereby we make life a little less terrible and a little less unjust in each generation.[3] This means that we need to help the weak, the sick, and those who suffer from oppression and injustice; we need to create employment opportunities and prevent crimes and war instigated by men who think they are gods.

## Spirit of Utopia

Be that as it may, such belief and good intention voiced by Popper already suggests utopianism. There is certainly the danger of utopia becoming a dystopia but, if we relinquish utopian thought, we lose the possibility to change our world for the better. We need to maintain our desire and determination to see that a better world is possible and to do this, humanity needs to have a utopian spirit. Paul Tillich expresses this aptly when he writes: "It is the spirit of utopia that conquers utopia."[4] Tillich believes that utopia is embedded in the nature of the person. It is not possible to understand history without utopia because historical consciousness implies a beginning and an end of history. For Tillich, "utopia is truth" in the sense that it expresses the person's essence, "the inner aim of his existence."[5] In other words, utopia reveals what a person essentially is and what his ultimate *telos* or purpose is.

---

1. Karl R. Popper, *Conjectures and Refutations* (London: Routledge & Kegan Paul, 1963), 360.
2. Ibid.
3. Ibid., 362.
4. Paul Tillich, "Critique and Justification of Utopia," in Manuel, ed., *Utopias and Utopian Thought*, 309.
5. Ibid., 296.

Further, utopia has the characteristic of "fruitfulness," open to possibilities which would be lost if we did not possess utopian spirit. Tillich writes: "Every utopia is an anticipation of human fulfillment, and many things anticipated in utopias have been shown to be real possibilities."[1] Without this anticipation of our self-actualization, many possibilities remain unfulfilled and we are left with a sterile society. With utopia, we can always work towards a different and better world. Jesuit martyr Ignacio Ellacuría is one who adopted the utopian spirit with genuine sincerity; these ideas will be explored in the following chapter.

1. Ibid., 297.

# 2
# Utopian Spirit

*A new spectre is haunting Europe. . . . An everyday postmodernism of the heart is spreading that is relegating the poverty and the destitution of the Third World to an even greater faceless remoteness.*[1]

One of the most disturbing developments lately is the recognition that ownership of the world's wealth and resources have been shrinking to a smaller and smaller number of individuals. In January 2016, the charity Oxfam International released its annual report, which revealed that the world's 62 richest billionaires have as much wealth as the bottom half of the world's population. Drawing from Forbes' annual list of billionaires and Credit Suisse's Global Wealth Databook, it says that the wealthiest have seen their net worth soar over the five years ending in 2015. And *the top one percent* own more than everyone else combined.

> The richest 1 percent have seen their share of global wealth increase from 44 percent in 2009 to 48 percent in 2014 and at this rate will be more than 50 percent in 2016. Members of this global elite had an average wealth of $2.7 million per adult in 2014. Of the remaining 52 percent of global wealth, almost all (46 percent) is owned by the rest of the richest fifth of the world's population.

1. Jon Sobrino, "Fifty Years for a Future that Is Christian and Human," *Concilium* 1 (2016), 69. Some material in this chapter appears in Ambrose Mong, "A Different World is Possible: Vision of Ignacio Ellacuría," *The Way*, A review of Christian spirituality published by the British Jesuits, July 2017, Volume 56, Number 3 (29 – 42).

The other 80 percent share just 5.5 percent and had an average
wealth of $3,851 per adult – that's 1/700th of the average wealth
of the 1 percent.[1]

"The scale of global inequality is quite simply staggering," warns
Oxfam's executive director Winnie Byanyima in the same report, "and
despite the issues shooting up the global agenda, the gap between the
richest and the rest is widening fast."[2]

Given the inability of our present economic and political systems to
provide everyone with the basic necessities to sustain life, there is an urgent
need to find alternative ways of organizing society that can provide all human
beings with a decent standard of living. Karl Marx said, "Philosophers have
hitherto only interpreted the world in various ways; the point is to change
it."[3] The question is how to transform this harsh and brutal world into a more
civilized and humane one. Many thoughtful people, including liberation
theologians, have acknowledged the shortcomings and weaknesses of our
neo-liberal capitalist economy and the adverse effects of globalization.[4]
Most rich and influential people, however, seem to refuse to acknowledge
the presence of poverty. They give the impression of being oblivious to
the sufferings of others.[5] The grim reality of poverty is confined to images
provided by the media, which the wealthy may watch in the comfort of their
television rooms. They are like people "having their own conscience seared
with a hot iron" (1 Timothy 4:2).

This chapter explores the implications of Ignacio Ellacuría's vision of
a new world in his own work and that of other theologians, reflecting
on the spirit of utopia, the civilisation of poverty, the centrality of

---

1. "Richest 1% Will Own More than all the Rest by 2016," https://www.oxfam.org/
   en/pressroom/pressreleases/2015-01-19/richest-1-will-own-more-all-rest-2016.
2. Ibid.
3. Karl Marx, *Theses on Feuerbach*, https://www.marxists.org/archive/marx/
   works/1845/theses/.
4. Neoliberalism refers to "ideology and policy model that emphasizes the value
   of free market competition . . . it is most commonly associated with laissez-
   faire economics. In particular, neoliberalism is often characterized in terms of
   its belief in sustained economic growth as the means to achieve human progress,
   its confidence in free markets as the most-efficient allocation of resources, its
   emphasis on minimal state intervention in economic and social affairs, and its
   commitment to the freedom of trade and capital." Encyclopedia Britannica,
   https://www.britannica.com/topic/ideology-society
5. For example, Bia Doria, wife of the millionaire, former mayor of São Paolo João
   Doria, sitting in her Porsche, said, "Brazil's poor just want hugs." Her crass comment
   exposed the vast gap between the Brazilian privileged few and the destitute of the
   rest of the population, *South China Morning Post*, Wednesday, 12 October 2016.

compassion and the mission of the Church. Ellacuría's understanding of Christianity is essentially messianic, with its focus on liberation of the whole person for the transformation of our society into a more humane one through a spiritual revolution.

On 16 November 1989, Ignacio Ellacuría, S.J., five fellow Jesuits, their housekeeper and her daughter were assassinated by soldiers from an elite army unit in El Salvador for their opposition to the Salvadorean government. The Jesuits were advocates of a negotiated settlement between the government and a guerrilla organization (the Farabundo Martí National Liberation Front) that had been fighting the government for over a decade.

As rector of *Universidad Centroamericana* (University of Central America), Ellacuría was committed to fighting for the poor by writing political analyses of the situation in the country, publishing and broadcasting them through various channels in the media. A liberation theologian, he sought to confront the social reality in Latin America in concrete and material ways. The presence of so much misery and poverty led Ellacuría to affirm that a different world is not only possible but necessary.[1]

The phrase "a different world is possible" does not refer to a blueprint for change; it indicates rather "a horizon or a time that is largely concerned with hope and with eschatology."[2] As it is a question of time, the focus is here and now: a different world is possible *here on earth*. Hope implies that we are not satisfied with the existing state of affairs and long for radical, utopian change. While eschatology is related to our Christian faith and deals with last things such as hell, purgatory and heaven, utopia is related to human action guided by practical reason. In Christianity we need a synthesis of eschatology and utopia.

## The Spirit of Utopia

According to another liberation theologian, José Maria Castillo, if we believe that a different world is possible, then we have "to regain a utopian consciousness," because we are not satisfied with our present world and

---

1. See Jon Sobrino, "On the Way to Healing: Humanizing 'a Gravely Ill World'," *America* (29 October 2014), available at http://www.americamagazine.org/issue/way-healing.

2. Luiz Carlos Susin, "Introduction: This World Can Be Different," in *A Different World is Possible, Concilium* (December 2004), 7-12, here 7. This phrase is a slogan of the World Social Forum and of the anti-globalization movement; it also forms the title for this important issue of *Concilium*, on which I draw extensively.

thus plan to be guided by "utopian reason" to construct a better one.[1] "Utopias have been the driving force of history" when charismatic individuals or groups refuse to maintain the status quo and seek to construct a more equitable and just society. "A society without utopias is a society without hope."[2] Utopian dreams, however, are not enough to develop something truly different from oppressive social structures. As Charles Villa-Vicencio, a former member of South Africa's Truth and Reconciliation Commission, writes:

> For the dreams of the oppressed to become a reality they are to be translated into political programmes and law-making that benefit those who have longed for, and fought for, the new age, while protecting the new society against the abuses which marked past oppression. This ultimately is what a liberatory theology of reconstruction is all about.[3]

The greatest danger, therefore, is to be satisfied with the present global system – to think we are living in the best of all possible worlds, as suggested by Gottfried Leibniz in 1710 (*Essays on the Goodness of God, the Freedom of Man and the Origin of Evil*), and do not want any other kind of world. For example, since the dissolution of the Soviet Union in December 1991, many people think that capitalism is the only feasible political system, that the market economy is the most efficient possible and thus "the effectiveness of the market has been elevated to the supreme criterion of values." Hence, people from the developed world often think that the poverty and destitution of the developing world are the result of corrupt politicians there – or that bad ethical behaviour is caused by a malfunction of the market economy.[4]

But in a capitalist world, the production and pricing of private goods is more important than social development for the common good, because society has evolved to satisfy the wants of the few rich individuals who dominate it. Promoting massive consumption and exploitation of natural resources, José Castillo argues, capitalism benefits the few at the expense of the many. A small number of rich people will always seek to perpetuate and protect their wealth and privileges, and to keep the majority of the

---

1. José M. Castillo, "Utopia Set Aside," *Concilium* (December 2004), 35-41, here 35.
2. Ibid., 38.
3. Charles Villa-Vicencio, *A Theology of Reconstruction: Nation-Building and Human Rights* (Cambridge: CUP, 1992), 29, quoted in Rudolf von Sinner, "Religion and Power: Toward the Political Sustainability of the World," *Concilium* (December 2004), 99.
4. Castillo, "Utopia Set Aside," 38.

population in subjugation and poverty.[1] This concentration of wealth produced by the global market and neoliberal capitalism "is causing more than 70,000 deaths daily from hunger, malnutrition, and their resulting pandemics." Its effects are worse than the brutalities of Nazism and Stalinism.[2] And, despite its emphasis on freedom, capitalism "in reality tolerates only the freedom of those who do not question the capitalist system." As such, much like Stalinist Communism and Hitler's Nazism, it only allows limited freedom on its own terms.[3]

According to Ellacuría, "Only a spirit of utopia and with hope can one have the faith and courage to attempt, together with all the poor and downtrodden of the world, to turn back history, to subvert it and launch it in a different direction."[4] Jon Sobrino, Ellacuría's friend and colleague, places this passage in the context of the "tradition . . . of following Jesus." "Central to this tradition," he writes, "is *honesty with reality and living in reality*, meaning overcoming deceit and lies . . . [and] *the absoluteness of compassion* for the suffering of others."[5]

The spirit of utopias, defined by Castillo as a public sense of duty to move society towards an idealized state of egalitarianism, has been the "driving force of history" when charismatic individuals or groups refused to abide by the status quo and sought to construct a more equitable and just society.[6] Purely utopian dreams, however, are not practical enough to develop something that is in reality different from the oppressive structures in society. Rudolf von Sinner holds that, for the hope of the oppressed to become a reality, utopian dreams must be translated into political actions and policies that are beneficial to all.[7]

---

1. Ibid., 39.
2. Ibid., 36.
3. Ibid., 37.
4. Ignacio Ellacuría, "El Desafío de las Mayorías Pobres," *Estudios Centroamericanos* (1989), 493-4, quoted as the epigraph to Jon Sobrino, "Turning Back History," *Concilium* (December 2004), 125. Complete English translation by Phillip Berryman as "The Challenge of the Poor Majority," in John J. Hassett and Hugh Lacey, eds., *Towards a Society that Serves Its People: The Intellectual Contribution of El Salvador's Murdered Jesuits* (Washington, DC: Georgetown University Press, 1991), 171-6. I have preferred Sobrino's translations here.
5. Sobrino, "Turning back History," 127 (italics in the original).
6. Castillo, "Utopia Set Aside," 38.
7. Rudolf von Sinner, "Religion and Power: Toward the Political Sustainability of the World," 99.

## Capitalism and Imperialism

Petras and Veltmeyer argue that, based on the exploitation of people and the degradation of the environment, capitalism almost always leads to "uneven development" and social inequalities and disparities, class conflict, and "a propensity towards crisis."[1] Capitalist development is fraught with internal contradictions. For example, in the 1930s the capitalist system collapsed in the wake of a financial crisis. This led to the development of the welfare state, which was introduced to slow down the strong impulse toward profit maximization. Welfare capitalism, based on a mixed economy, was designed to solve the problem of uneven development and to promote a more equitable distribution of resources, thus narrowing the gap between the rich and the poor. Unfortunately, by the end of 1970s, the cost of maintaining a welfare state resulted in a "fiscal crisis" in the north and a "debt crisis" in the south.[2] This gave rise to a new order in some countries where the forces of market were let loose, and the protection given by the welfare state was removed; as a result of which big corporations benefitted but a large section of the population was impoverished.

According to Wim Dierckxsens, after a decade of economic growth and capital accumulation, neoliberalism since the 1970s and 1980s has been seeking financial capital growth at the expense of local markets throughout the world. This model of neoliberal capital accumulation is called globalization, a policy that has resulted in labor exploitation and the destruction of local economies. Eventually this is detrimental to economic growth. For example, in Latin America, since the 1980s, there has been a crisis of external debt and loss of economic dynamism.[3]

Emerging from the violent era of military dictatorship in the 1980s, Latin Americans hoped that democracy would bring about social justice for the poor. Unfortunately, this did not happen. Petras and Veltmeyer argue that weak governments in Latin America were forced to accept free market capitalism dictated by the United States, which benefitted only the elite and the influential sector of the society. In fact,

---

1. James Petras and Henry Veltmeyer, *Imperialism and Capitalism in the Twenty-First Century: A System in Crisis* (Farnham: Ashgate Publishing Company, 2013), 19-20. For a comprehensive understanding of economic history, see Thomas Piketty, *Capital in the Twenty-First Century* (Cambridge, MA: The Belknap Press of Harvard University Press, 2014).
2. Ibid., 6.
3. Wim Dierckxsens, "The End of Neo-Liberalism, Unsustainable Capitalism, and the Need for a New Utopia," *Concilium* (December 2004), 15-16.

poverty increased from 40 to 44 percent by the 1990s. Workers suffered the most because of low wages and rising inflation.[1] Time and again, capitalism has shown itself incapable of a reform that would lead to a more humane and just society. Capitalism "provides a very poor model for changing society in the direction of social equality, participatory democratic decision-making, and human welfare – 'another world,' as proponents of an emerging radical consensus understand it, *i.e.* as beyond both neoliberalism and capitalism."[2] Dierckxsens baldly concludes that, capitalism has reached a point in history where it is impossible to link investment to production with profitable outcome.[3] This means that, under the existing economic framework and social relationships, improvement of people's standard of living, especially among the poor, is no longer possible, in spite of investments by multinational corporations.

In the opinion of Petras and Veltmeyer, in Latin America, a more humane form of development can be achieved by adopting socialism, which involves re-organizing the economy in the direction of social equality. Socialism also includes the "socialization of consumption if not production" so as to ensure a more equitable distribution of wealth. This involves providing social welfare for the poor, reforming taxation policy, promoting "participatory democracy" in the workplace, the "nationalization of the big banks" and the "regulation of financial institutions" in the interest of the public. [4]

According to Petras and Veltmeyer, "socialism would begin the transition from a capitalist economy directed by mercenary predators and swindlers and a state at their command, to an economy of public ownership under democratic control."[5] This would ensure that the dictatorship of money and the rule of the capitalist class would not dominate society. One of those who fought against such dictatorship in Latin America and paid for it with his life was Ellacuría.

---

1. Petras and Veltmeyer, *Imperialism and Capitalism in the Twenty-First Century*, 8. By the end of the 1990s, the income of the 300 wealthiest people in the world is more than the income of the two million poor people. Dierckxsens, "The End of Neo-Liberalism, Unsustainable Capitalism, and the Need for a New Utopia," 21.
2. Petras and Veltmeyer, *Imperialism and Capitalism in the Twenty-First Century*, 148.
3. Dierckxsens, "The End of Neo-Liberalism, Unsustainable Capitalism, and the Need for a New Utopia," 24.
4. Petras and Veltmeyer, *Imperialism and Capitalism in the Twenty-First Century*, 149.
5. Ibid.

## Confrontation with Social Reality

Ellacuría was committed to fighting for the poor; he sought to confront social reality in Latin America in more concrete and material ways; his belief was that a different world was not only possible but necessary.

First, Ellacuría emphasizes that human knowledge has an essentially biological function, which is the preservation of life. Therefore, if the theologian speaks of "life in abundance," as promised in the Gospel, he must understand it in the context of biological life. The point is that we should not spiritualize nor idealize the teachings of Christ. Ellacuría writes:

> Only from the senses and in references to the senses, which are, more than anything else, biological functions and serve primarily to keep the living being alive, can human intelligence be effective. Moreover, human intelligence is, of itself and formally, a biological activity, insofar as its initial function, for which it emerged, as well as its permanent exercise, are oriented towards assuring the biological viability of the human being, both as individual and as species.[1]

Second, due to its biological orientation, the fundamental aim of human knowledge is not about finding meaning, which is a derivative activity, but to understand reality. If we indulge in this search for meaning, we disregard the formal condition of knowledge. For Ellacuría, real knowledge involves: "a confrontation of the human being with himself/herself and with other things as real things – things which only through their essential relation to human beings can have this or that meaning for them. To confront oneself with things as real things means that one 'confronts things as they are.'"[2] This confrontation can be carried out by facing the reality of things instead of getting lost in ideas about things; by taking charge of the demands of reality as an ethical duty; by taking the cause of reality seriously by committing oneself to a "praxis" or guided action. Ellacuría also points out that theological knowledge is not only contemplative but is also "praxis-oriented."[3]

---

1. "Hacia una Fundamentación del Método Teológico Latino-Americano," *Estudios Centroamericanos* (1975): 418-19, quoted in Georges de Schrijver, "The Distinctive Contribution of Ignacio Ellacuría to a Praxis of Liberation," *Louvain Studies* 25, no. 4 (2000), 321. Ellacuría's philosophy of liberation was influenced by Xavier Zubiri, the supervisor for his doctoral dissertation.
2. Quoted in de Schrijver, "The Distinctive Contribution of Ignacio Ellacuría to a Praxis of Liberation," 322.
3. Ibid.

Third, human knowledge is not only historical but that "historicity belongs to its essential structure." This means "the content of our knowledge always has a very precise, historical character." Further, theological knowledge, which is part of human knowledge, "is woven into a specific social structure and social interests." Knowledge is supposed to be autonomous but Ellacuría wanted to reveal how knowledge is being used and for whom. In other words, "a hermeneutical reading of normative texts should critically examine and uncover the social roots and intentions of certain statements, without immediately blocking the road to creative breakthroughs."[1]

The social reality that Ellacuría had to confront is the enormous gap between the rich and the poor, developed countries and developing countries, the Global North and the Global South, social exploitation and environmental degradation. He saw capitalism as a calculating power that cared little about the welfare of the people – in other words, that capitalism could not guarantee a decent standard of living for humanity. In fact, in his final days before he was killed, Ellacuría had concluded that "our civilization is gravely ill." [2]People in many parts of the globe are being threatened with economic inequalities, military conflicts and forced migration which exposes the harshness and brutality of this world. While many people welcomed the prospect of globalization, Ellacuría held that those tributes to globalization were parochial, misleading and self-serving.

While Ellacuría thought of globalization as parochial, Felix Wilfred also denies its claim of universality. Wilfred holds that many people are disenchanted by past utopias because they "mystify human consciousness" and fail to help victims to attain their realistic goal. Today, globalization is playing the same "mystical role" as a project bent on restoring capitalism.[3]

Unlike revolutions led by the masses, the wealthy nations are keen to promote globalization to expand their markets. Through globalization, the elites enriched themselves at the expense of the majority, which eventually resulted in conflict and domination. Wilfred holds that "globalization is a mystification which is naked violence dressed up in respectable apparel for public appeal."[4] The widening gap between the rich and poor, the economic inequalities between nations, have exposed the falsity and supremacy of the market system.

---

1. Ibid.
2. Sobrino, "On the Way to Healing," 21.
3. Felix Wilfred, "Searching for David's Sling: Tapping the Local Resources of Hope," *Concilium* (December 2004), 86.
4. Ibid.

## Wealth and Poverty

According to Ellacuría, the theme of wealth and poverty is not just a religious issue, it is also a sociological issue, and, thus, it has to do with the human relationship with God. He perceives wealth as one of the greatest hindrances to the building of the kingdom of God on earth. The history of salvation reveals to us that the locus of God's revelation and salvation is poverty and not wealth. Before the prophets appeared in the Old Testament, material wealth was viewed as a blessing from God. However, the material prosperity of a few came to be seen as the result of the exploitation of the defenceless poor. The prophets spoke against wealth insofar as wealth was the actual cause of poverty and this denunciation reaches its high point in the New Testament. Jesus' poverty gives Him absolute freedom in relation to the powers of this world.[1] The theme of poverty and wealth is thus for Ellacuría a significant socio-theological term, as we shall see.

Ellacuría was convinced that wealth causes and produces poverty, and, thus, one is forced to choose to be with the oppressor or with those being oppressed. It is very clearly stated in the scriptures that the locus of God's revelation is among the poor. The Evangelist, Luke, regards wealth as dishonest (Luke 16:9): "The Pharisees, who were lovers of money, heard all this, and they ridiculed him." So, he said to them, "You are those who justify yourselves in the sight of others; but God knows your hearts; for what is prized by human beings is an abomination in the sight of God" (Luke 16:14-16). The text here allows no compromise – it not just condemning unjust wealth, but wealth itself because of its connection with poverty.[2] In other words, someone becomes wealthy always at the expense of the poor.

The denunciation of wealth is also related to our relationship with God: "No slave can serve two masters; for a slave will either hate the one and love the other, or be devoted to the one and despise the other. You cannot serve God and wealth" (Luke 16:13). According to Luke, prosperity and wealth cause people to forget God's rule because wealth has the tendency to become an absolute value, which eventually leads people into idolatry.

In Ellacuría's opinion, idolatry is not just denying God's existence or worshipping wealth, it takes the form of viewing God as "the Lord of the Wealthy."[3] This gives people excuses for accumulating wealth for

1. Ignacio Ellacuría, *Freedom Made Flesh: The Mission of Christ and His Church*, translated by John Drury (Maryknoll, NY: Orbis Books, 1976), 34.
2. Ibid., 36.
3. Ibid.

themselves. Hence, a capitalist interpretation of Christianity goes against the real meaning of Christ's message: "As for what was sown among thorns, this is the one who hears the word, but the cares of the world and the lure of wealth choke the word, and it yields nothing" (Matthew 13: 22). Hence, wealth makes it difficult for the Word of God to flourish in people's lives as the example of the rich young man in the gospel reveals to us (Mark 10:17-31 and Matthew 19:16-30).

The story reveals to us that merely keeping the commandments does not make us Christian: "The Christian is not an ethical creature engaged in keeping commandments."[1] He is someone who follows Christ by giving up his wealth and distributing it to the poor. Thus, only those who are free of wealth can have the freedom to follow Jesus. The young man's wealth did not prevent him from hearing God's call but it did prevent him from making a commitment. Thus, "it is easier for a camel to go through the eye of a needle than for someone who is rich to enter the kingdom of God" (Matthew 19:24).

Possessing wealth is definitely an obstacle to gaining eternal life. Convinced that the sickness of this world is caused by the "civilization" of wealth, Ellacuría desired a change in direction in the way society is organized in order, as he saw it, to avoid a major catastrophe; he proposed a "civilization" of poverty.

## The Civilization of Poverty

Ellacuría wished for an entirely different world, superior to the civilization of wealth pushing our planet towards its destruction. In what he called the "excremental historical analysis" or "the study of the faeces of our civilization," he exposed the sickness of society resulting from widespread inequality and injustice.[2] Ellacuría called for a "civilization of poverty" which "rejects the accumulation of capital as the motor of history. . . . It makes the satisfying of basic needs the principle of development."[3] Poverty no longer meant deprivation of necessities. This new civilization would guarantee the satisfaction of basic needs, the freedom of individuals and the creativity of the community. The civilization of poverty allows for the emergence of new ways of life and forms of culture where new relationships between human beings and nature, as well as with the divine, are cultivated.

---

1. Ibid., 38.
2. Ellacuría, "El Desafío de las Mayorías Pobres," quoted in Sobrino, "Fifty Years for a Future That Is Christian and Human," 73.
3. Ellacuría, "Utopia y Profetismo," *Revista Latinoamericana de Teologia*, 17 (1990), quoted in Sobrino, "Fifty Years for a Future That Is Christian and Human," 74.

Ellacuría viewed poverty by contrast with and in opposition to wealth, which drives and defines our present civilization. In a world of wealth and crass materialism, poverty can act as an antidote to a sick civilization where the gap between the rich and the poor is widening. The present global economy is driven by "capital-wealth dynamism," marked by sin and leading to death.[1] Poverty offers a different kind of dynamism:

> This poverty is a poverty that really gives the spirit space, no longer swamping it with the desperate need to have more than the next person, by the desperate lust for all sorts of superfluous things, when most of the human race lacks the basic necessities. Then it will be possible for the spirit to flourish, and the immense spiritual and human wealth of the poor and peoples of the Third World, which is today choked by desperate poverty and by the imposition of cultural models that may in some ways be more developed but for all that are not more fully human.[2]

As the Indian theologian Felix Wilfred testifies:

> Affluence creates a weak person and a fragile culture. On the other hand, the confrontation with human suffering and response in terms of compassion has developed in the victims some of the values we require to sustain a different world – solidarity, humanness, the spirit of sharing, the technique of survival, readiness to take risks and steely determination in the midst of adversities.[3]

These values are embodied in the lives of the poor and marginal, who can offer resistance to the existing global system that promotes an expansionist and assimilationist ideology, denying pluralism and human uniqueness. Although the expansion of the market and capitalism is taking place all over the world, it is not *universal*, for universality is "a spiritual quality of transcendence:" "universality . . . is not to be confounded with ubiquity."[4]

"True universality is possible only where there is sacrifice and renunciation." This requires the ability to move beyond one's own cultural, ethnic or national identity. The universal is present "at the local level in the

---

1. Ibid., 75.
2. Ignacio Ellacuría, "Misión Actual de la Compañia de Jesus," *Revista Latinoamericana de Teologia*, 29 (1993), quoted in Sobrino, "Fifty Years for a Future That Is Christian and Human," 76.
3. Wilfred, "Searching for David's Sling," 88.
4. Ibid., 92.

experience of subordinated peoples, the illiterate villagers and powerless identities." Subordinated people are more willing to make sacrifices than the wealthy: "The poor are attuned to the spirit of genuine universality promising hope for our world, while the worldwide expansion of selfish pursuit is not. The latter is the enemy of universality."[1] Consequently, poor and marginal people can be considered: "guardians of peace and . . . defenders of genuine universalism. At the grassroots level the common struggle for survival brings people together." The xenophobia of the West towards immigrants and refugees "stands in stark contrast to the compassion and deep humanity with which simple people accept each other and help each other . . . without regard to ethnic, religious or linguistic background."[2]

The Church is deeply involved with both of the two sectors of civilization, that of wealth and that of poverty. The old Christendom of wealth and empire may have disappeared in modern times but, as Johann Baptist Metz has shown, a bourgeois Christianity has taken its place.[3] Left to themselves, Churches and religions tend to forget their messianic vocation because of institutional concerns, political interests, and bureaucracy. Nonetheless, messianic impulses at times emerge in spirituality and mysticism, social reform movements and even in martyrdom, as in the case of Ignacio Ellacuría. The Church in Latin America has revealed to us that living faith and religious practice can be revolutionary and transformative, so that a different world, where compassion prevails, becomes possible.

## The Centrality of Compassion

Metz argues that, for Christianity to be authentic, it must emphasize the centrality of compassion at the heart of its teaching. As Jon Sobrino explains:

> For Metz compassion is . . . a primary reaction to another person's suffering. It possesses a political dimension, in that a merely private attitude . . . is not enough. And since it has to be exercised in the midst of oppression and repression, it has to become *justice*.[4]

---

1. Ibid.
2. Ibid., 93.
3. On bourgeois Christianity, see Johann Baptist Metz, *The Emergent Church: The Future of Christianity in a Postbourgeois World*, translated by Peter Mann (London: SCM, 1981).
4. Sobrino, "Fifty Years for a Future That Is Christian and Human," 70.

In the Gospels, Metz observes, Jesus is more attentive to the sufferings of others than to their sins. He is, nevertheless, very critical of the sin of hypocrisy committed by the scribes and Pharisees – the religious authorities. Unfortunately, however,

> Christianity very soon began to have serious difficulties with this fundamental sensitivity to other people's sufferings, which is inherent in its message. The worrying question about justice for the innocent who suffer, which is at the heart of the biblical traditions, was transformed, with excessive haste, into the issue of the salvation of sinners.[1]

Perhaps this rapid shift from focussing on sufferings to sins gave the Church more power over the souls of its members. But as a result, the messianic-prophetic elements in the Gospel have increasingly been ignored, and the messianic-prophetic elements in Christianity have been domesticated by political, economic and technological developments in a globalized world.

## Messianic Christianity

The Dominican Claude Geffré has argued that, while Christianity stresses the political character of Jewish messianism, it has also over-emphasized the spiritual character of Jesus' messianism and thus seems to neglect the historical nature of salvation. It is a good sign that the Church since the 1960s has begun to rediscover the messianic aspect of the Christian faith:

> the power to transform history which implies the announcement of the kingdom of God in word and deed. Exegetes and theologians have shown in particular how the eschatology of the New Testament transforms the promises of the First Testament, which announces the future of a kingdom of justice and peace on earth, without abolishing them. The kingdom proclaimed by Jesus is not of this world, but it can already have its anticipation in the course of history.[2]

---

1. Johann Baptist Metz, "La Compasión: Un Programa Universal del Cristianismo en la Época de Pluralismo Cultural y Religioso," *Revista Latinoamericana de Teologia*, 55 (2001), 27, quoted in Sobrino, "Fifty Years for a Future That Is Christian and Human," 70. Translated as "Towards a Christianity of Political Compassion," in María Pilar Aquino, Kevin F. Burke and Robert Anthony Lassalle-Klein, eds., *Love That Produces Hope: The Thought of Ignacio Ellacuría* (Minnesota: Michael Glazier, 2006), 250.
2. Claude Geffré, "The God of Jesus and the Possibilities of History," *Concilium*

The messianic elements in the Gospel entail standing by the poor and the disenfranchised against the rich and powerful; as Mary proclaims in the Magnificat: "He has brought down the powerful from their thrones, and lifted up the lowly; he has filled the hungry with good things, and sent the rich away empty" (Luke 1:51-53). The Vatican II document *Gaudium et Spes* attempts to align the Church with the contemporary world by taking the side of the poor and afflicted:

> The joys and the hopes, the griefs and the anxieties of the men of this age, especially those who are poor or in any way afflicted, these are the joys and hopes, the griefs and anxieties of the followers of Christ. Indeed, nothing genuinely human fails to raise an echo in their hearts.[1]

Unfortunately, what we still have today in many places is a bourgeois Christianity that ignores the plight of the poor.

## Bourgeois Christianity

According to the German political scientist Iring Fetscher,

> The rise of the "bourgeoisie" is accompanied by: the triumph of the modern sciences and technology, the individualistic calculation of utility as the basic rule of life, the legitimation of individual love as the basis of communal life, the rejection of any non-democratic foundation for state power, a high regard for work, industry and thrift as typical "bourgeois" virtues (to which cleanliness and tidiness are subsequently added).[2]

Such individualism, he writes, can lead to: "egoism and cold calculation. 'Every man for himself – and God for all.'"[3] For the bourgeoisie, diligent work is a means of accumulating wealth, and they are also interested in possessing more and more – what counts is what they have, the level of income that ensures they live well, at least in the material sense. This means that buying power is very important to them, and they thrive in a modern industrial society driven by capitalism. Thus, the bourgeois principle is essentially destructive because it turns human beings into

---

(December 2004),73.

1. *Gaudium et Spes*, n. 1.
2. Iring Fetscher, "The 'Bourgeoisie' ('*Bürgertum*,' Middle Class): On the Historical and Political Semantics of the Term," *Concilium*, 125 (December 1979), 9.
3. Ibid., 10.

competitors and undermines human solidarity. This bourgeois ideology has had a pervasive influence on Christianity in the West and has also spread to other parts of the world.

Karl Barth holds that the bourgeois person interprets the Gospels to suit his or her comfortable lifestyle and endorses what God has taught "as a matter for consideration, which he can accept, but of which he is fundamentally the master, which does not cause him any inconvenience, indeed in the possession of which he is doubly secure, justified and rich." Regarding the danger of "making the Gospel respectable" and the domestication of Christ's teaching in the Church, Barth also speaks of how such a person may accept the Gospel message "peacefully and at once make himself its lord and possessor, thus rendering it innocuous." He can thus justify all his actions by "being a believer along with all the other things he is, by making even the Gospel into a means of his self-preservation and self-defence!"[1] The bourgeois person tailors the Word of God according to his or her will and interests. Barth calls this "natural theology."

Focussing on the United States, the theologian and sociologist Gregory Baum considers how bourgeois Christianity emphasizes personal salvation:

> Middle class individualism has its spiritual counterpart: the emphasis on personal salvation. Here Jesus is seen as the saviour who rescues us one by one from the catastrophe of history. . . . This approach can lead to such a concentration on the individual that life after death becomes the entire religious preoccupation.[2]

This approach leads to a tendency to neglect the social dimension of Christianity. It is predominantly Protestant, although Catholicism has shown some elements of it with its emphasis on sin and guilt. Middle-class Christianity tends to view sin as a very private notion and thus the injustices that are prevalent in our institutions and society are largely overlooked. The disadvantaged in society are also ignored, because bourgeois Christians are focussed only on their own community and concerned only about their own salvation. As Baum continues:

> Middle-class piety overlooks the enormous social gaps between people and believes that the Christian message has the same meaning for all, beyond the differences of class. . . . To respond to

---

1. Karl Barth, *Church Dogmatics: Volume 2 – The Doctrine of God*, translated by T.H.L. Parker *et al.* (Edinburgh: T. & T. Clark, 1964 [1934]), n.26, 141.
2. Gregory Baum, "Middle-Class Religion in America," *Concilium*, 125 (December 1979), 21.

world hunger a preacher will ask people to opt for a more modest life and a simpler diet without any awareness that some families in the congregation are unable to feed their children properly.[1]

Bourgeois Christianity, Baum concludes, "easily speaks of unity and reconciliation. It disguises the real conflicts in the community and the inequality of power and pretends that love can unite all people in a common humanity."[2] It naively believes that love conquers all, even the gap between rich and poor nations. To counteract this distorting process, a political theology has developed, which attempts to expose the largely individualistic and utilitarian ideological nature of bourgeois Christianity.

## Political Theology

Theology is defined as God-talk and the relationship of the human person with God. Politics refers to the use of structural power to organize our society and community. In this sense, political theology is "the analysis and criticism of political arrangements (including cultural-psychological, social, and economic aspects) from the perspective of differing interpretations of God's ways with the world."[3] Theology tends to reflect and affirm unjust political structures, and thus, the aim of political theology is to expose the ways in which theological teachings actually reinforce economic and social inequalities. In exposing these inequalities, political theology aims to serve the cause of justice. In this section, I would like to focus on the political theology of Johann Baptist Metz.

Regarding Metz's theological approach, he embraces modernity and supports the "formal re-orientation of thought away from the world towards man, away from nature towards history, away from substance to the subject and its free subjectivity, in short, away from a more 'cosmocentric' towards an 'anthropocentric' way of thinking, the historical beginning of which we commonly connect with the beginning of the modern period."[4] As Barth has observed, Christianity has often been domesticated to serve the interest of the ruling party and wealthy elites. Christianity has also been used as a tranquilizer to numb the pain and sufferings of the oppressed. But, in actual fact, our Christian faith

1. Baum, "Middle-Class Religion in America," 21.
2. Ibid., 21-2.
3. Peter Scott and William T. Cavanaugh, "Introduction," in *The Blackwell Companion to Political Theology* (Oxford: Blackwell Publishing Ltd, 2004), 1.
4. Johann B. Metz, *Theology of the World*, translated by W. Glen-Doepel (London: Burns & Oates/Herder & Herder, Inc., 1969), 57.

should bear witness to the true spirit of the Gospel and challenge the status quo of the establishment. Through his interest in the Frankfurt School, Metz's theology has become markedly political.[1] He is convinced that theology must utilize the tools of social and political science, such as Marxism, to gain a better insight and understanding of divine revelation.

Metz adopts a positive approach towards the secular and sees in the secularization process the redemptive work of God within human history. And so, he maintains a keen interest in the social and political implication of the Gospel. He challenges those who view secularization as contrary to the Christian faith. For Metz, these so-called "anti-secularists" treat salvation history as something outside history and therefore fail to recognize the working of the Spirit in the contemporary world. For him, secularization does not mean "Christianity is disappearing, but that it has become truly historically effective."[2] In other words, the spirit of Christianity is embedded in world history.

Christology forms the basis of Metz's understanding of the process of secularization. According to him, the theology of history is primarily concerned with an understanding of the world as constituted in Christ and this understanding in turn "lives from the historical power of the framework for the world given in Christ."[3] Christianity is not against secularization; in fact, "a genuinely Christian impulse is working itself out historically in this modern process of an increased secularization of the world."[4]

Regarding the Pauline injunction, "Do not be conformed to this world" (Romans 12:2), Metz argues that this teaching should not be interpreted as abandoning the world, but as a constructive involvement marked by a readiness "to be prepared for a painful estrangement from the present world situation."[5] In its engagement with the world, the Church must adopt a militant theology with its hopes for "an eschatological order of justice, the humanizing of man and the establishing of a universal peace."[6] Metz also views Christian asceticism not as a flight from the world but rather as taking responsibility for the plight and suffering of humanity. For him, true asceticism involves sacrifice, service, solidarity, and "a mysticism of fraternity."[7]

---

1.  John Marsden, "The Political Theology of Johannes Baptist Metz," *Heythrop Journal* 53, no. 3 (May 2012), 440. See also Walter Benjamin, "On the Frankfurt School," *Cités*, 2010, 149-59.
2.  Metz, *Theology of the World*, 16.
3.  Ibid., 33.
4.  Ibid., 35.
5.  Ibid., 93.
6.  Ibid., 96.
7.  Ibid., 104.

In Metz's political theology, he attempts to formulate an eschatological message in the context of our present society. In other words, the eschatological message must be proclaimed in the midst of social and political realities. Further, if theology fails to see human existence as political, then it cannot perform a critical function that "delivers faith up to modern ideologies."[1] A transcendental, personal, and existential theology that focusses on the individual would tend to neglect the eschatological promises of justice, peace, and reconciliation. To counteract this individualistic tendency, Metz insists that "the deprivatizing of theology is the primary critical task of political theology."[2]

Christ's identification with the poor and oppressed and his announcement of the kingdom of God still have a powerful effect in our present times. Metz considers this solidarity with the poor a dangerous and subversive memory because it "anticipates the future as a future of those who are oppressed, without hope and doomed to fail."[3] This memory should jolt us out of our complacency and help us to enter into solidarity with suffering humanity. Regarding those who ignore the plight of the poor and suffering, Metz writes: "the imagination of future freedom is nourished from the memory of suffering, and freedom degenerates wherever those who suffer are treated more or less as a cliché and degraded to a faceless mass."[4] In other words, human suffering cannot be ignored. In fact, the memory of suffering "brings a new moral imagination into political life, a new vision of others' suffering which should mature into a generous, uncalculating partisanship on behalf of the weak and unrepresented."[5]

Metz understands Christianity as "dangerous memory" and therefore as Christians we cannot "remain neutral in the struggle for worldwide solidarity for the sake of the needy and the underprivileged."[6] The memory of Christ is also a "dangerous memory" for those who take part in evil doings. With this kind of political theology, liberation theology in Latin America cannot remain politically neutral: the Church is either on the side of the poor or on the side of the rich, those without power or those with power. Ignacio Ellacuría insists that the mission of the Church today is to proclaim liberation, justice and love for the poor and disinherited.

---

1. Ibid., 111.
2. Ibid., 110.
3. Johannes B. Metz, *Faith in History and Society: Toward a Practical Fundamental Theology*, translated by David Smith (New York: A Crossroad Book, The Seabury Press, 1980), 90.
4. Ibid., 112-13.
5. Ibid., 117-18.
6. Ibid., 235.

## The Mission of the Church

Ellacuría believed that the Church could proclaim liberation, justice and love without falling into either what he called "angelism" or "secularism." The Church, he said, "is above the danger of a wholly inner and subjectivist interpretation of salvation, and also above the danger of a wholly secularist and politicizing interpretation."[1] Liberation is a historical process in which we encounter the God who saves us. "People came to feel that development, even integral development, could not serve today as the mediating tool of salvation; that liberation would have to play the role instead."[2] Although "liberation" does "move into the whole area of political and societal behavior," Ellacuría held that the term is more than just political because it proclaims "a salvation that runs through history but also goes above and beyond history."[3]

In the Old Testament, it is clear that the chosen people understand the meaning of salvation through a political experience of liberation. Ellacuría believes this is the way God chose to reveal his true nature to his people. The Exodus is in actual fact an experience of political liberation because it was concerned with the socio-political oppression of the Hebrew people who had begun to learn about God and his ways. The theology of the chosen people began when they tried to figure out their own role in history. According to Ellacuría, "One can scarcely overstress the importance of the Exodus in giving configuration to Yahweh's revelation to his people, nor the reality of socio-political experience in mediating the salvation demonstrated in the Exodus."[4]

The prophets in the Old Testament also advance the religious experience of the chosen people by attacking oppressors and oppression. They condemn rulers, priests, unjust judges and those in power who were oppressing and exploiting the people. The prophets also criticize economic inequalities as well as foreign imperialism. It was the prophets' heightened sense of awareness of human beings' closeness to God that

---

1. Ellacuría, *Freedom Made Flesh*, 95.
2. Ibid., 96. "Integral development" is expounded in Paul VI's encyclical *Populorum Progressio*, n.14, which states: "The development we speak of here cannot be restricted to economic growth alone. To be authentic, it must be well rounded; it must foster the development of each man and of the whole man."
3. Ellacuría, *Freedom Made Flesh*, 98.
4. Ibid., 99. Jung Mo Sung reminds us that the Exodus did not result in the end of oppression in the Old and New Testaments. Faith in Christ's resurrection gives Christians hope that the kingdom of God will be fully realized one day: Jung Mo Sung, "Economics and Spirituality: Towards a More Just and Sustainable World," *Concilium* (2004), 109.

enabled them to attack inequalities and exploitation. Hence, those who claim that the Church has misunderstood its vocation or has "lost the inner tension and thrust of faith" because of its commitment to socio-political issues should re-read the prophetic literature of the Old Testament to re-evaluate their own judgment.[1]

The psalmists too speak of the importance of liberation, which is not confined to the socio-political sphere but in fact touches on every aspect of oppression. The psalmists speak of liberation from sin, death, sickness, and enemies. In the psalms, we experience the cry of liberation, which seems to suggest that human beings in history have been oppressed by all kinds of unjust domination and exploitation. The psalms suggest that liberation and salvation are one and the same thing. It is a good sign that human liberation is now understood as part and parcel of salvation. Within the liturgy, the psalms have a distinctive socio-political emphasis, although it is addressed directly to God himself. The socio-political arena seems to be "the privileged locale for encountering God."[2] Thus it is the "historical responsibility" of all Christians and "anonymous Christians" to provide history with "a human face."[3] In other words, Christians and all people of goodwill have the responsibility to create a more humane world.

Ellacuría warns that an excessively pietistic and personal reading of the New Testament would lead us to overlook the important connection between the two testaments and also the socio-political character of the New Testament. Luke gives us a very good hermeneutical device to help us understand the relationship between the Old and New Testaments. In his first public teaching, Jesus invokes the prophetic tradition by quoting from the text of Isaiah: "The Spirit of the Lord is upon me, because he has anointed me to bring good news to the poor. He has sent me to proclaim release to the captives and recovery of sight to the blind, to let the oppressed go free, to proclaim the year of the Lord's favour" (Luke 4:18-19). Jesus proclaims that these words are fulfilled in his person. Thus, the interrelationship between the Old and New Testaments "is made clear in the fact that Jesus frames his public life in the prophetic line of the Isaiah text, for that prophetic tradition proclaims the yearning of the nation for restoration and liberation."[4]

As we have observed, there is no doubt that Jesus' life has an essentially socio-political character although it is not limited to it. However, according to Ellacuría, "the fact remains that the overall incarnation

---

1. Ibid., 100.
2. Ibid.
3. Geffré, "The God of Jesus and the Possibilities of History," 73.
4. Ellacuría, *Freedom Made Flesh*, 101.

of his message in the contemporary situation led him into continuing collision with those in power who were oppressing his people; and he never evaded this confrontation."[1] Ellacuría adds that, in criticizing the priests and the Pharisees, Jesus was fighting against the existing socio-economic powers by his emphasis on the "dialectic of wealth versus poverty."[2] Indirectly, Jesus was fighting against the state that was perpetuating the unjust condition. It was a threefold fight that gave Jesus' activity a political dimension and he was ultimately killed for political reasons. In other words, Jesus' activity was seen as "meddlesome" to those who held power in a situation that was unjust. Ellacuría puts it this way: "It seemed to represent interference in the political realm – which was really the objectification of a sinful condition."[3] In other words, Jesus was indirectly fighting against a sinful structure that perpetuates injustice and oppression of the poor.

In the Sermon on the Mount, the socio-historical dimension of Jesus' teaching is clearly revealed – those who enjoy power and wealth in this world have no place in the kingdom of God because they refuse to share their resources with the majority of humanity who are hungry, thirsty, and naked. Ellacuría says Jesus' blessings and condemnation are framed within this "dialectical relationship."[4] In the Epistle to James, "faith by itself, if it does not have works, is dead" (James 2:17). Emphasizing the socio-political aspect of this teaching, Ellacuría holds that Christians should rejoice because liberation, a historical necessity, gives theological foundation to the themes of progress and development: "If theology and pastoral concern want to proclaim Christian liberation, they need only immerse themselves in salvation history. Liberation is absolutely essential to the Gospel message."[5] Thus liberation is now understood as salvation, which the Church has a duty to proclaim.

## Christian Liberation

In the interaction between liberation and salvation, Christian liberation avoids the two extremes of viewing liberation in purely immanent terms and purely transcendental terms. "The distinctive character of Christian liberation is to be found in the fact that it entails liberation from something and liberation for something." In this way, liberation has a positive direction, moving towards something new. Liberation

1. Ibid.
2. Ibid., 102.
3. Ibid.
4. Ibid.
5. Ibid., 103.

is liberation from sin, which is not merely "a purely spiritual fault that only indirectly affects the world of human beings." According to Ellacuría:

> There is an historical objectification of sin, and it is absolutely necessary to maintain the distinction between personal sin and objectified sin. In the concrete, anything that positively and unjustly stands in the way of human liberty is sin. It is sin because it prevents a human being from being a human being, depriving him or her of the liberty that properly belongs to a child of God. Sin is the formal exercise of an act of radical injustice.[1]

Sin is not just something that is personal, interior and subjective, it affects the whole community. "Sin is seen as the absolute negation and denial of the absolute in reality."[2] There is such a thing as structural sin, a state of sin that perpetuates injustice and oppression.

## A Sign of Credibility

The work of Christian liberation, which involves the struggle against injustice and the effort to facilitate love, is a sign of credibility for the Church. Ellacuría wrote: "The Church dedicates itself to liberation because it is the very essence of its mission, because it is an inescapable obligation in its service to the world."[3] Furthermore, "The only limits on the Church in its service to the world are those limits which are intrinsic to its mission itself. It is senseless to worry about whether the Church is meddling in politics when it is carrying out its liberative mission." Jesus never shirked the responsibilities of his mission, even when the religious and political authorities condemned him for interfering in the secular world.[4]

The Church has not always been faithful to its mission of fighting against injustice. In fact, it has contributed much towards injustice and oppression in the world. Ellacuría said:

> The Church has contributed to injustice by acts of commission and omission, abetting oppression to a greater or lesser degree. It must face this fact and acknowledge it. It is a fact within the Church itself, where respect for the human person and personal rights [have] often been subordinated to other, inferior values,

---

1. Ibid., 104.
2. Ibid., 105.
3. Ibid., 110.
4. Ibid., 111.

with the result that the institutional aspect has often stifled the primary and essential aspect of interpersonal communion and community. The Church's words have proclaimed one thing while its deeds have proclaimed something very different. As a result, it has gradually lost credibility in the eyes of many.[1]

The Church has been serving the established order rather than making an effort to bring about a new order where justice can prevail. Its failings are obvious and have been increasing, Ellacuría lamented. "The Church has often done more to serve the preservation of the natural order than to abet the social transformation of history."[2] It has reinforced unjust structures instead of trying to alleviate injustice and has adopted, not a civilization of poverty, but a civilization of wealth.

Ellacuría also believed that the Church "has not gone far enough to face up to its sinful character." All of us who make up the Church must admit this. Sin resides not only in its members but also in the Church as an institution. "As such [the Church] should serve as a concrete sign of conformation to Christ, but it has frequently conformed itself more to the world of sin." It has not always been "a radiant sign of God's justice and Christ's *kenosis*." Thus, Ellacuría held that, if the Church "does not effectively undergo . . . painful conversion, if it does not endure the humiliation of Good Friday, then it cannot expect the glory of resurrection or its acceptance by the world."[3] But, if the Church can undergo this conversion, then salvation resides in it.

In addition, the Church must "take positive action in the fight against injustice." It must direct its activity towards battling against the sin of injustice and oppression. The Church must also *denounce* injustice as sin "publicly, incessantly and forthrightly," and at the same time *announce* the necessity of dying to oneself in order to experience the resurrection. "This calls for a radical conversion in history, for *metanoia* in the individual and revolution in existing structures. . . . Personal conversion must have impact in the area of structural change if this conversion is to attain its full objectification in history."[4]

History, as well as the Bible, has shown us that:

> it is the oppressed that will liberate the oppressor. . . . The active nay-saying of the oppressed is what will redeem the sin-laden yea-saying of the oppressor. There is real interaction between

---

1. Ibid., 113.
2. Ibid., 114.
3. Ibid.
4. Ibid., 115.

oppressor and oppressed, but the activity of the former tends to maintain the state of oppression whereas that of the latter tends to eliminate it rather than merely seek revenge.[1]

The Church, thus, must "identify itself with the struggle of the oppressed." Naturally it will end up in conflict with those in power. But this in itself is a real sign that the Church is dedicated to the cause of justice and "the clearest proof of its Christian character. In acting thus, the Church will be following the purest strain of salvation history. That is what the prophets did; that is what Jesus himself did."[2] In practical terms, this means embracing a civilization of poverty, allowing Jesus Christ to reign over human beings so that the world becomes more human. This would bring about a world very different from the existing one.

## Possibilities of History

Claude Geffré suggests four ways to help create a better world. The first way is a purification of the memory. Following the example of John Paul II, the Church is called to repent for the sins of the past, such as the schisms in Christianity, the Crusades, the exclusions of the Jews, the wars of religions, and the treatment of black people. This approach must involve historical discernment to discover the real cause of deviation from Christian teaching. The sins of the past include false conversion of people of other venerable faiths. Vatican II emphasizes religious freedom, which includes dialogue among various religious traditions. Dialogue has led to the realization that religions do not exist to serve their own limited interests but are called upon to "serve the great causes which prod the universal conscience."[3] In other words, the role of religions is to promote peace in our globalized world.

The second way is to show respect for true humanity. Globalization has led to the dehumanization of society in many parts of the world. In view of this, followers of Christ must create a counter-culture in order to create a more humane society by promoting a global ethic on a planetary scale. The dialogue among religions is a real breakthrough. However, the building of a better world requires morality based on religious and secular ethics. All religions, including Christianity, must listen to "the call of universal human conscience and the legitimate aspiration" towards freedom and happiness.[4] This means that religions must reinterpret

1. Ibid.
2. Ibid., 116.
3. Geffré, "The God of Jesus and the Possibilities of History," 74.
4. Ibid., 75.

their teachings if they are found to be inhuman and, at the same time, secular ethics must learn from the wisdom of religious traditions. The great monotheistic religions, Judaism, Christianity, and Islam, must show that belief in a personal God and respect for true humanity are complementary.

The third way is the law of superabundance. Christianity has no monopoly over truth, justice, and solidarity. Therefore, Christians must rejoice at the triumph of humanitarian movements. Christians, non-Christians, and those who have no religion have observed the Golden Rule: "Do not do to others what you would not want them to do to you." At the same time, human conscience is fragile if left to its own devices or "inner demons."[1] Even a society with a strict rule of law can become oppressive and exploitative. When this happens, it needs to be replaced by a culture of peace and love. This means moving "beyond the rules of justice, which are the rules of equivalence, to another logic, that of the law of superabundance which takes us back to the paradox of the Gospel."[2] Thus, a different world is possible if we practise forgiveness, compassion, over and above the requirements of law or ethics, so that the disadvantaged can be protected. This is the best way to write history with a human face so that the kingdom of God can be realized.

The fourth way is an ecological justice. We are now just discovering that we need to defend human rights and respect the rights of the earth. The powers of science and technology are capable of destroying the ecological balance that sustains human life on this planet. In view of the destruction of environment caused by industrialization and modern living, we are called upon to "act in such a way that the effects of your actions are compatible with the permanence of an authentically human life on earth."[3] In sum, for the world to be different, it has to remain sustainable in two areas: ecology and ethics. This means protecting our planet and living together in peace and harmony by embracing pluralism.

Further, in the face of ecological disaster, we are called upon to renew our confidence in God who desires human beings to be His co-creators so that we can make this world more habitable. Just as God rested on the seventh day, humankind must learn "a sabbatical wisdom," which means to stop plundering and exploiting our natural resources.[4] The protection of our natural environment with gratuitousness, restraint, and silence is not a luxury but a matter of survival.

---

1. Ibid.
2. Ibid., 76.
3. Quoted in Geffré, "The God of Jesus and the Possibilities of History," 76.
4. Ibid., 76.

## Environmental Crisis

The importance of proclaiming a different world arises not only from a political and theological position of denying the absolute character of our existing world, but primarily from the very serious social, political, economic, and environmental crises brought about by globalization and neoliberal capitalism, so says Jung Mo Sung.[1] In other words, the existing socio-economic system is unjust and cannot be sustained.

The obsession with increasing economic growth and consumption is one of the main causes of the environmental crisis. The minority of affluent people in poor countries adopt the consumerist lifestyle of wealthy nations and this has led to the exploitation of poor people in their own countries and a decrease in social spending. Jon Sobrino warns us that a civilization of wealth is not possible because our limited world resources do not allow everyone to live like Europeans or North Americans. It is immoral to have a civilization of wealth for a few people because what "cannot be universalized cannot be a human solution" according to Kant.[2] Thus, "to the extent that the pressure of the global capitalist economy and the desire to imitate its pattern of consumption push economic and social processes in this direction of levelling up consumer spending and the frenetic quest for higher consumption, so social and environmental crises become worse."[3]

Advocates of capitalism claim that science, technology, and the free market will be able to give us a better life and overcome the limits of nature. In many developing nations, this has proven to be false and has led to the sufferings of countless people and the destruction of the earth. In fact, the unrestrained consumption of the affluent has led to the suffering, death of many human beings and the destruction of our environment. In other words, the capitalist system is unjust and harmful to our environment. In view of this, Christianity and other religions must develop theological or religious positions that can combat the worship of the market system and the false ideology of human progress.

---

1. Jung Mo Sung, "Economics and Spirituality: Towards a More Just and Sustainable World," 106.
2. Sobrino, "Turning Back History," 126.
3. Jung Mo Sung, "Economics and Spirituality: Towards a More Just and Sustainable World," 107.
3. Ibid., 109-10.
4. Ibid.

## Sustainable Systems

To have a different world, we need to ensure that our economic and social systems and environment are sustainable. The economic system must be capable of giving every human being a decent standard of living, beyond the minimum that can sustain life. Further, our society must promote social relationships and institutions that help all human beings to flourish. Jung Mo Sung, a Korean theologian living in Brazil, speaks of the need for "a cultural convergence and a spirituality"[3] that gives the individual a sense of belonging in society. There must exist "symbols, rites and myths" that unite people.[4] Unfortunately, the modern capitalist model idolizes the market and promotes it through mass media. Everything is reduced to the desire and not the need to consume: the philosophy seems to be "I consume, therefore I am" or "I shop, therefore I am."

## True Spiritual Revolution

It is not enough just to oppose capitalism, continues Jung Mo Sung, we need a true spiritual revolution that helps us to discover and accept the real human condition:

This spirituality both allows us to share and is found through our sharing in the sufferings, fears, and insecurities of other individuals and groups (compassion), and also in their hopes, struggles and joys (solidarity). Without this encounter with persons who are suffering, without the encounters found in compassion and in struggles, there can be no encounter with oneself or with the Spirit who breathes over us, and without these encounters there can be no reconciliation.[1]

If Christianity and other religious traditions do not take up this task of changing the world through spirituality, others will not be able to do so:

Without spiritual revolution there will be no real economic revolution, since capitalism is, in fact, an economic system based on and motivated by deep spiritual beliefs, and consumerism is a form of religious expression in our daily lives.[2]

A different world is possible through such a genuine spiritual revolution. The Church does not possess an ideal model for constructing a better world or a more equitable society to live in peace and harmony. However, it has the hope that the Spirit of God is at work to renew the face

---

1. Ibid., 113.
2. Ibid.

of the earth. Each time we put the teaching of the Gospel into practice, we make the world a better place to live and we anticipate the coming of God's kingdom in our midst. In his life and writings, Ignacio Ellacuría showed that constructing a better world where justice and peace prevail is possible.

# 3
# Globalization

Thomas More's vision of utopia is presented as a story of exploration of an unknown place. It seeks out new people and brings the Old World into contact with the New. Utopia is associated with the desire to cross borders, to encounter and connect with people and places. Thus, utopia and globalization are linked.[1] Globalization can be viewed as a distinct mode of utopian representation when it emphasizes free trade, a world without borders, the power of technology, and equality among nations.

In the positive sense, globalization is associated with a range of utopian ideas such as human rights, peace, and global governance. Culturally, globalization gives "the vision of an increasingly cosmopolitan orientation amongst world citizenry, where everyone is connected instantly with everyone else, a global village of mutual understanding and constructive interchange, where people can pick and choose from the wealth of humanity's diverse, rich cultures."[2]

In the negative sense, globalization suggests the widening gap between the rich and the poor, the global domination of multinational corporations and the relentless pursuit of profit that threatens the environment. Politically, globalization is associated with "the idea of a new imperialism centred on US military might and plans for a new American Century; and, culturally, in notions, such as cultural imperialism, Westoxification, and Coca-colonization."[3]

---

1. Patrick Hayden and Chamsy el-Ojeili (eds), *Globalization and Utopia: Critical Essays* (Basingstoke: Palgrave Macmillan, 2009), 51.
2. Ibid., 6-7.
3. Ibid., 7.

In chapter two, we observed that Ignacio Ellacuría and Felix Wilfred were suspicious of what globalization claims to promise – improved standards of living for everyone on earth. Ellacuría believed the so-called advantages of globalization were parochial, misleading and served the interests of only the rich. Wilfred denies globalization's claim to universality.

This chapter attempts to argue that the disadvantages of globalization far outweigh the advantages and that globalization has left many of its grand promises unfulfilled. In fact, the majority of Christians who are engaged with the ethics of globalization perceive it as a negative phenomenon. Arguably, while globalization has provided employment and investment in developing countries, this process has ironically also impoverished and undermined the livelihoods and cultures of many people in the Third World and thus globalization has become a pejorative term. The Church, through its social teaching, can promote the humanization of market economies and the protection of local cultures against the threat of a globalized economic culture that claims to be beneficial.

Globalization can be defined as an economic phenomenon that promotes the increased flow of goods, services, and money across nations as the result of reduced taxes, growth of multinational corporations, and advances in technology and communication networks. This process is often accompanied by a migration of people looking for jobs in the fast-developing industries. Globalization has often been equated with Westernization or Americanization – the attempt to impose Western cultural norms on developing nations. To facilitate global economic integration, organizations such as the International Monetary Fund (IMF) and the World Trade Organization (WTO) were established by the United States and her Western allies.

A complex process, globalization's main aim is the removal of barriers to the movement of people, capital, and goods. Globalization leads to the "rapid integration of international markets for commodities, manufactures, labor, and capital."[1] With the collapse of Communism, the market system dominates virtually everywhere on this planet.

Assisted by new technology, the desire for wealth drives the process of globalization and promotes the liberalization of the person and the market simultaneously. Frederic Jameson maintains that "the concept

---

1. Niall Ferguson, *The Ascent of Money* (London: Penguin Books, 2009), 287. Negative consequences of free trade include harm to small farmers, local manufacturers and businesses, spread of consumerist values, the undermining of democracy, increased conflicts and ecological crises. See John Sniegocki, "Neoliberal Globalization: Critiques and Alternatives," *Theological Studies* 69, no. 2 (June 2008), 325-27.

of globalization reflects the sense of an immense enlargement of world communication, as well as of the horizon of a world market, both of which seem far more tangible and immediate than in earlier stages of modernity."[1] People are brought closer to one another under a common corporate vision. José Casanova puts it this way:

> Globalization is the new philosophy of space that has come to replace the modern philosophy of history. In a sense, with globalization the spatial metaphor has begun to replace the dominant temporal-historical metaphor of Western secular modernity. It is a short trip indeed from the most traditional village to the most modern global metropolis and back.[2]

Regarding the movement of people, I have personally experienced the joy of living in a multi-racial society in Singapore with a mixture of Malays, Chinese, Indians, Europeans, and other minority races. Living harmoniously in a multicultural society can be regarded as one of the "richest exchanges of humans ever to occur."[3] However, at the present time, when over 40 million people are migrating to countries where they can have a decent standard of living to bring up their families, the phenomenon of vast migration is causing cultural, social and economic tensions in many parts of the world, especially in Europe and the United States.

## Historical Background

Globalization has in fact appeared in different forms since ancient times. The Roman-Hellenistic world experienced an early form of globalization. Christian missionary activity became associated with globalization when it accompanied the colonial expansion of Europe in the fifteenth and sixteenth centuries. In fact, European expansion in the fifteenth and sixteenth centuries can also be regarded as a modern form of globalization. In more modern times, the British industrial revolution, the development of the digital age and the collapse of the Soviet Union can also be viewed as part of the globalization process.[4]

---

1. Quoted in Gerard McCann, "Globalization and the Need for a 'Moral Economy'?" *The Furrow* 57, no. 5 (May 2006), 293.
2. José Casanova, "From Modernization to Secularization to Globalization: An Autobiographical Self-Reflection," *Religion and Society (New York, NY)* 2 (2011), 33
3. Mary Evelyn Tucker, "Globalization, Catholic Social Teaching, and the Environment," *Journal of Catholic Social Thought* 4, no. 2 (2007), 357.
4. John Pawlikowski, "Creating an Ethical Context for Globalization: Catholic

One of the earliest modern ideas of globalization was promoted by media theorist Marshall McLuhan. While working as lecturer in the University of Toronto, he postulated the idea of a global village in a 1962 book, called *The Gutenberg Galaxy,* which was released just as the television was starting to become popular. He predicted the world was entering the fourth, electronic age, which would be characterized by a community of people brought together by technology. He called it the "global village" and said it would be an age when everyone had access to the same information through technology. In his follow-up book, *Understanding Media,* he expanded the theory to show the method of communication rather than the information itself would come to be the most influential fact of the electronic age.

The political dimension of globalization, however, was started at the tail-end of World War II during the 1944 economic forum in Bretton Woods. At this conference in New Hampshire in the United States, representatives from forty-five countries established the International Monetary Fund (IMF) and the World Bank (WB), both based in Washington, D.C. Promoting extensive free trade and the breaking down of economic barriers, the IMF and WB have been credited with being the engines of modern globalization.[1] This form of globalization enables the free flow of capital across continents and has led to the rise of transnational corporations.

Globalization promotes interdependence and communication, and "its practice is underwritten by an ideal of consumer and cultural homogeneity."[2] This is touted as a kind of liberalization but it actually leaves individuals and societies subject to the dictates of the market, which has become the sole determinant of human conduct. Many people, especially the poor and the marginalized, experience it as something that has been imposed on them. It is not a process in which the poor can freely participate and hence they become the victims of this "liberalism," supposedly guided by the "invisible hand," the term famously coined by Adam Smith, of the market. For example, although the Mass Rapid Transit in Singapore was established as a public service venture, its drive for profits has caused cuts in its service levels and frustration in the primary constituents that it is supposed to serve – commuters, some of whom do not have cars. Corporations tend to want to maximize profits to serve their shareholders. Many of the public goods that earlier economists thought should be provided to society have become controlled by profit-maximizing, global organizations.

Perspectives in an Interreligious Context," *Journal of Ecumenical Studies* 42, no. 3 (2007), 363.

1. Ibid., 364.
2. McCann, "Globalization and the Need for a 'Moral Economy'?" 293.

## The Invisible Hand

Adam Smith introduced the idea of the "invisible hand" in his seminal book, *An Inquiry into the Nature and Causes of the Wealth of Nations* (1776), generally shortened to *The Wealth of Nations*. The invisible hand is simply the unobservable market force that enables the supply and demand of goods in a free market to reach equilibrium automatically, thus promoting the common good. However, concern about contemporary western lifestyle, the environmental crisis, and the recent global financial crisis challenged the idea of an "invisible hand" regulating our market. In fact, the market seems out of control. People are beginning to question the moral basis of liberal capitalism and the ethical foundation of markets.[1]

Wen Jiabao, Prime Minister of China from 2003 to 2013, spoke of the "visible hand" of the state guiding the economy and regulating the market. He believed that socialism can guide a market economy:

> The complete formulation of our economic policy is to give full play to the basic role of market forces in allocating resources under the macroeconomic guidance and regulation of the government. We have one important piece of experience of the past 30 years: that is to ensure that both the visible hand and the invisible hand are given full play in regulating the market forces.[2]

Having read Adam Smith, Premier Wen understands well that, if only a few individuals possess wealth, conflict and instability are inevitable. The premier strongly believed in the need for the visible hand of the state to promote social justice and equality. Needless to say, supporters of full-blown liberal capitalism are against such interference in the market.

Capitalism insists that all barriers such as regulations, customs duties, and restrictions on the market be reduced or even removed in order to promote economic growth. There should be free movement of goods, services, and capital. According to one of the World Trade Organization's principles, "lowering trade barriers is one of the most obvious ways of

---

1. Paul S. Williams, "A Visible Hand: Contemporary Lessons from Adam Smith," in Paul Oslington, ed., *Adam Smith as Theologian* (New York: Routledge, 2011), 133. Stefano Zamagni holds that: "the economy does not run by means of its own mechanisms only, and Adam Smith's 'invisible hand' that would reconcile the sum of individual self-interests with the common good is valid under conditions that are so hard to respect that they have practically never been met." Zamagni, "Financial Integrity and Inclusive Capitalism: Civilizing Globalization," *Journal of Catholic Social Thought* 12, no. 2 (2015), 208.
2. Transcript of interview with Chinese Premier Wen Jiabao, http://edition.cnn.com/2008/ WORLD/asiapcf/09/29/chinese.premier.transcript/.

encouraging trade; these barriers include customs duties (or tariffs) and measures such as import bans or quotas that restrict quantities selectively."[1] Barriers are regarded as limitations to economic growth. Thus, says Paul S. Williams, "all moral visions of the 'good' that they may embody are relativized in favour of increasing the range of choice over which *individual* expressions of utility can be maximized."[2]

However, he warns that such "freedom" would only lead to "increased inequality and instability."[3] Already there is increased inequality as the result of the concentration of market activities in rich nations at the expense of the poor. There is also an increase in instability because of the movement of capital and labor. In fact, "these processes actively undermine the possibility of rooted communities. This systemic logic of capitalism undermines the connections between people and places and, in doing so, also encourages the objectification and use of the environment as nothing more than a resource to serve the consumption needs of humanity."[4]

Instead of condemning the market mechanism outright, Stefano Zamagni, Professor of Economics at the University of Bologna and a member of the Pontifical Academy of Social Sciences (Vatican City) writes:

> humanize the market, don't demonize it: this is the slogan that describes the challenge confronting us today. That is why we cannot consider any solution to the many and grave problems now afflicting our societies that would delegitimize the market as a social institution. If people continue to demonize the market, it really will become hell.[5]

---

1. World Trade Organization, https://www.wto.org/english/thewto_e/whatis_e/what_stand_for_e.htm.
2. Williams, "A Visible Hand: Contemporary Lessons from Adam Smith," 136.
3. Ibid.
4. Ibid. Joseph Stiglitz holds that: "the issue is that this global economic crisis has a *Made in USA* label on it. We exported not only the deregulatory philosophy that enabled the spread of the crisis around the world but also many of our toxic mortgages." International structures such as the IMF and WTO have "the effect of simultaneously exposing developing countries to more volatility, therefore putting at risk the citizens of those countries to the depravation of their basic economic human rights, while at the same time undermining the ability of the state to respond to those problems." Stiglitz, "Human rights and Globalization: The Responsibility of States and Private Actors," *Journal of Catholic Social Thought* 10, no. 1 (2013), 87-88, 89.
5. Zamagni, "Financial Integrity and Inclusive Capitalism: Civilizing Globalization," 215.

For this reason, national and international bodies need to regulate market forces to promote the common good.

Emphasizing the importance of control over free trade, Pope Paul VI commented in his encyclical *Populorum Progressio*:

> It is evident that the principle of free trade, by itself, is no longer adequate for regulating international agreements. It certainly can work when both parties are about equal economically; in such cases it stimulates progress and rewards effort. That is why industrially developed nations see an element of justice in this principle. But the case is quite different when the nations involved are far from equal. Market prices that are freely agreed upon can turn out to be most unfair. It must be avowed openly that, in this case, the fundamental tenet of liberalism (as it is called), as the norm for market dealings, is open to serious question.[1]

Besides this inadequacy of free trade and open market, the removal of economic and social barriers has also affected and marginalized local cultures.

## Erosion of Culture

There is a fear that globalization has rapidly become a cultural phenomenon in which "the market as an exchange mechanism has become the medium of a new culture."[2] The market has imposed itself on our way of life, affecting our manner of thinking and acting. It has led to the commoditization of everything. As Oscar Wilde said about a cynic, we have become like a "man who knows the price of everything, and the value of nothing" (*Lady Windermere's Fan*, 1892).

Many people who have been unwillingly subjected to globalization see it as a threat to their way of life, "a destructive flood threatening the social norms which had protected them and the cultural points of reference which had given them direction in life."[3] This happens when culture cannot catch up with rapid changes in technology and the

---

1. Pope Paul VI, *Populorum Progressio*, http://w2.vatican.va/content/paul-vi/en/ encyclicals/documents/ hf_p-vi_enc_26031967_populorum.html, 58.
2. Ibid., 3. See John Paul II's *Centesimus Annus* (*cf.* 34, 58) regarding how the market economy needs to be controlled by the community in order to respond to people's need while respecting free initiatives. http://w2.vatican.va/content/ john-paul-ii/en/encyclicals/documents/hf_jpii_enc_01051991_centesimus-annus.html.
3. Ibid. For an overview of current realities, see Sniegocki, "Neoliberal Globalization: Critiques and Alternatives," 327-29.

common good is threatened. Globalization therefore also crosses into the social and cultural spheres with deleterious effects. "Every aspect of the processes of globalization is discretionary, that is, based on human choices, and is thus based on values and value judgments."[1]

The possibilities of travel and communication have led to frequent contacts between communities. The popularity of television and cheap air travel means greater exposure to foreign cultures. This creates the sense of cultural relativity when we realize that culture is a changeable human construct.[2] Further, the process of globalization has the tendency to impose a single culture – like a prolonging of European imperialism or the reduction of cultural diversity into one consumerist way of life. It is a cultural colonization spread through marketing with the aid of technology-driven communication. Vincent Miller writes: "Hegemony is pre-packaged in Los Angeles, shipped out to the global village, and unwrapped in innocent minds."[3] Globalization, thus, seems like Americanization when we see McDonald food chains, Coke and iPhones spreading everywhere.

Driven by profit, globalization is rooted in Mammon rather than the humane values that should govern human relationships. Globalization promotes consumerism, individualism and exploitative capitalism. Globalization is elusive and ambiguous, which makes the process all the more sinister and threatening. Teresa Okure, a Nigerian Catholic religious sister, says, "globalization is an ill wind that blows no culture any good."[4] It destroys local cultures not just in Africa but also in other Third World countries.

José Casanova points out that:

> globalization also represents a great threat insofar as it implies the de-territorialization of all cultural systems. Globalization threatens to dissolve the intrinsic link between sacred time, sacred space and sacred people common to all world religions, and with it the seemingly essential bonds between histories, peoples and territories which have defined all civilizations.[5]

---

1. Charles M.A. Clark, "Greed Is Not Enough: Some Insights on Globalization from Catholic Social Thought," *Journal of Catholic Social Thought* 2, no. 1 (2005), 25.
2. Neil Ormerod, "Theology, History and Globalization," *Gregorianum* 88, no. 1 (2007), 39.
3. Quoted Vincent Jude Miller, "Where is the Church? Globalization and Catholicity," *Theological Studies* 69, no. 2 (June 2008), 413-14.
4. Teresa Okure, SHCJ, "Africa: Globalization and the Loss of Cultural Identity," *Concilium* 293/5 (2001), 68.
5. José Casanova, "Religion, the New Millennium, and Globalization," *Sociology of*

Globalization threatens to destroy local and native cultures by promoting a hyper-culture and a way of life that is based solely on consumption.

The philosophy "I consume, therefore I am" distorts what it means to be human because consumerism is not a natural human characteristic but "a cultural construct created artificially" by the profit-oriented capitalistic global economy.[1] The human person is looked upon solely as a consumer who finds meaning and satisfaction in consuming without any thought of sustainability of our environment. Businesses are keen to raise the level of consumption of the people because it means greater profit. The purpose of business is, of course, the maximization of profits. To achieve this goal, businesses attempt to create false expectations with a promise of satisfying them. With all these false expectations, people are still waiting for the grand promises of globalization to come true.

## Still Waiting

Advocates of globalization believe that this process would raise productivity and output, and thus, improve the standard of living and reduce poverty worldwide. The reality, however, is very different: poverty in the world remains high and is worsening in many places. The standard of living for most people has stagnated or even fallen and the wealth that has been created is in the hands of a few people.

According to Credit Suisse and Oxfam, half of the world's wealth is now possessed by one percent of the population.[2] This concentration of wealth is caused by globalization. Our environment and local cultures have also been adversely affected by globalization.

Likewise, supporters of the free-market assure us that "in the final analysis, it will produce far more winners than losers because economic growth will one day provide sufficiently for all and include everyone in its rewards. We shall all be beneficiaries."[3] Such claims are continually made by those from the International Monetary Fund and the World Trade Organization to justify harsh policies that lead to increased

---

*Religion* 62, no. 4 (2001), 430-31.

1. José Ignacio González Fau, "The Utopia of the Human Family: The Universalization of the Truly Human as Real Globalization," *Concilium* 293/5 ( 2001), 100.

2. "Richest 1% own half the world's wealth, study finds," https://www.theguardian.com/inequality/2017/nov/14/worlds-richest-wealth-credit-suisse and "Oxfam Says Wealth of Richest 1% Equal to Other 99%," http://www.bbc.com/news/business-35339475.

3. Quoted in Xavier Alegre, "The Sin of the World: The Devil is a Liar, a Deceiver and a Murderer," *Concilium* 293/5 ( 2001), 51.

unemployment and human suffering. Politics in the twenty-first century is not concerned about sharing the resources of this world but about remaining competitive.

Champions of globalization believe that, in the long run, its benefits will reach the less fortunate. Pope Francis, however, is not convinced of this argument:

> In this context, some people continue to defend trickle-down theories which assume that economic growth, encouraged by a free market, will inevitably succeed in bringing about greater justice and inclusiveness in the world. This opinion, which has never been confirmed by the facts, expresses a crude and naive trust in the goodness of those wielding economic power and in the sacralized workings of the prevailing economic system. Meanwhile, the excluded are still waiting.[1]

With its destructive impact on the environment, globalization gives new meaning to John Maynard Keynes' famous remark, "in the long run we are all dead."[2]

## Fallacies of Globalization

Globalization offers us efficient ways to communicate and exchange ideas through the use of technology. However, efficient means of communication do not necessarily create a greater solidarity among humankind. In fact, globalization is a kind of illusion that creates a make-believe world through advertisements and marketing strategies which offer instant gratification or the solution to all our needs and desires. This kind of illusion is beneficial to the rich and powerful but is harmful to the poor and dispossessed.[3] The poor of this world struggle

---

1. Pope Francis, *Evangelii Gaudium*, https://w2.vatican.va/content/francesco/en/apost_exhortations/documents/papa-francesco_esortazione-ap_20131124_evangelii-gaudium.html, 54.
2. Clark, "Greed Is Not Enough," 23. Ecology is a key global issue because nobody will survive if our planet is destroyed. We have seen the destruction of rain forests, the depletion of the protective ozone layer and the rise in the sea level as a result of global warming. Further, we have also witnessed the destructive effect of acid rain in many places. Hence, we must deal with this environmental crisis on an international level. John Pawlikowski, "Creating an Ethical Context for Globalization," 386.
3. Jon Sobrino and Felix Wilfred, "Introduction: The Reasons for Returning to this Theme," in Jon Sobrino and Felix Wilfred, eds., *Globalization and its Victims*, *Concilium* 5 (London: SCM Press, 2001), 11.

for food, water, shelter, basic education, medical help, and so on – a harsh reality in stark contrast to the ostentatious advertisements that the media promotes. Globalization has not made the world a better place to live; rather, the poor become poorer and the rich become richer.

Instead of becoming more united as globalization has promised, the world has become more fragmented because it excludes many people who cannot take part in its benefits. Globalization offers greater profit-maximizing opportunities for a few by making labor cheap and accessible through labor mobility. This exploitation of laborers comes in the form of low wages, long working hours and poor working conditions. The poor are not wanted if they do not have the skills required by industry, further marginalizing them.

Factories are moving out of China to Bangladesh, Laos, Cambodia and Myanmar for manufacturing as these countries have lower wages. In 2016, *China Labour Bulletin* reported that:

> China would actually lay off around six million workers from its ailing state-owned industries. These redundancies, combined with the millions of private sector workers in the manufacturing and construction industries who had already been laid off during the economic slowdown, triggered renewed fears of mass unemployment and social unrest. Those worst affected by the lay-offs are likely to be older low-skilled workers.[1]

Aware of the consequences of increased labor mobility and migration as the result of the interconnectedness of markets, Pope Benedict XVI has observed that:

> The process of globalization taking place in the world entails a need for mobility that obliges numerous young people to emigrate and live far from their home countries and their families. This brings about an unsettling feeling of insecurity that undoubtedly has repercussions on their ability not only to dream and build up a project for the future, but even to commit themselves to matrimony and start a family.[2]

---

1. *China Labour Bulletin*, Unemployment, http://www.clb.org.hk/content/wages-and-employment#%E2%80%8B. See also "How China Is Changing Its Manufacturing Strategy," http://www.wsj.com/articles/how-china-is-changing-its-manufacturing-strategy-1465351382.
2. Benedict XVI, "Message of His Holiness Benedict XVI to the Participants in the 9th International Youth Forum," https://w2.vatican.va/content/benedict-xvi/en/messages/pont-messages/2007/ documents/hf_ben-xvi_mes_20070328_rylko-forum-giovani.html.

Globalization has a corrosive impact on families as its appetite for increased movement of labor leads people to leave their homes in search of employment. In addition, living in foreign countries with very different cultures and languages alienates migrant workers, discouraging them from starting families of their own.

Adherents of globalization promise unity but it actually divides people by creating an underclass of the unemployed and the under-employed. Many people are now much poorer while a relatively small group has become hugely rich. We have witnessed the great divide between the developed countries of the North and the undeveloped countries of the South: "Globalization promises unity, but does not achieve it because it lacks justice, and that is why it cannot be a credible unity of the world."[1] The problem is not the modernization of the world, but the lack of opportunity for modernization and improvement. Further, as a cultural process, globalization calls for uniformity of culture, consumption and production. Thus, it works against pluralism and cultural diversity. This cultural-homogenization provokes resentment and conflicts.[2]

Unity can be forged only through hard struggle and pain, not through mandating a ready-made programme. The global is not to be equated with the universal, Felix Wilfred has emphasized.[3] The universality that globalization promotes is the universality of capital and the unity of the wealthy, based on economic ends and self-interest. The social critic and journalist Thomas L. Friedman, in his influential book on globalization, *The World is Flat: A Brief History of the Twenty-first Century* (2005), remarked that while communism was a great system for making people equally poor, capitalism made people unequally rich. Ultimately, globalization leads to the disintegration of traditional communities and the widening chasm between the very rich and the poor. In other words, globalization offers no hope for any universal communion.[4]

---

1. Sobrino and Wilfred, "Introduction: The Reasons for Returning to this Theme," *Concilium* 5 (2001), 12.
2. Ibid.
3. An attempt to claim universality is made by the Coca-Cola company. Coca-Cola was invented in 1886 by a pharmacist called John Pemberton and sold as soda-fountain drink. Asa Griggs Candler bought the business and became the sole owner of Coca-Cola in 1891. He made great efforts to make the soft drink a national brand through advertising, even promoting it as a medicine that would cure fatigue and headaches. Later he realized that "only some people have headaches and only for some of the time; on the other hand, there is something everyone has all the time: thirst." See Fau, "The Utopia of the Human Family," 100.
4. Felix Wilfred, "Religions Face-to-Face with Globalization," *Concilium* 293/5 (2001), 39.

Presenting itself as good and beneficial to humankind, unbridled globalization has actually caused an increasing impoverishment of the majority of the people on this planet. It is therefore important to expose the fallacies of globalization and promote resistance to it in order to promote true solidarity that will help eradicate poverty through honest sharing.

Concerned that globalization's increased market access should reach small farmers, Pope Benedict XVI asserts that: "It must not be forgotten that the vulnerability of rural areas has significant repercussions on the subsistence of small farmers and their families if they are denied access to the market."[1] Benedict objects to poor farmers being denied access to markets, calling for unconditional access to markets by poor nations.[2] He writes:

> The adoption of a single customs union for the member nations is indeed a positive sign of the progress being made in this important undertaking. Communal solidarity at this level not only assists in the integral development of the region, but also develops a level of rapport and mutual concern.[3]

Benedict is aware that globalization as currently practiced, leads to inequality and monopolistic power in the hands of just a few individuals in a few nations. He writes that: "It is indeed essential that the constantly developing bonds of interdependence between peoples be accompanied by an intense commitment to prevent consequences of the disastrous escalation of the marked inequalities that persist between developed and developing countries." Benedict believes that, while globalization "benefits the great family of humanity" to some extent, it also "brings with it the risk of vast monopolies and of treating profit as the supreme value."[4] It is thus important that globalization be directed ethically and

1. Benedict XVI, "Address of His Holiness Benedict XVI to the Participants in the Thirty-Third Conference of the United Nations Food and Agriculture Organization (FAO)," https://w2.vatican.va/ content/benedictxvi/en/speeches /2005/november/documents/hf_ben_xvi_spe_20051124_conference-fao.html.
2. Joseph Anthony Burke, "Pope Benedict on Capitalism, Marxism, and Globalization," *The Catholic Social Science Review* 14, (2009), 182.
3. Benedict XVI, "Address of His Holiness Benedict XVI to Mr Ali Abeid A. Karume, Ambassador of Tanzania Accredited to the Holy See," https://w2.vatican.va/content/benedict xvi/en/speeches/2005 /december/documents/hf_ben_xvi_spe_20051201_ambassador-tanzania.html.
4. Benedict XVI, "Address of His Holiness Benedict XVI," Inaugural Session of the Fifth General Conference of the Bishops of Latin America and the Caribbean, http://w2.vatican.va/content/benedict-xvi/en/speeches/2007/may/documents/

placed at the service of humanity. The ethics of globalization must deal with the question of how economics affects people from poor nations, and how the systems that support it should foster true human progress.

## Moral Obligations

Albino Barrera raises three moral issues arising from globalization. First, the very rapid flow of information makes the plight of faraway people instantly known, causing "a much lower threshold for what constitutes moral failures of omission."[1] Second, globalization increases the ability of rich nations to accumulate surpluses which must be shared with those in need. Third, our increased interdependence requires us to attend to the different effects of price changes for the rich and the poor.[2]

Globalization has made us more morally transparent in the way our economic system is operating. Our economic decisions are no longer private affairs; they have social consequences on others who are powerless to protect themselves. Barrera says: "Greater economic interdependence has made us one another's indirect employers and employees. Better access to information has led to a much improved capacity to provide assistance."[3]

## Responsibility of the Church

Through Catholic social teaching (CST), the Church seeks to address the harmful effects of capitalism on humanity. For example, in 2009, Pope Benedict XVI's *Caritas in Veritate* presented a critique of capitalism in light of globalization. He observed that the dominance of capitalism has led to a "downsizing of social security systems" as countries strive to compete in the global market.[4] The demise of Soviet communism seems to reveal the superiority of capitalism. Catholic social teaching, however, maintains its reservations about the free market.

---

hf_ben-xvi_spe_20070513_conference-aparecida.html.

1. Albino Barrera, "Globalization's Shifting Economic and Moral Terrain: Contesting Marketplace Mores," *Theological Studies* 69, no. 2 (June 2008), 292.
2. Ibid., 294.
3. Ibid., 295.
4. Pope Benedict XVI, *Caritas in Veritate*, http://w2.vatican.va/content/benedict-xvi/en/encyclicals/documents/hf_ben-xvi_enc_20090629_caritas-in-veritate.html, 25. Catholic social teaching is both critical of communism as well as unrestrained free markets found in capitalism. See David Golemboski, "The Globalization of Catholic Social Teaching," *Journal of Catholic Social Thought* 12, no. 1 (2015), 99.

Based on faith and reason, CST is derived from the Gospel, the writings of the Early Church Fathers, the Scholastics of the medieval ages, especially St Thomas Aquinas, in addition to contributions from modern philosophy and social sciences. These insights are the fruits of 2000 years of reflection on society and fall within the natural law tradition.[1] As such, CST is also addressed to non-Christians and can be defended on secular principles and reason.

CST comprises seven fundamental principles: first, respect for human dignity and the pursuit of the common good; second, promotion of solidarity among people; third, distribution of wealth to enhance the dignity of the people and the community; fourth, ethical governance based on a moral vision; fifth, advancement of social justice and human rights; sixth, economic empowerment for all; and, seventh, the principle of subsidiarity – that a central authority should have a subsidiary function, performing only those tasks which cannot be performed at a more local level.[2] With these principles in mind, the Church has pursued a "prophetic model" to deal with the financial and political crises that the world is experiencing. Through theological reflection, the Church attempts to develop "an ethical monetary and governance vision" for the world.[3]

This prophetic approach of the Church to dealing with globalization has two important components: upholding the dignity of the human person and promoting the common good. The Church believes all humans are created in the image and likeness of God and thus possess a spiritual dimension. It supports a genuinely humane capitalism characterized by freedom and morality. Such a system empowers people to seek the common good. It proposes a reward mechanism that satisfies the needs of people rather than institutions and would advance the interests of stakeholders rather than the interests of stockholders.

---

1. Clark, "Greed Is Not Enough," 28.
2. Jo Renee Formicola, "Globalization: A Twenty-First Century Challenge to Catholicism and its Church," *Journal of Church And State* 54, no. 1 (2012), 111-12. The principle of subsidiarity "suggests generally that smaller, hierarchically 'lower' bodies are better equipped to address individual and social needs, are the most appropriate agents to address such needs, and ought to be given priority in doing so." Thus, functions that are proper to smaller entities should not be absorbed by larger entities. In other words, local associations should not be subsumed under structures of rigid government. This suggests that the common good is best served when individual and local associations maintain authority and autonomy. Golemboski, "The Globalization of Catholic Social Teaching," 102.
3. Formicola, "Globalization," 108.

Based on theological reflections and practical considerations, such a mechanism could be implemented through cooperation with governments.[1]

## Human Dignity

The foundation of Catholic social teaching is a theological anthropology that understands the person in relation to the mystery of God and his/her rightful place in creation. Pope John Paul II in *Centesimus Annus* declares: "man's true identity is only fully revealed to him through faith, and it is precisely from faith that the Church's social teaching begins."[2] Further, in the celebration of World Day of Peace in 1999, John Paul declared:

> The dignity of the human person is a transcendent value, always recognized as such by those who sincerely search for the truth. Indeed, the whole of human history should be interpreted in the light of this certainty. Every person, created in the image and likeness of God (*cf.* Genesis 1:26-28) and therefore radically oriented towards the Creator, is constantly in relationship with those possessed of the same dignity. To promote the good of the individual is thus to serve the common good, which is that point where rights and duties converge and reinforce one another.[3]

Thus, having an appropriate understanding of the human condition (the concept is from *La Condition Humaine*, the title of André Malraux's 1933 novel on the failed workers' insurrection in April 1927 in Shanghai that led to a widespread massacre of Communist Party members) is crucial to the survival and flourishing of human societies.

Similarly, Pope Paul VI in *Populorum Progressio* holds that human development runs the risk of being reduced to little more than economic progress: "The development we speak of here cannot be restricted to economic growth alone. To be authentic, it must be well rounded; it must foster the development of each man and of the whole man." Quoting an eminent scholar on this issue, he states: "We cannot allow economics to be separated from human realities, nor development from the civilization in which it takes place. What counts for us is man – each individual man, each human group, and humanity as a whole."[4]

---

1. Ibid., 109.
2. John Paul II, *Centesimus Annus*, 54.
3. John Paul II, For the Celebration of World Day of Peace, https://w2.vatican.va/content/john-paul-ii/en/messages/peace/documents/hf_jp-ii_mes_14121998_xxxii-world-day-for-peace.html, 2.
4. Paul VI, *Populorum Progressio*, 14.

Economic growth is important but it should not be achieved at the expense of other aspects of human development. Paul VI speaks of a new and true humanism:

> What are truly human conditions? The rise from poverty to the acquisition of life's necessities; the elimination of social ills; broadening the horizons of knowledge; acquiring refinement and culture. From there one can go on to acquire a growing awareness of other people's dignity, a taste for the spirit of poverty, an active interest in the common good, and a desire for peace.[1]

Thus, human existence consists not just in the satisfaction of material needs but includes opportunities for education, appreciation of cultures and working for peace and the common good. We also need to acknowledge the existence of moral and transcendent values, the gifts of faith, hope and charity.

## Common Good

The common good is a fundamental tenet in Catholic social teaching. The Church urges the state to regard the common good as its primary responsibility. As Pope John XXIII wrote: "The attainment of the common good is the sole reason for the existence of civil authorities. In working for the common good, therefore, the authorities must obviously respect its nature, and at the same time adjust their legislation to meet the requirements of the given situation."[2] Understanding the inherent difficulties in promoting the common good, he added:

> Today the universal common good presents us with problems which are world-wide in their dimensions; problems, therefore, which cannot be solved except by a public authority with power, organization and means co-extensive with these problems, and with a world-wide sphere of activity. Consequently, the moral order itself demands the establishment of some such general form of public authority.[3]

In the past, the common good was associated with the hierarchical social order comprising the sovereign and the delegated lower authorities. Society was conceived as unified and homogeneous where the subjects

---

1.  Ibid., 21.
2.  John XXIII, *Pacem in Terris*, http://w2.vatican.va/content/john-xxiii/en/encyclicals/documents/hf_j-xxiii_enc_11041963_pacem.html, 54.
3.  Ibid., 137.

contributed to the common good according to their duties and station in life. Such a view of society has long disappeared: "egalitarian and participatory aspirations have advanced; central authority has been relativized; societies have become dynamic with social and geographic mobility; and individuals have adopted life plans reflective of pluralistic worldviews and value systems."[1]

Nonetheless, in this age of globalization, the concept of common good is still relevant because certain goods, food staples, and social and healthcare services are necessary for the commonweal: "basic human goods are required by human nature and known by human reason; they also define justice as social relations in which material and social goods are distributed fairly, conflicts resolved and violations compensated."[2] With the advent of aggressive globalization that promotes corporate greed rather than the common good, the Church must continue to search for what is beneficial for the individuals as well as for communities through dialogue and open conversation.

## The Third Way

Through theological reflection, the Church questions the efficacy of globalization, and examines the adverse economic, cultural, and political effects on poor nations that have emerged from this global financial integration. Critical of both communism and capitalism, the Church calls for a more humane and ethical form of economic development known as the "Third Way."[3]

In his 1967 encyclical, *Populorum Progressio*, Pope Paul VI asserts that wealthy nations have three major obligations towards poor nations: first, mutual solidarity – the aid that the richer nations must give to developing nations; second, social justice – the rectification of trade relations between strong and weak nations; and, third, universal charity – the effort to build a more humane world community, where all can give and receive, and where the progress of some is not bought at the expense of others. The matter is urgent, he says, for on it depends the future of world civilization.[4] Paul VI also calls upon nations to protect life, respect

1. Kenneth R. Himes, "Globalization with a Human Face: Catholic Social Teaching and Globalization," *Theological Studies* 69, no. 2 (June 2008), 283.
2. Quoted in ibid., 283. See Lisa Sowle Cahill, "Globalization and the Common Good," in John A. Coleman, S.J., and William F. Ryan, S.J., eds., *Globalization and Catholic Social Thought: Present Crisis and Future Hope* (New York: Orbis Books, 2005).
3. Ibid., 113.
4. Pope Paul VI, *Populorum Progressio*, 44. Pope John Paul II further developed

cultures, and support both moral and economic developments that benefit the whole human race. For the pontiff, integral development is "the new name for peace."

In *Caritas in Veritate*, Pope Benedict XVI calls for an ethical economic system that seeks a higher goal than mere profit:

> Economic life undoubtedly requires contracts, in order to regulate relations of exchange between goods of equivalent value. But it also needs just laws and forms of redistribution governed by politics, and what is more, it needs works redolent of the spirit of gift. The economy in the global era seems to privilege the former logic, that of contractual exchange, but directly or indirectly it also demonstrates its need for the other two: political logic, and the logic of the unconditional gift.[1]

Benedict also urges government and economic institutions to protect the rights of people to participate in economic policy formulations to ensure justice and peace.

Aware of the pervasive (and often pernicious) influence of globalization, Pope Francis, in his 2013 Apostolic Exhortation, *Evangelii Gaudium*, asserts: "As children of this age, though, all of us are in some way affected by the present globalized culture which, while offering us values and new possibilities, can also limit, condition and ultimately harm us."[2] In this text, he highlights the rise of a "globalization of indifference" when "almost without being aware of it, we end up being incapable of feeling compassion at the outcry of the poor, weeping for other people's pain, and feeling a need to help them, as though all this were someone else's responsibility and not our own."[3] Francis laments that the culture of prosperity numbs us as we focus just on what the market can offer us. The sufferings of others fail to move us to compassion.

## Local versus Global

When individuals of different cultures come into contact, there is tension from competing claims to priority of the particular (local) and the universal (global). Aware of this tension, the Church seeks to reconcile the local and the global. Pope Francis has affirmed the importance of both:

---

these ideas in *Laborem Exercens* (1981), <u>Sollicitudo Rei Socialis</u> (1987) and *Centesimus Annus* (1992).

1. Pope Benedict XVI, *Caritas in Veritate*, 37.
2. Pope Francis, Apostolic Exhortation, *Evangelii Gaudium*, https://w2.vatican. va/content/francesco/en/apost_exhortations/documents/papa-francesco_ esortazione-ap_20131124_evangelii-gaudium.html, 77.
3. Ibid., 54.

An innate tension also exists between globalization and localisation. We need to pay attention to the global so as to avoid narrowness and banality. Yet we also need to look to the local, which keeps our feet on the ground. Together, the two prevent us from falling into one of two extremes.[1]

In other words, there are people who are too obsessed with the abstract and globalized world, while others are not capable of appreciating God's beautiful creation beyond their own precincts.

Globalization offers us the opportunity to live in solidarity with other people as a family. Pope John Paul II wrote:

The exercise of solidarity within each society is valid when its members recognize one another as persons. Those who are more influential, because they have a greater share of goods and common services, should feel responsible for the weaker and be ready to share with them all they possess. Those who are weaker, for their part, in the same spirit of solidarity, should not adopt a purely passive attitude or one that is destructive of the social fabric, but, while claiming their legitimate rights, should do what they can for the good of all. The intermediate groups, in their turn, should not selfishly insist on their particular interests, but respect the interests of others.[2]

At the same time, Francis reminds us that we need not delete differences that make humans unique: "The global need not stifle, nor the particular prove barren."[3] As we experience a more integrated world with its relentless marketing and promotion of Western (Hollywood) values, the challenge for us is to protect our national and cultural identities that have provided richness and variety in our lives.

The Church must attempt to help people forge a richer and more humane identity so that local cultures may not be absorbed by the globalized economic culture. Catholic social teaching must fight against the false cultural universalism that globalization tends to promote.[4] This means the Church must develop moral values and norms that transcend any particular place and time, such as its past euro-centric culture.

---

1. Ibid., 234.
2. John Paul II, *Sollicitudo Rei Socialis*, http://w2.vatican.va/content/john-paul-ii/en/encyclicals/documents/hf_jp-ii_enc_30121987_sollicitudo-rei-socialis.html, 38.
3. Pope Francis, Apostolic Exhortation, *Evangelii Gaudium*, https://w2.vatican.va/content/francesco/en/apost_exhortations/documents/papa-francesco_esortazione-ap_20131124_evangelii-gaudium.html, 235.
4. Himes, "Globalization with a Human Face," 281.

Religions have often been a source of division and conflicts, but today they can have a unifying potential because every religious tradition possesses "a universal vision of unity" and at the same time each is rooted in a particular social and cultural context.[1] To bring about solidarity, religions should align themselves to new social movements, such as the liberation of women, nature conservation, and the defence of the rights of indigenous and exploited peoples. These movements embody universal, ethical values and promote a utopian consciousness. They advance justice and peace by engaging daily in "the art of resistance."[2] It is important that religions seek to work closely with these movements by providing spiritual and moral support. The new social movements in turn can help religious traditions achieve unity through concrete acts of solidarity, thus giving expression to their commitment to the poor and oppressed.

1.  Wilfred, "Religions Face-to-Face with Globalization," 39-40.
2.  Ibid., 40.

# 4
# Confucianism

It has been claimed that utopia is not a universal concept – it arose only from the Hellenistic-Christian world. There are versions of the ideal or perfect society found in non-Western culture, usually of religious significance, but they cannot be called utopia.[1] The assumption is that a secular and literary genre of utopian writing did not exist outside Christian Europe. Perhaps this is because Europe has accumulated enough textual materials to establish an intellectual tradition of utopian writing as a literary genre.[2] After all, it was Thomas More who coined the word "utopia" and thus defined the terms of reference. In fact, Roland Schaer says utopia is strictly speaking a sixteenth-century European invention.[3] Krishnan Kumar also holds that a secular utopia does not exist in non-Western culture.[4]

Be that as it may, the idea of utopia suggests a vision for a better life, which implies a certain degree of dissatisfaction with the present state of things. This desire for change is deeply embedded in our human nature and is thus ubiquitous. There are, of course, differences between Eastern and Western concepts of utopia. Western utopias are identified with life in the city or *polis*, whereas Eastern utopias, especially those of the early

---

1. Kumar, *Utopianism*, 33.
2. Claeys, *Searching for Utopia*, 45.
3. Zhang Longxi, "The Utopian Vision, East and West," *Utopian Studies* 13, no. 1 (2002), 1.
4. Krishnan Kumar, *Utopia and Anti-Utopia in Modern Times* (Oxford: Basil Blackwell, 1987), 19-20.

Daoists, are closely associated with the rural and agricultural way of life. The Eastern vision of a perfect society lies not in the future but in the memory of the past – "nostalgia for a state of primitive happiness for mankind and for a Golden Age."[1] Influenced by Christianity, Western utopia generally looks toward the future and the world to come. There were future-looking Chinese utopias, such as the White Lotus Society.

Thomas More's *Utopia* maintains that through the use of reason, a different and better world is possible. Here rational self-interest is the motivating force in human behavior. Self-interest, however, cannot be relied upon to promote a harmonious society. "Inner morality" which means "doing the right thing when no one is watching" is what matters most.[2] What we need is not just competent and rational government, but ethical and virtuous leaders motivated by the desire to work for the common good.

In this chapter we will explore Confucian understanding of the ideal society because the Sage's moral and political philosophy has served as the cultural foundation of a number of East and South East Asian societies for centuries till now. Mainland China applied Confucianism to its government bureaucracy for almost two thousand years until the Chinese revolution led by Mao Zedong in 1949. In spite of Marxist criticisms, Confucian philosophy continues to influence virtually every aspect of Chinese culture and the Chinese understanding of human nature. China may have abandoned Confucianism when the Communists took over this vast nation, but the success of tiger economies, such as South Korea, Taiwan, Hong Kong, and Singapore, have been linked to the Master's influence. This essay concludes that a Confucian utopia can be realized to some extent as revealed by the success story of Singapore.[3]

---

1.  Jean Chesneaux, "Egalitarian and Utopian Traditions in the East," *Diogenes* 62 (1968), 100. See Jan Nattier, *Once Upon a Future Time: Studies in a Buddhist Prophecy of Decline* (Nanzan Studies in Asian Religions) (Berkeley, CA: Asian Humanities Press, 1991).
2.  Kim Young-oak and Kim Jung-kyu, *Great Equal Society: Confucianism, China and the 21st Century* (Singapore: World Scientific Publishing Co. Pte Ltd, 2013), 8.
3.  *National Geographic Magazine* reports that Singapore, together with Denmark and Costa Rica, are the world's happiest places because people in these three countries "feel secure, have a sense of purpose, and enjoy lives that minimize stress and maximize joy." The researchers in this magazine conclude that happiness is caused by six factors: "strong economic growth, healthy life expectancy, quality social relationships, generosity, trust, and freedom to live the life that's right for you." These factors come about through the nation's government policies and its cultural values. This suggests that "the happiest places incubate happiness for their people." *National Geographic*, https://www. nationalgeographic.com/magazine/2017/11/worlds-happiest-places/.

## Confucius (551-479BC)

The name "Confucius" was actually coined by European Jesuits who entered China in the late 1500s, although they did not manufacture "Confucianism."[1] His real name was Kong Qiu (孔丘) and the Chinese call him Kongzi (孔子). Confucius was born in the eastern part of China in the state of Lu, which today is the city of Qufu (曲阜) in Shandong province. During the time of his birth, China was split into nine or ten rival states. The Zhou dynasty had ruled the Northern part of China for over 500 years but those peaceful days were gone during Confucius' time. The great house of Zhou was divided into competing regional families headed by princes, each one claiming to be the legitimate Zhou successor, and to rule by "divine right" given by the spirits of their ancestors. Officials from powerful families appointed by these princes formed networks of allies and fought to expand their political influence. In such political turmoil, there was always the threat of conflict and warfare. This historical era is known as the Spring and Autumn period (722-481BC), a term which reflects the rise and fall of various warring states.[2]

The ruler of Lu claimed to be a descendant of the Zhou Dynasty and was thus able to maintain some kind of legitimacy. Confucius's father held some political or military post in this regime and thus his family was accepted as coming from a minor aristocratic class. In China at that time, the people were divided into the ruling aristocracy who were educated and the common people who were illiterate and had to do manual work. The aristocrats saw themselves as preservers of traditions and as the natural governing class. As a member of the elite class, Confucius could associate easily with people of privileged families as well as government ministers. He was often consulted on public and official matters.[3]

In 501BC, at the age of fifty, Confucius was given a high government post, which he held for several years. For most of his life, however, he was a teacher who attempted to transmit the "Way" (his vision of life) to his disciples and students who hoped to gain political office. However, the way of dao (道) is a bit more expansive than Confucius' own vision of life – he linked it with the proper human way of moral and political development, grounded in the social and political institutions of the Zhou.

---

1. See Nicolas Standaert, "The Jesuits Did NOT Manufacture 'Confucianism,'" *East Asian Science, Technology, and Medicine*, no. 16 (1999), 115-32.
2. Ronald Suleski, "Confucius: The Organization of Chinese Society," in David Jones, ed., *Confucius Now: Contemporary Encounters with the Analects* (Chicago: Open Court, 2008), 254-55.
3. Ibid., 255.

It was his role as a teacher that gained him a unique position in the history of the Chinese civilization. In fact, he was China's "first private thinker" who conveyed his vision directly to his disciples, thus avoiding official scrutiny or censorship.[1] Many people regarded Confucius as an embodiment of the Chinese culture and mind-set.

Confucius was respected for his profound understanding of the ancient rites and ceremonies that played a crucial role in official life. These ceremonies were centuries old and existed long before Confucius was born. Thus, strictly speaking, Confucius is not the founder of Confucianism. It was developed during the civilization of the Zhou Dynasty (1046-256BC).

In fact, "Confucianism" is not a Chinese term. Confucius was a *ru* (儒) scholar (an expert in the ancient history and culture of China), and the *ru* tradition is far older than Confucius. Association of the *ru jia* (儒家) or *ru* school with Confucius as its most important sage has a long tradition, but the reference to this school as "Confucianism," associating it with the name of Confucius, is a Western innovation.[2]

The key concepts that are central to Confucianism, such as *ren* (仁), *yi* (義), *li* (禮), *zhi* (智), *xin* (信), were not constructed by Confucius himself. In fact, Confucius has said, "I do not voice my own original ideas but just narrate and expound the ideas of the ancients whom I like most and have deeply believed in."[3]

Tu Wei-ming, a prominent Confucius scholar, argues that just as Shakyamuni, Jesus Christ, and Muhammad founded a new realm in their respective religious traditions:

> Confucius also founded a new realm, but his new realm included large parts of the traditional teachings of people like Yao (堯), Shun (舜), Yu (禹), Tang (湯), Wen (文) and Wu (武). He believed he himself could not reach the moral conduct and achievement of these people. Moreover, he believed he was only a translator, an intermediary.[4]

Confucius' plan to restore Lu to its former glory as a ducal state failed, and he was forced to leave his home state. Confucius spent fifteen years with his disciples traveling from state to state in Eastern China, looking

1.  Benjamin I. Schwartz, *The World of Thought in Ancient China* (Cambridge, MA: Harvard University Press, 1989), 60, and ProQuest ebrary.
2.  See Lionel Jensen, *Manufacturing Confucianism: Chinese Traditions and Universal Civilization* (Durham: Duke University Press, 1977).
3.  Gu Zhengkun, "Confucian Family Values as Universal Values in the 21st Century Family – Nation – World," in Klaus Mühlhahn and Nathalie van Looy, eds., *The Globalization of Confucius and Confucianism* (Zurich: Lit Verlag, 2012), 43.
4.  Tu Wei-Ming, "Confucian Encounter with the Enlightenment Mentality of the Modern West," *Oriens Extremus* 49 (2010), 299.

for a ruler who would employ him and adopt his political philosophy. Eno points out that "the *Analects* pictures some key moments in these travels, which ultimately proved fruitless."[1] Eventually Confucius was able to return to Lu (魯), where he lived his final years teaching young men in the literary, ritual and musical arts which he believed were central to the Zhou (周) tradition. In spite of Confucius' failure to restore the state of Lu with his philosophy, the *Analects* can inspire those who wish to shape a better future because of its utopian spirit.

## Secular Philosophy

There exists a secular account of an ideal society in *The Analects of Confucius* (論 語) and *Book of Rites* (禮 記), which proposes a harmonious society where rulers are just and subjects are obedient, where the old are respected and rituals regarding the principles of order are observed. Confucian utopian view is essentially secular in that Confucius is concerned with the reality of this life rather than the life to come. Confucius was never a founder of a religion as Christ founded Christianity or as Muhammad founded Islam. Confucianists describe themselves as followers of "the way of the sages," or "the way of the ancients."[2]

In fact, Confucius is rather ambivalent about the gods as he is more interested in serving human beings than spirits. Even though the *Analects* mentions *tian* (天) or heaven, Confucius is more concerned with ethical rather than religious issues. Confucianism is a secular tradition that subordinates the concern for the afterlife to the search for a harmonious society in this present life by means of "individual and collective moral self-rectification."[3] Thus, I have argued that Chinese culture is more open to other religious beliefs, except perhaps to Christianity because of its association with Western imperialism.[4] Confucianism is essentially a code of behavior and therefore, followers of Confucius can choose a number of different religious commitments, for example, one can be a Christian and Confucianist at the same time.

Some scholars, however, argue that Confucianism has been the source of much resistance to non-Chinese religions, such as Buddhism, Islam, and Christianity, through Chinese history. The "Neo-Confucians" often

---

1. Robert Eno, *The Analects of Confucius: An Online Teaching Translation*, http://www.indiana.edu/~p374/Analects_of_Confucius_(Eno-2015).pdf, iii.
2. Paul H. Beattie, "The Religion of Confucius: The First Humanist," *Religious Humanism* 22 (1988), 11.
3. Claeys, *Searching for Utopia*, 50.
4. See Ambrose Mong, *Guns and Gospel: Imperialism and Evangelism in China* (Cambridge: James Clarke & Co., 2016).

endorse Confucianism as a clear response and challenge to Buddhism. [1]
The idea that Confucianism is compatible with other religions (and,
thus, potentially Christianity) is largely the invention of the Jesuits, who
recognized the near impossibility of uprooting Confucianism in China,
and instead moved to the strategy of trying to install Christianity in a
Confucian context.

In Confucianism there is no sharp division between the material and
spiritual worlds. A prominent Confucius scholar, Tu Wei-ming writes:

> In the future, every spiritual civilization will have to develop two
> worlds of meaning, you can also call it two kinds of languages,
> one is a special language derived from a particular civilization's
> religious traditions, and the other is a common language derived
> from the need of addressing the many contesting and problematic
> developments that exist today. Yet Confucianism has always had
> just one language.

Tu holds that Confucianism is "inner-worldly" which means it has no
special language nor has it any absolute dogma.[2]

Confucius certainly has a more secular outlook on life; he emphasizes
serving the people first, before the spirits, and understanding life
first, before trying to figure out what death means (*Analects* 11:12).
Preoccupied with improving the political conditions of his time by
teaching people to pay more attention to moral standards, Confucius'
focus is on this world, on the ills of society, which can be remedied by
sound teachings.

## New Utopia

Confucius admired the ancient dynasty of Zhou especially under
King Wen (文帝). Zhang Longxi (張 隆 溪) holds that "this nostalgia
for a wonderful time in antiquity, the adoration for the benevolence
of ancient sage kings, constitute in the Chinese tradition something
almost parallel to the lost paradise of Eden."[3] In the chaotic and
corrupt world of his time, Confucius could not find any state that

---

1. Neo-Confucianism is "the synthesis of Taoist cosmology and Buddhist
   spirituality around the core of Confucian concern with society and government,
   a synthesis which predominated in the intellectual and spiritual life of China,
   Korea, and Japan prior to the modern period." *Neo-Confucianism, https://faculty.
   washington.edu/mkalton/NeoConfucianism.htm.*
2. Tu Wei-Ming,"Confucian Encounter with the Enlightenment Mentality of the
   Modern West," 253-54.
3. Longxi, "The Utopian Vision, East and West," 8.

might resemble the Zhou state where there was peace and harmony as described in the sacred records and ancient texts such as the *Book of Document* (書 經) and *Book of Poetry* (詩 經). These texts describe long periods of "relative tranquillity" in China and give us a glimpse of the idyllic past.[1]

Inspired by these ancient classical texts, Confucius wanted to recreate the early Zhou society through its ritual known as *li* (禮), which forms the foundation of his virtue theory. Hagop Sarkissian explains: "the *li* comprised religious rites (ancestor worship) and formal ceremonies (weddings, funerals), as well as the manners and customs, the strictures and prerogatives, the protocols and functions of each social, political and familial station. The *li* would indicate, for example, appropriate dress for ceremonial occasions, as well as appropriate conduct for a father or a son."[2] They are norms that allow for proper social interaction.

Confucius also understands that strict adherence to conventional rules of propriety is not enough to guarantee a virtuous life. He recognises that there is a difference between acting appropriately and acting virtuously. In fact, strict adherence to rule could be wrong and offensive (*Analects* 3:18) Thus he adds that the individual observing propriety must be sincere in his behavior (*Analects* 3:12, 3:26). It is more important to be honest than to appear to be honest (Analects 3:4, 7:11). Confucius is concerned with moral development of the person, his emotional and psychological maturity.

Confucius' determination to restore the early Zhou tradition:

> seems to be based, however, not only on this shared memory [of an idyllic past] but on a blending of this memory with a conception of the good socio-politico-cultural order which he already finds envisioned in the *Book of Documents* and the *Book of Poetry*. When positive memories based on experience are fused with conceptions of an achieved normative order found in the sacred literature, one can readily understand the all-inclusive idealization to which this may lead.[3]

Roberto Eno holds that "the details of what Confucius saw as legitimate Zhou culture and why he thought its patterns were tools for building a new utopia are the principal subjects of the *Analects*."[4]

---

1. Schwartz, *The World of Thought in Ancient China*, 45, and ProQuest ebrary.
2. Hagop Sarkissian, "Confucius and the Effortless Life of Virtue," *History of Philosophy Quarterly* 27, no. 1 (2010), 2.
3. Schwartz, *The World of Thought in Ancient China*, 65, and ProQuest ebrary.
4. Eno, *The Analects of Confucius*.

It is likely that Confucius believed there had been an ideal primitive society before civilization and he was committed to re-creating that utopia. For him, restoring the culture of an ideal society is not brought about by any divine intervention but through human effort. The purpose of reviving the ancient past is for the perfection to be achieved in the future and in this sense, the "ideal past has an important presence in social life, it can, and indeed often does, serve as a measure against which the present is judged and criticized."[1] Confucius' vision of an ideal society, known as the "Grand Union," is further outlined in the *Book of Rites*:

> When the Grand course was pursued, a public and common spirit ruled all under the sky; they chose men of talents, virtue, and ability; their words were sincere, and what they cultivated was harmony. Thus, men did not love their parents only, nor treat as children only their own sons. A competent provision was secured for the aged till their death, employment for the able-bodied, and the means of growing up to the young. They showed kindness and compassion to widows, orphans, childless men, and those who were disabled by disease, so that they were all sufficiently maintained. Males had their proper work, and females had their homes. They accumulated articles of value, disliking that they should be thrown away upon the ground, but not wishing to keep them for their own gratification. They laboured with their strength, disliking that it should not be exerted, but not exerting it only with a view to their own advantage. In this way selfish scheming was repressed and found no development. Robbers, filchers, and rebellious traitors did not show themselves, and hence the outer doors remained open, and were not shut. This was the period of what we call the Grand Union.[2]

This vision of Confucian utopia is defined as a community where people place the common good above self-interest. In other words, it is "a society where public-mindedness prevails over selfishness."[3] In this society, the government is honest and competent and the people are disposed to look after the welfare of the community. It is a society that is filled with goodwill and mutual trust. This Grand Union, Confucius believed, can be achieved by cultivating the right leadership through education.

---

1. Longxi, "The Utopian Vision, East and West," 8.
2. The Lî Kî (*The Book of Rites*) Part I, Book 7, Translated by James Legge (1885), http://www.sacred-texts.com/cfu/liki/liki07.htm.
3. Kim Young-oak and Kim Jung-kyu, *Great Equal Society*, ix.

Unfortunately, when the Grand Union breaks down we see people pursuing their own self-interest at the expense of the common good. Once public trust is lost, people become suspicious of one another – not only do people lock their doors, but rulers begin to build walls and stronger defences. Further, the rich and powerful have no qualms about exploiting others to enhance their wealth. Obviously, widespread litigation is a sign that people do not trust one another in a highly materialistic society: "A society without lawsuits is a society where the spirit of cooperation prevails over narrow self-interest; this, in turn, is the very definition of the Great Equal Society."[1]

## Influence of Confucius

During the many years of teaching and conferring with government officials, Confucius spelt out a number of principles that many Chinese still follow to this day. He believed that human beings are basically optimistic, willing to improve their life through hard work. In a class-conscious society, Confucius taught that one's social status at birth and one's innate abilities were less important than this "basic attitude of perseverance."[2]

Believing that formal education was instrumental in uplifting people to higher social and personal status, Confucius insisted that it should be available to everyone without discrimination. The goal of a Confucian education was to cultivate a true gentleman or *junzi* (君子) – sometimes translated as wise and virtuous person. This concept can be applied to anyone who seeks to act with propriety and dignity. Thus, in Confucius' opinion, if our society were filled with *junzi*, there would be order, stability and justice.

Confucius insists that young people should respect their elders. In other words, the young should have filial piety or *xiao* in order to receive guidance from their elders who are more experienced in life. As the result of Confucius' influence, folks in the East tend to show great deference to their elders. These basic principles developed by Confucius have become the core values that guide many people in East and South East Asian societies. Values such as the importance of proper behavior, the respect for education, persistence in the face of hardship, diligence and self-improvement, have withstood the test of time. These values are explicated in *The Analects*.

---

1. Ibid., 6.
2. Suleski, "Confucius: The Organization of Chinese Society," 256.

## Universal Values

*The Analects* of Confucius reflects not only Chinese values from a particular era, but is also universal, an embodiment of sentiments that are relevant to everyone. It has retained its validity for more than two thousand years. In fact, economically advanced societies in Asia, such as Japan, South Korea, Taiwan, Hong Kong, Singapore, and even China recently, have been influenced by Confucian philosophy. Beyond the economic benefits, the utopian spirit in Confucian teaching spurs us to establish a harmonious society by improving our relationship with one another. Confucius is not as dogmatic and authoritarian as often depicted. As we have seen, he is neither stubborn nor ego-centric (*Analects* 9:4); he is not concerned with personal advantage (*Analects* 4:16); and he dislikes competition (*Analects* 3:7).

Confucius' concern for the equitable distribution of wealth parallels Thomas More's concern for social justice in *Utopia*. Advising rulers to develop virtues and culture, Confucius says:

> As for me, I have heard that the ruler of a state or the head of a household: Does not worry that his people are poor, but that wealth is inequitably distributed; does not worry that his people are too few in numbers, but that they are disharmonious. Does not worry that his people are unstable, but that they are insecure. For if wealth is equitably distributed, there is no poverty; if the people are harmonious, they are not few in number; if the people are secure, they are not unstable (*Analects* 16:1).

In Confucius' thought, the leader or ruler plays a crucial role in shaping the community.

## Leadership

Only wise and virtuous leaders can govern a civilized society. Leaders need to be educated. Due to the scarcity of resources and personal limitations, most peasants do not have the opportunity to acquire learning that would qualify them for leadership positions. At the same time, not all men of learning are fit to govern. There are also some who inherit positions of power but have no love for learning. Confucius was convinced that only those who possess true knowledge can participate in government.[1] Confucius distinguishes two levels of knowledge: recognizing or memorizing and reflection. The virtuous person should

---

1. Schwartz, *The World of Thought in Ancient China*, 96, and ProQuest ebrary.

have reflective knowledge before acting. The Master said, "There may be those who act without knowing why. I did not do so. Hearing much and selecting what is good and following it; seeing much and keeping it in memory – this is the second style of knowledge [or a lower level of knowledge]." (*Analects* 7: 28) Like Thomas More, Confucius believed in cultivating intellectually gifted and morally advanced persons from all classes of society to be leaders.

The *Analects* describes two types of leadership: the first is that which seeks to make people obey by law and regulations; the second is that which seeks to develop their moral virtues. The Master said:

> Lead the people with administrative injunctions (*zheng*) (政) and keep them orderly with penal law (*xing*) (行), and they will avoid punishments but will be without a sense of shame. Lead them with excellence (*de*) (德) and keep them orderly through observing ritual propriety (*li*) (禮), and they will develop a sense of shame, and moreover, will order themselves (Analects 2:3).

Needless to say, Confucius prefers the ruling of society through virtue and ritual propriety. This method allows the members of the community to develop a sense of shame when they transgress the social contract. When they develop a sense of shame, they will strive to be virtuous:

> The principle of righteousness (*yili*) (義 理) is universally innate within the human mind. Therefore, the recognition of goodness and the rejection of evil is the same in every Human heart. To teach people through virtue and courtesy is to show them what they themselves already have equally, so that they can reject evil and find their own path to goodness, and thus the ruler does not have to enforce the people's obedience. If one rules only through laws and prohibitions, and forcefully coerces the people, they cannot but be obliged to follow, knowing it is ordered by the high officials; but since they are not aware of the principle innate in their own mind in the first place, they will never realize the hatefulness of evil – how, then, shall they ever make their way to goodness![1]

Thus, when a society is led by virtue, people will be motivated to be good and will feel ashamed when they do something bad. A virtuous leader will encourage his followers to be good. The Master said:

---

1. Quoted in Choi Young-jin and Lee Haeng-hoon, "The Confucian Vision of an Ideal Society Arising out of Moral Emotions, with a Focus on the Sishu Daquan," *Philosophy East and West* 66, no. 2 (2016), 397.

"Governing with excellence (*de*) can be compared to being the North Star: the North Star dwells in its place, and the multitude of stars pay it tributes" (*Analects* 2:1). In fact, Mencius (372-289BC or 385-c.303BC, a Chinese philosopher often described as second only to Confucius) holds that the sense of shame is the foundation of moral behavior. Shame is a motivation for us to be moral.[1]

Confucian understanding of an ideal society is essentially a moral community where the selfish desires of the individual are held in check by his innate moral instinct and thus he is enabled to work towards the common good. Although economic and military powers are needed to sustain a society, Confucius holds that the most important condition to establish a peaceful and harmonious society is trust (*xin*). In sum, the requirements to maintain a moral society are good leadership with the ability to distribute resources equitably and to control the selfish ambition of its population.[2]

The Confucian ideal world is also "a life community in which all the things living under heaven actualize their nature to the fullest degree possible, so as to form a great, harmonious whole with the Universe."[3] Its ruler plays an important role by living a virtuous life and thus inspiring the people to be virtuous as well.

## Criticizing Confucius

The Chinese Communist Party (CCP) was swept into power in 1949 and established the People's Republic of China (PRC). It seems that Confucian philosophy could be adapted to support Marxism because Confucius demands obedience from citizens towards their government. The early Communist leaders were not overtly anti-Confucianism as they saw the Master as a great teacher and philosopher who had something positive to offer to Chinese socialism. Marxist thinkers, however, regard Confucianism as a product of feudal society based on class exploitation. With its distinct hierarchical relationships, sharp distinction between the aristocracy and the common people, Marxists regarded Confucianism as backward and harmful to China's future development as a socialist state.[4]

In fact, there was a political campaign (1973 – 1976) started by Mao and led by the Gang of Four to criticise Confucius and Lin Biao (1907-71), a general of the People's Liberation Army who posed a threat to Mao

---

1. Ibid., 398.
2. Ibid., 399.
3. Ibid., 407.
4. Suleski, "Confucius: The Organization of Chinese Society," 268.

Zedong's supremacy. The campaign accused Confucius of accepting and endorsing oppressive class division during his time. In the same way, Lin Biao was portrayed as a leader, who like Confucius, seemed to work for the interest of the State but in actual fact was only working for his own advantage.[1]

The campaign pointed out that Confucius was a product of the aristocratic class in China who ignore the plight of the poor. Confucius' emphasis on hierarchical relationships as natural means that class division is normative. The class of *junzi* would rule over the people because of their education. Class struggle thus exists between the *junzi* (gentleman) (君子) and *xiao ren* (common person) (小人). Confucius' teaching of *ren* (仁) was considered self-serving and idealistic. Furthermore, Confucius' emphasis of *li* (禮), proper conduct, was a means to separate the privileged class, bourgeoisie, from the masses, proletariats, who toiled for a living. Although Confucius encouraged education, he never took any initiative to extend it to the common people.[2]

Marxist scholars regarded Confucius as a "political swindler" and "a feudal reactionary thinker" who invented the idea of a benevolent government to keep the masses under control.[3] Compared to Confucianism, Communism was presented as a superior form of government that works towards the common good. The campaign to discredit Confucius only reveals how widespread Confucianism was in China. Mao's followers knew that the virtues taught by Confucius were recognizable symbols that would evoke strong emotions among the people. Even after several decades of attempting to abolish Confucianism in Communist China, Confucius' ideas still persist in the collective consciousness of the Chinese. At the official level, there is a revival of Confucianism in the nation. President Hu Jintao has developed the idea of a "Harmonious Socialist Society," drawing on Confucian ideas. The Chinese government has established a number of Confucius Institutes around the world.

## Promoting Confucius

While Communist China sought to abandon Confucianism as feudal and reactionary, between the 1970s and the 1990s Asian economies, such as Japan, South Korea, Taiwan, Hong Kong, and Singapore, experienced an economic boom. Confucian philosophy forms the bedrock of these

1. Ibid., 269.
2. Ibid.
3. Ibid.

societies. In fact, many Asian leaders believed that the growth and prosperity enjoyed in their burgeoning economies were made possible by sound Confucian values that formed the basis of Asian culture. Influenced by Confucius' teaching on the importance of family as a basic unit of society, Asians tend to see themselves not as individuals but as members of a community. This helps to promote social cohesion and discourage individualism. Compared to Europeans and Americans, Asians in general tend to work harder to provide for their families and strive to live up to the expectations of their elders. Seeing themselves as members of a wider society, Asians are willing to work for lower salaries, and to avoid strikes for the sake of stability and harmony. [1]

Confucianism, of course, is not one coherent thing straddling different cultures in East Asia throughout millennia. I am suggesting that the Confucian values mentioned earlier were operative, maybe, in some cases central, in the economic success of certain East Asian nations.

The economic success of Confucian societies in countries such as those mentioned above prompts Kim Young-oak and Kim Jung-kyu to write: "We believe both the Asian model and Asian values theories contain elements of truth. . . . But we would like to offer a simpler explanation for the Asian miracle: the quality of leadership, which is another way of saying that it is all about people."[2] Regarding the importance of leadership in Asian countries, these two authors have in mind Lee Kuan Yew who was prime minister of Singapore from 1959 to 1990.

Lee Kuan Yew (1923-2015) was one of the leading advocates of Confucianism. For years Lee worked hard to promote Confucian values in Singapore, a multiracial society with a Chinese majority. He was convinced that Singapore's rapid economic growth was due to its inculcation of Asian values, such as diligence, hard work, and the spirit of self-sacrifice. In the 1980s, Singapore established the East Asian Institute to do research on Confucian ethics and its link to modern society.

---

1. "Longer hours, worse jobs: are Asians turning into working machines," https://www.scmp.com/week-asia/politics/article/2022099/longer-hours-worse-jobs-are-asians-turning-working-machines.

2. Kim Young-oak and Kim Jung-kyu, *Great Equal Society*, 38. The late Lee Kuan Yew, the *National Geographic Magazine* reports, was responsible for developing this place where happiness and satisfaction flourished. Under Lee's government, all the people in Singapore, including lowly paid workers, were ensured decent housing and healthcare. Singaporeans possess "life satisfactions" which experts regard as the third strand of happiness – this includes being financially secure, having a high degree of status and feeling a sense of belonging. *National Geographic*, https://www.nationalgeographic.com/magazine/2017/11/worlds-happiest-places/.

Believing that the secret of success in the country lies in the leader's abilities to channel the economic, social and political energies of the people, Lee formed a strong and paternalistic government. He created a team of technocrats to control and guide the economy towards prosperity for all. As a leader, he did not suffer fools patiently and had little tolerance for dissent. Following the Confucian tradition, Lee believed he knew what was best for the country and he worked hard to achieve those goals that he thought would make people happy and satisfied. According to Confucius, citizens must obey their rulers, who will guide them towards their best interests. In governing, Lee tolerated no opposition, just as a father would not welcome any criticism from his children. A paternalistic ruler, the city-state was like his extended family.

Needless to say, this kind of autocratic and benevolent government is anathema to Western liberal thinking. Critics may regard Singapore as "Disneyland with the Death Penalty."[1] Many people thought that Lee was using Confucian traditions in Singapore to consolidate his power but Chan Heng Chee (Singapore's Ambassador to the US between 1996 and 2012) has remarked that he was "a leader who understood the constraints of a cultural system. He used the positive aspects of it. He also tried to correct aspects of the system too."[2] One may or may not agree with Lee's governing philosophy, but the success of Singapore is obvious.

## Singapore's Success

Under the leadership of Lee Kuan Yew, Singapore's government has been wildly successful in many areas, for example, maintaining almost full employment, providing affordable public housing, healthcare, transport, and first-class education for all. The city-state is ranked one of the leading financial centres after London and New York and is considered the most competitive economy in the world. These spectacular achievements drew praise from no less than the late paramount leader of China, Deng Xiaoping, who remarked, "There is good social order in Singapore. . . . We should draw from their experience, and do even better than them."[3]

---

1. "Disneyland with the Death Penalty" is an article about Singapore written by William Gibson, first published as the cover story for *Wired* magazine's September/October 1993 issue.
2. Tu Wei-ming, ed., *The Triadic Chord: Confucian Ethics, Industrial East Asia and Max Weber* (Singapore: The Institute of East Asian Philosophies, 1991), 408.
3. "Go East, Young Bureaucrat," *The Economist*, 19 March 2011, 10. "One of the first things that Xi Jinping did after being anointed in 2010 as China's next leader was to drop in (again) on Lee Kuan Yew, Singapore's minister-mentor, who ran the island from 1959 to 1990, and his son, Lee Hsien Loong, who has been

A former British colony, originally populated by poor immigrants from Southern China, India, and the neighbouring countries, Singapore's success is all the more spectacular because this little island, a mere dot on the map, has practically no natural resources.

Modern Singapore enjoys a low tax rate and a balanced budget. The country has a very successful public housing programme and manages its limited water resources efficiently. Its highly competitive education system caters for students of various abilities, including offering vocational training for those less gifted academically. It has a superb and affordable healthcare system and its infant mortality is one of the lowest in the world.

The success of Singapore is mainly due to its ability to attract top talent to its civil service and to the ruling party (the People's Action Party). Besides being highly educated and competent, those recruited to the government must also be people of high integrity. Lee said, "You need people who are inoculated against corruption. . . . Once we are corrupt, we are finished."[1] Some of the candidates the Singapore government has recruited have excellent track records in the private sector and have made sacrifices to join the civil service or to enter politics. The high caliber of Singapore's leaders has given people great confidence in the government, to the extent of being too dependent on official initiatives.

Success, of course, comes with a price. It is a "fine" city: there are fines imposed for offences such as littering, spitting and not flushing public toilets after use. There is growing income inequality and limited freedom of expression. Be that as it may, the success of Singapore is enviable. Certainly Confucius' philosophy has a role to play in promoting the kind of political climate that produces leaders who are competent and free from corruption. It is a philosophy that emphasizes the importance of family in nation-building which Lee sought to implement.

## Family-Nation

Confucius showed how the ancient values from the rites (*The Rites of Zhou*) would build the sort of character that is required by a family-oriented society. Confucius' view of good government is described as "family-like" in that it embodies the values of clans and tribes. Nurtured by *ren* or love,

---

prime minister since 2004. The Chinese are looking at other places, too – most obviously Hong Kong, another small-government haven. But it is hard to think of any rich-country leader whom China treats with as much respect as the older Mr Lee." Ibid.

1.  Lee Kuan Yew and Han Fook Kwang, *et al.*, *Lee Kuan Yew: Hard Truths to Keep Singapore Going* (Singapore: Straits Times Press, 2011), 124.

members of the society would see themselves as belonging to one big family guided by ethics and rites. In times of crisis, members who adopted these family-oriented attitudes display a high degree of unity.[1]

In Singapore, families have been urged by the government to seek to preserve cultural values and to inculcate in their children the virtues of a "rugged society," such as resilience, diligence, the spirit of sacrifice, and the quest for excellence. Taking on the intermediary role between the individual and the state, the family is seen as serving as an important tool for achieving economic and social progress in the nation. In this way, the family has become an active agent of economic and social planning.[2]

In Confucius' tradition, the government was not chosen by regular elections, but by recruiting people possessing the highest level of virtues. To qualify for positions in the civil service, potential candidates had to sit the rigorous imperial examinations to test both their intellectual and moral qualities, and so this Chinese-style technocracy is "a government ruled mainly by virtues."[3] Thus in Ancient China, the family-like government had an emperor who acted like the head of a household. He had thousands of officials, drawn from the common people, who had passed the imperial examinations. This examination system ensured that only highly intelligent and morally upright persons would be chosen for the civil service. The civil service examination system had its origin during the Sui dynasty (581 – 618 BC) and was fully established during the Qing Dynasty. It played an important role in education, government and society throughout the Qing period. The examination system during this period was based on the Confucian classics and authorized commentaries on the classics.

Although Singapore holds regular elections, the system Lee created reflects the Confucian model in many ways. In an interview with Fareed Zakaria, Lee said, "Again, we were fortunate we had this cultural backdrop [Confucianism], the belief in thrift, hard work, filial piety, and loyalty in the extended family, and, most of all, the respect for scholarship and learning."[4] Lee also suggested that cultures that do not possess Confucian values would not be able to compete successfully:

---

1. Gu Zhengkun, "Confucian Family Values as Universal Values in the 21st Century Family – Nation – World," in Mühlhahn and van Looy, eds., *The Globalization of Confucius and Confucianism*, 57.
2. Trevor O. Ling, "The Weberian Thesis and Interpretive Positions on Modernisation," in Tu Wei-ming, ed., *The Triadic Chord: Confucian Ethics, Industrial East Asia and Max Weber*, 75.
3. Ibid.
4. Fareed Zakaria and Lee Kuan Yew, "Culture Is Destiny: A Conversation with Lee Kuan Yew," *Foreign Affairs* 73, no. 2 (1994), 114.

Getting the fundamentals right would help, but these societies will not succeed in the same way as East Asia did because certain driving forces will be absent. If you have a culture that doesn't place much value in learning and scholarship and hard work and thrift and deferment of present enjoyment for future gain, the going will be much slower.[1]

Some scholars have put forward the "post-Confucius thesis," which holds that the set of values with which people grow up, conventionally labelled Confucian, provides them with the right mentality and work ethic believed to be conducive to economic development."[2] While Western individualism worked well during the early years of industrialisation in Europe and the United States, "post-Confucian collectivism" may be more appropriate to the age of mass-production.[3] Protestant work ethic is said to have contributed to the success of Western capitalism in the past. I believe Confucian work ethic has the same effect on Asian economies in the twentieth century. Confucian ethic pushes the individual to work hard for the welfare of his family and the society in which the person belongs.

Further, Western-style democracy does not seem to be working very well in many parts of the world, especially in Third World countries. Perhaps this family-oriented kind of government with its strict examination system to recruit civil servants may be more suited to developing countries. Humane and rational, this system is based on the collective effort of millions of people who desire a peaceful place to work and raise their families.

Confucian values, a heritage of East Asia, can help to unify the world because they help us to see the world as one family. Globalization has sharpened our awareness that we are interconnected. The Confucian spirit certainly merits our consideration. We may not agree with Lee Kuan Yew's draconian style of government. Nevertheless, the nation-state he created shows that the wisdom of Confucius is still relevant and can help to make this world a better place to live. The spectacular success of Singapore reveals that a Confucian utopia is not a far-fetched idea.

---

1. Ibid., 116-17.
2. Ambrose Y.C. King, "The Transformation of Confucianism in the Post-Confucian Era: The Emergence of Rationalistic Traditionalism in Hong Kong," in Tu Wei-ming, ed., *The Triadic Chord: Confucian Ethics, Industrial East Asia and Max Weber*, 204. Chinese intellectuals, during the 1915-21 New Culture Movement (or May Fourth Movement), however, asserted that China's backwardness was largely due to the feudal Confucian family value system. Ibid., 205.
3. Hwan Kwang-kuo, "Dao and the Transformative Power of Confucianism: A Theory of East Asian Modernization," in Tu Wei-ming, ed., *The Triadic Chord: Confucian Ethics, Industrial East Asia and Max Weber*, 232.

# 5
# Mohism

In chapter four, we saw how Confucian values can help to unify society by seeing the world as one big family. In this chapter we shall focus on Mo Tzu (470-391BC) and his vision of an ideal society. Mo Tzu rose to prominence in the third and second centuries BC and his thought briefly rivalled Confucianism as the leading school of thought in ancient China. "Among the nine major schools of thought, only Confucius is qualified to contend against Mo-tse [Mo Tzu]. And the other schools have no qualification to contend against him."[1] Like Confucius, Mo Tzu also faced the same volatile political environment and sought to discover the best path to law and order. While Confucius idealized the aristocratic past, Mo Tzu looked back to an earlier period, the Xia Dynasty (夏朝) (2183-1752BC), when human beings lived in relative equality without class distinction or rank.[2]

Mo Tzu (墨子) believes that, at the dawn of civilization, human beings were not divided into clans and tribes but co-operated with each other in what he describes as universal love, which resembles the teaching of Christ. Mo Tzu writes: "If men were to regard the states of others as they regard their own, then who would raise up his state to attack the state of

---

1. Quoted in Qi Zhou, "On Volunteer Spirit and Thought of 'Universal Love,' by Mo-tse," *Asian Social Science* 7, no. 9 (2011), 185.
2. Schwartz, *The World of Thought in Ancient China*, 154, and ProQuest ebrary. Mo Tzu's greatest hero was the sage king called Yü, the founder of the Xia Dynasty, who spent his life building water control projects for his people in spite of his presumed high position and great wealth. Ibid.

another? It would be like attacking his own."[1] It should be noted that the philosopher's name, Mo Tzu, is also the name given to a book compiled by his followers. It is a work that attempts to present a vision of utopia and suggests ways to attain it through a systematic application of Mo Tzu's thought known as Mohism (墨家).

Mo Tzu's ideal world is a simple society with a functional culture originally started by the sage kings. These wise rulers, for example, built houses to protect people from cold and heat. They even had inner walls so that male and female occupants could have their own privacy. In other words, the houses were functional, built for living and not for show. Mo Tzu's ideal society provides basic necessities in abundance but there are no frills and luxuries. The ruler and his people live a simple and frugal life. Mo Tzu forbids extravagant living because he believes it is only at the expense of the poor that the rich live luxuriously.[2]

Born in Shandong Province, Mo Tzu's profound understanding of Confucianism indicates that he might have studied under a disciple of Confucius. Like Confucius, he claimed to offer no new knowledge but merely to follow the traditional teachings of the ancient sage kings. He also travelled widely in the country, sharing his ideas with those in authority, hoping to help them to resolve the various political and social crises that were plaguing the country. While his ideas might seem impractical, unrealistic and even naive, Mo Tzu's teachings received credibility because of his personal integrity, moral uprightness, and political courage. Frugal and austere in his lifestyle, he worked with his hands to support himself and thus upheld the dignity of labor. Besides his philosophical knowledge, Mo Tzu was also an engineer who invented mechanical machines for the defense of cities. He did his best to prevent wars among the rulers of the warring states. In fact, Mo Tzu considered his work a divine vocation to restore the world to its pristine stage. His work can be regarded as a blueprint for a Chinese utopia.[3]

This chapter examines Mo Tzu's vision of an ideal society by focussing on the following topics: "Honouring the Worthy," "Identifying with One's Superior," "Universal Love," "Against Offensive Warfare" and "The Will

---

1. Mo Tzu, *Basic Writings*, translated by Burton Watson (New York: Columbia University Press, 1966), 40. The text is not a single book by Mo Tzu himself, but a collection of essays of uncertain authorship, most likely containing the thoughts of the teacher. Mo Tzu's life is not as well documented as that of Confucius.
2. Schwartz, *The World of Thought in Ancient China*, 154, and ProQuest ebrary.
3. Augustinus A. Tseu, *The Moral Philosophy of Mo-Tze* (Taipei: China Printing Ltd., 1965), 23-29. See also Scott Lowe, *Mo Tzu's Religious Blueprint for a Chinese Utopia: The Will and the Way* (New York: The Edwin Mellen Press, 1992).

of Heaven." Mo Tzu is not interested in creating an egalitarian society but one that emphasises meritocracy. Nonetheless, it appears that his kind of government is an elitist and benevolent leadership that seeks to identify the needs of the people. This style of leadership has proven to be quite successful in uniting a multi-racial society like that which exists in Singapore. The economic success of Singapore is partly based on the Mohist-style leadership of the country and the Confucian values and ethics system of its people.

## Mohism Versus Confucianism

Though Mo Tzu's followers criticize Confucians, they nevertheless share some important common beliefs. Both Mo Tzu and Confucius believe that societies are naturally stratified and hierarchical, but that there should be opportunities open to all for upward mobility. Both also stress social and political stability. However, the two philosophers have very different views regarding the source of moral values. Confucius teaches that moral values are based on tradition. Emphasizing the importance of families as the basic unit of society, Confucius holds that personal virtues can be cultivated by following the rules of propriety, and that such rules govern rituals which facilitate our familial, social or professional relationships, whereas Mo Tzu thinks that Confucian ritual observed for its own sake yields only "unreflective morality."[1]

As a rival to the thought of Confucius, Mo Tzu is dissatisfied with the Sage's emphasis on ceremony and loyalty to family ties at the expense of the common good. He is opposed to the frivolity, music, and other amusements, which distract a person from following the "will of heaven." Similar to Christianity, Mo Tzu preaches that heaven desires all human beings to love one another. The righteous ones will be rewarded with eternal life but those who do not follow this path of righteousness will be punished. Many people, however, thought that Mo Tzu's teaching was impractical and eventually after the second century BC his school was forgotten.[2]

Unlike Confucius, Mo Tzu insists on reward and punishment as a method to motivate people to behave. This kind of strict social control resembles that of legalists. His society is strictly hierarchical and regimented. Thus "only in the condition of the ruled is anything resembling egalitarianism to be found."[3] The rulers and ministers have

1. Diane Collinson, Kathryn Plant, and Robert Wilkinson, *Fifty Eastern Thinkers* (Routledge Key Guides)(London: Routledge, 2000), 228.
2. Mo Tzu (470-391BC), http://oll.libertyfund.org/pages/mo-tzu-c-470-391-bc#_ftn1.
3. Lowe, *Mo Tzu's Religious Blueprint for a Chinese Utopia*, 16. On the issue of

all the power, prestige, and respect. In Mo Tzu's ideal world, equality is lacking but there is adequate food, clothing and shelter for all, without luxuries. Regarding the purpose of clothing, Mo Tzu insists that the purpose is to keep out the cold in winter and the heat in summer. Thus, any decorative element that does not contribute to this function is to be avoided. In this we are reminded of Thomas More's *Utopia*, where everyone wears the same kind of clothing to reduce class distinctions, and houses are built to keep out the elements, and thieves. Mo Tzu is against fashion or decoration that does not add anything to the utility of goods. For him, wealth is not to be wasted on trivialities. He wants rulers to give up their passion for collecting jewels, birds, horses, clothing, boats, weapons, and so on, so as to lessen taxation on people and thus bring about more benefits to the nation.[1]

Mo Tzu's ethical principles on social economy are as follows: (i) The right use of wealth. This means to use goods according to their natural purpose; for example, the purpose of eating is to nourish one's body. Eating excessively is gluttony. Everything we enjoy is created by heaven for our benefit, created to satisfy our natural needs and not for luxurious purposes. (ii) The right to private property. Mo Tzu wishes all people to share the benefits of heaven but he is not in favour of abolishing private property. In fact, he believes in the inviolability of private property when he teaches against aggressive war, which he regards as theft and robbery. For Mo Tzu, the violation of private property is a criminal act. (iii) The dignity of labor. For Mo Tzu, men must work hard to live. It is the capability of working that distinguishes human beings from animals.[2]

Mo Tzu and his disciples, known as Mohists, were much more critical of the ruling class than the followers of Confucius and other philosophical schools. In fact, the Mohists condemned the pastimes of the aristocrats, such as music, dances, luxurious lifestyle, which were made possible through taxing the poor. They also denounced expensive warfare because it was a burden on the people and brought little material benefit to the nation. Furthermore, the Mohists condemned extravagant funeral services, and fatalistic thinking. They believed such practices and ideas had to be abolished before there would be peace and order in society.[3]

----

    equality for Mo Tzu, see Evan Osborne, "China's First Liberal," *The Independent Review* 16, no. 4 (Spring, 2012), 536-39.

1.  Mo Tzu, *Basic Writings*, trans. Burton Watson, 62-64.
2.  See Tseu, *The Moral Philosophy of Mo-Tze*, 325-31.
3.  Mo Tzu, *Basic Writings*, trans. Burton Watson, 6.

Regarding Mo Tzu's anti-Confucianism, Benjamin Schwartz writes:

> it is the burning conviction of Mo Tzu that there is much that
> is not true and that the latter-day Confucianists embody this
> untruth. What he notes in them first of all is their enormous
> passivity in the face of fate (*ming*) – a passivity which he cannot
> disassociate from their entire attitude toward the universe,
> toward the whole area which we call religion.[1]

Mo Tzu was against four tenets of the Confucianists which he believed
would destroy the world: (i) they believe that heaven and the spirits do
not manifest their power nor do they speak; (ii) they spend too much
money on rites of mourning; (iii) they indulge in music and dances; and
(iv) they believe in fate and destiny regarding life, death, poverty, and
wealth.[2]

To have a better grasp of Mo Tzu's thoughts, it is important to have some
knowledge of the historical context in which he formulated his ideas. Mo
Tzu's life spanned the last years of the Spring and Autumn period (722-
481BC) and the early decades of the period of the Warring States (475-
221BC). Unfortunately, almost nothing is known about the life of Mo Tzu
except that he was the founder of the Mohist school of philosophy.

## Historical Background

After the death of Confucius in 479BC, the corruption deplored by the
Sage accelerated. There was fierce struggle for survival and domination
among the states and eventually a few large states dominated the rest. A
decline of the old aristocracies led to the formation of a more bureaucratic
form of government. Positions in the government were filled by elements
from the "floating stratum" – people that were drawn from the group
between the peasantry and the older nobility. One of the elements was
the emerging mercantile class, which reflected the development of a
currency-based economy, growth in production, and improvements in
transportation.[3] These were periods of great technological and social
change that led to the collapse of the feudal system.

Not everyone, however, benefitted from such changes. In fact, the rich
got richer and the poor got poorer because the peasants lost their lands
to the wealthy when they moved into urban areas seeking employment
in industries and commerce. Further, improvement in the "art of war"

---

1. Schwartz, *The World of Thought in Ancient China*, 138, and ProQuest ebrary.
2. Ibid., 139.
3. Ibid., 135.

also led to more battles being fought between the states. As we shall see, Mo Tzu was against aggressive warfare that led to much suffering and death. Military service provided opportunities for social mobility for a few individuals but the devastation caused by war afflicted many more people. "For those of humble origin, opportunities for personal advancement had never been greater, yet at the same time the peril and uncertainty of the ages left many longing for peace."[1] Witnessing this political and social turmoil, the growing population of literati developed religious scepticism, and new schools of thought attempted to offer solutions to this complex situation where there was widespread chaos. During this time, literacy began to spread to the sons of merchants, landlords, industrialists, and even to some talented commoners. This group of educated elite came to be known as *shih* (士) or knights, a title that formerly belonged to the aristocratic class. Confucius, who started schools to train administrators and scholars for the civil service, belonged to this class of *shih*. Mo Tzu too, pioneered a school that was distinct from the Confucian tradition. In fact, many such academies began to flourish at this time under different thinkers. Even though they held different philosophical and political positions, their main focus was on statecraft, which sought to answer questions associated with the ideal society, the social order, the conduct of ministers, and the role of the sage ruler. These academies also promoted their versions of the ideal gentleman. During the late Warring States period, there were a hundred of such schools but the most influential ones were those of Confucius and Mo Tzu.[2] Mo Tzu's vision of utopia is not so much an attempt to establish a new order but a desire for "worthy" persons to join the government service

## Honouring the Worthy

An ideal society, according to Mo Tzu, means that the people respect and honour their leaders – "honouring the worthy." Therefore, it was important for the rulers to recruit wise and honest men for employment in the government service. This may seem reasonable to us but, during the time of Mo Tzu, the aristocratic class controlled ministerial positions in the feudalistic government. However, such practices had already been challenged and many rulers were gathering men chosen from the lower classes less encumbered by family ties. Unburdened by family connections like the aristocrats, these common people would prove to be very loyal to the rulers who raised them up.[3]

1. Lowe, *Mo Tzu's Religious Blueprint for a Chinese Utopia*, 27.
2. Ibid., 28-29.
3. Mo Tzu, *Basic Writings*, trans. Burton Watson, 7.

Mo Tzu believed that rulers and high officials were unfit to govern the country because they failed to honour and employ the "worthy." This means they failed to engage educated, competent, and virtuous people to run the civil service. He held that the nation must promote righteous persons irrespective of their family background and thus set a good example for the rich and influential people in the country. Such righteous persons would be promoted, honoured with titles, given a good salary, and entrusted with great responsibilities. The "worthy" person in Mo Tzu's view must be a diligent and conscientious bureaucrat.

Competence and honesty are qualities that an ideal government official should possess:

> When a worthy man is given the task of ordering the state, he appears at court early and retires late, listens to lawsuits, and attends to the affairs of government. As a result, the state is well ordered and rewards and punishments are justly administered. When a worthy man heads a government bureau, he goes to bed late and gets up early, collecting taxes on the barriers and markets and on the resources of the hills, forests, lakes, and fish weirs, so that the treasury will be full.[1]

Recalling the ancient days of sage kings who were successful in the affairs of government, Mo Tzu writes:

> So, among the officials who enjoyed high rank and generous stipends in those days, there were none who were not unfailingly cautious and respectful, none who did not encourage and strive with each other in honouring virtue. It is gentlemen of true worth, therefore, who must act to assist and carry on the government.[2]

It is to be noted that, in keeping with these ideas, the Singapore government today pays high salaries to its ministers to ensure good performance and to avoid corruption.[3]

These worthy persons in ancient times, according to Mo Tzu, serve their lord with all their strength and heart and, when they were successful in carrying out their duties and responsibilities, they gave credit to their rulers: "Thus all that was beautiful and good came to reside in the ruler, while all grudges and complaints were directed against his subordinates. Peace and joy was the portion of the ruler, care and sorrow

---

1. Ibid., 23.
2. Ibid., 21.
3. See Lee Kuan Yew and Han Fook Kwang, *Lee Kuan Yew: Hard Truths to Keep Singapore Going*, 120-27.

that of his ministers."[1] This was how the wise kings ruled ancient China. Unfortunately, in the days of Mo Tzu, worthy men were given titles but they were poorly paid. Thus, they failed to inspire confidence in the people. The ministers would feel that they were being made use of by the rulers and thus had no affection for their superiors. Eventually, only the unworthy would fill the ranks of the civil service. Corruption would set in: "Put in charge of a government bureau, they steal and plunder; assigned to guard a city, they betray their trust or rebel."[2] The lesson Mo Tzu teaches is that the ruler must employ capable people to run the country and not depend on their family members, relatives and friends. Mo Tzu also adds that rich and attractive persons are not necessarily wise and alert in office. Good government requires competent and honest personnel.

When the country is run by worthy men, some of whom are recruited from very humble backgrounds, the people will not go hungry, cold or naked. Mo Tzu writes: "The ancient sage kings, in giving all their thought to honouring the worthy and employing the capable in government, were patterning their actions on the ways of Heaven."[3] Heaven also shows no discrimination between rich and poor, eminent or humble folks. Rich and eminent people who strive to be worthy are able to practice universal love. In other words, they work hard to benefit all people and teach the people to honour heaven and the spirits. Regarded as "Sons of Heaven," they act like parents to their subjects.[4] It should be noted that the word, "benefit," has a pejorative sense in Confucius' *Analects* – it means a concern for self-interest and is the opposite of righteousness. Perhaps Mo Tzu used it as a "gesture of defiance."[5]

Virtuous and enlightened leaders would rule people with justice, regulate water and land for the common good. "They served Heaven above, and Heaven responded to their virtues. They acted for the sake of the people below, and the people received benefit their whole life through."[6] Mo Tzu also warns us that there were also wealthy and eminent people who became wicked kings like the Three Dynasties of Old (Xia, Shang

---

1. Mo Tzu, *Basic Writings*, trans. Burton Watson, 25.
2. Ibid., 26-27.
3. Ibid., 30.
4. These are the sage kings of the Three Dynasties of Old, Yao, Shun, Yü, T'ang, Wen, and Wu. Ibid. The Three Dynasties of Old – Xia, Shang and Zhou – were perceived as ideal, a golden age. See Ching-I Tu, *Interpretation and Intellectual Change : Chinese Hermeneutics in Historical Perspective* (New Brunswick, N.J.: Transaction Publishers, 2005), 278.
5. Schwartz, *The World of Thought in Ancient China*, 145, and ProQuest ebrary.
6. Mo Tzu, *Basic Writings*, trans.Burton Watson, 32.

and Zhou), Chieh, Chou, Yu and Li.[1] They failed to "honour the worthy," instead they oppressed and tyrannized their subjects and caused them to curse heaven and abuse the spirits. Heaven thus punished these evil kings with execution and death, scattered their sons and grandsons, destroyed their homes, and prevented them from having descendants. Thus, for Mo Tzu, honouring the worthy by appointing able and honest ministers and paying them their due, is the foundation of good government.

Throughout the text, *Mo Tzu*, we discover the author's concern for the welfare of the world. The ultimate concern of Mo Tzu is to promote actions and policies that are beneficial to all the peoples in the world and at the same time eliminate those that are harmful to the common good. Concretely, the aims of Mo Tzu are as follows: to restore good government, to increase population and to achieve harmony among people – in other words, to bring about an ideal society.

Mo Tzu is not interested in creating an egalitarian community but rather a meritocratic society where competent and honest persons would rise to the top of the social and political system. They would be rewarded with high position in the government and receive a good salary. Mo Tzu also provides an account of humble people like cooks and fishermen who were promoted to high positions when they were discovered to be talented as well as being honest and good workers. The emphasis here is on employing and promoting the virtuous who will ensure that those who are hungry will be fed and those who are naked will be clothed. Recalling the ancient sage kings who prudently exalted the virtuous and employed them to govern the country without regard for their social rank, Mo Tzu taught that these monarchs were modelling themselves on heaven. In other words, the kings were imitating the impartiality of heaven.

For Mo Tzu, the norm of morality is heaven or the will of God. Heaven in Mo Tzu's thought appears to be like a personal God who is capable of loving people and also demands that people love each other. Mo Tzu's understanding of heaven is synonymous with *Shang Ti*, "a personal and intelligent God, Creator and Supreme Ruler of the Universe."[2] In fact, Mo Tzu thinks of heaven as a personal being with a mind and heart, a being capable of reflection, formulating intentions, and having emotions such as love and anger.[3] Scholars generally believe that Mo Tzu was a theist who believed in the existence of a personal God whose will is the norm of morality.

---

1. Ibid., 31.
2. Tseu, *The Moral Philosophy of Mo-Tze*, 80.
3. Geoffrey MacCormack, "The Legal Philosophy of Mo Tzu," *Archiv Für Rechts-Und Sozialphilosophie/Archives for Philosophy of Law and Social Philosophy (ARSP)* 79, no. 3 (1993), 335.

Confucius' teaching, too, emphasized the importance of character and ability rather than birth. It is about statecraft and the need to recruit talented and honest people to government since proper management of human resources is crucial for the welfare of the nation. The former Prime Minister of Singapore, Lee Kuan Yew, also believed that "having exceptional talent in charge is critical. Without men of integrity and ability helming key institutions and government, the place would go down." He said, "Once you have weaker people on top, the whole system slowly goes down. It's inevitable."[1] Lee adds, "I am against a feudal society where your birth decides where you stay in the pecking order."[2] Lee's style of government is actually a kind of elitism that seeks to implement an egalitarian society from above via a benevolent leadership which "identifies its interests with the poor and marginalized in society."[3] To this day, the Singapore leadership style reflects Mo Tzu's teaching on identification with one's superior.

## Identification with One's Superior

Good governance is about securing benefits for society and preventing harm being done to it. Mo Tzu's vision of an ideal society includes prosperity, a flourishing population, and a stable government that promotes peace and harmony among the people. A state of anarchy and chaos would be abhorrent to Mo Tzu:

> Within the family, fathers and sons, older and younger brothers grew to hate each other and the family split up, unable to live in harmony, while throughout the world people all resorted to water, fire, and poison in an effort to do each other injury. Those with strength to spare refused to help out others, those with surplus wealth would let it rot before they would share it, and those with beneficial doctrines to teach would keep them secret and refuse to impart them. The world was as chaotic as though it was inhabited by birds and beasts alone.[4]

In such a chaotic world, there are no distinctions between lord and subject, superior and subordinate, elder and younger brother, no proper relationship between father and son. This is because there is no ruler able

---

1. Lee Kuan Yew and Han Fook Kwang, *Lee Kuan Yew: Hard Truths to Keep Singapore Going*, 19.
2. Ibid., 50.
3. Ibid., 150.
4. Mo Tzu, *Basic Writings*, trans. Burton Watson, 34.

to unify the view of the world. According to Mo Tzu, thus, heaven would step in and select the most virtuous, clever and capable person to be the emperor so that he could unify the views of the empire. The emperor, however, could not do the job alone; he had to appoint the wisest and ablest men as dukes to help him to unify the states. Similarly, the dukes would also select virtuous people to help them in the task of governing, as generals, officials, and village chiefs.

In the midst of political and social turmoil, Mo Tzu urges his followers to identify with their superiors rather than hold fast to their own personal views. Through "a series of progressively more universal identifications," individuals can expand their sphere of loyalty to the clan, to the district, to the state, then to the emperor, and, finally, to heaven itself. In this way, at each stage of allegiance, "the wills and standards of the people are united in ever widening circles of allegiance, producing the desired social cohesion and harmony."[1]

The ideal society presented by Mo Tzu is one of harmony achieved by the standardization of thoughts and actions. Anyone who strays from the norms set by his superior is disciplined and punished. A system of rewards and punishment ensures that there are checks and balances. Informers are also employed to make sure that the culprits are reprimanded and the good rewarded. The ultimate source of this system is not the emperor but heaven. Mo Tzu assumes that identification with the superior is desirable because the superior is following the dictates of heaven. Moreover, "the will of the people has a force of its own that is based on a sort of ethical consensus; the people cannot long be subjected to arbitrary decrees that clash with their ingrained, Heaven-ordained standards of right and wrong."[2] For Mo Tzu, heaven is the foundation of social order.

Chinese philosophy has a great deal of authoritarianism and thus a doctrine like Mo Tzu's "identifying with one's superior" is not as controversial as one might imagine. The lower class did not have much independence of thought and action. Chinese society is basically hierarchical, a pyramid with the "Son of Heaven" at the top. Thus, it was natural for Mo Tzu to insist that people take their orders from the class above them. Human beings imitate the speech patterns and practices of their elders. Mo Tzu seeks to exploit this disposition to emulate and to modify it. Utilitarianism would be the norm to guide social and ethical behavior.[3]

---

1. Lowe, *Mo Tzu's Religious Blueprint for a Chinese Utopia*, 86.
2. Ibid., 90.
3. Chad Hansen, "Mo-Tzu: Language Utilitarianism," *Journal of Chinese Philosophy* 16,

The doctrine of utilitarianism holds that actions are neither intrinsically right nor wrong. Actions are right if they increase benefits or decrease harm; actions are wrong if they decrease benefits or increase harm. In other words, actions are to be judged by their consequences. Utilitarianism according to Mo Tzu is not for the satisfaction of desire nor for pleasure or happiness. Mo Tzu thinks of utilitarianism as beneficial for the material well-being of all people in the state.[1]

Confucius teaches that, if the ruler were to go astray or go awry, then a ruler with superior virtue would rise up to take his place, simple as that. Mo Tzu follows this principle but he is more focussed on the supernatural power of heaven in this process of change.[2] The power of heaven includes the command to love everyone without discrimination.

## Universal Love

Universal love is referred to as the action of the sage: "It is the business of the benevolent man to try to promote what is beneficial to the world and to eliminate what is harmful."[3] Thus, the sage must be able to control disorder, which is caused by the lack of mutual love, according to Mo Tzu. Mutual love is equivalent to filial piety or *xiao*. In Mohism, it is applied to a wide range of relationships between superiors and subordinates. This means that sons must love their fathers, but fathers must also show their affection for their sons. In the same way, ministers should love their lords and the lords must also show affection for their ministers. Both parties in this relationship must live up to their responsibilities if we are to have social order.[4] Disorder arises when individuals seek to benefit only themselves, their families or their state at the expense of others. According to Mo Tzu, this disorder stems from the lack of mutual love.

---

no. 3 (1989), 359-60. Regarding Mo Tzu as a consistent utilitarian who is committed to a divine command theory, see Kristopher Duda, "Reconsidering Mo Tzu on the Foundations of Morality," *Asian Philosophy* 11, no. 1 (March 2001), 23-31.

1. Ibid., 379. Both David Soles and Dennis Ahern argue that Mo Tzu is not a utilitarian. Soles says that Mo Tzu is "a consistent Voluntarist or Divine Will theorist who believes that utilitarian considerations are reliable indicators for determining Heaven's will." David E. Soles, "Mo Tzu and the Foundations of Morality," *Journal of Chinese Philosophy* 26, no. 1 (1999), 47. See also Dennis M. Ahern, "Is Mo Tzu a Utilitarian?" *Journal of Chinese Philosophy* 3, no. 2 (1976), 185-93.
2. Mo Tzu, *Basic Writings*, trans. Burton Watson, 8.
3. Ibid., 39.
4. Lowe, *Mo Tzu's Religious Blueprint for a Chinese Utopia*, 92.

Universal love is actually an aspect of "identification with the superior" mentioned earlier. It occurs when we expand our loyalties from individual self-interest to include the interest of the clan, the state, the emperor, and heaven.[1] Thus, instead of worrying about our own self-interest, Mo Tzu teaches us to identify with the interest of society at large and eventually with the will of heaven. Further, Mo Tzu's universal love suggests regarding other states, their families, and their people as our own. If there is universal love, there will be no wars and all relations will be harmonized. All abuses and exploitations of the poor and weak will come to an end as well.

Critics say that universal love is idealistic and impractical. Mo Tzu, however, believes that, if rulers understand what benefits universal love would bring, they will work hard to foster it. They will choose their assistants carefully and reward them generously for good service. They will use both reward and punishment to get the desired result. Mo Tzu sees universal love in terms of physical feats or acts of control and not in terms of emotion or spiritual state. Thus, "if one acts *as if* he regards another's person as his own, then he is practicing universal love."[2] An ascetic, Mo Tzu is concerned with outward behavior and not the psychological or spiritual disposition of the person. His idea of universal love is not based on emotion but is rather a style of acting out one's conviction. It is a style characterized by magnanimity, righteousness and impartiality.[3] For Confucius, however, love "is a kind of total inner excellence of soul from which all the other virtues flow." It is a particular love that occurs in degrees - "graded love."[4]

Christine Swanton holds that "the virtue of universal love is a *preparedness* to manifest love towards any human individual regardless of attractiveness, merits, and so forth, and is expressed by actual manifestations where appropriate."[5] This preparedness is an orientation towards the world at large and is manifested in virtues such as grace, benevolence, forgiveness, and mercy.

Refuting Mencius' teaching, Mo Tzu points out that universal love is not contrary to filial piety because filial sons, too, desire others to love their parents as well. Essentially the *Dao* or way of the ancient sage kings, universal love will bring wealth to people who practice it. Universal love

---

1. Ibid., 93.
2. Ibid., 95.
3. Ibid., 99.
4. Schwartz, *The World of Thought in Ancient China*, 146, and ProQuest ebrary.
5. Christine Swanton, "A Challenge to Intellectual Virtue from Moral Virtue: The Case of Universal Love," in Heather Battaly, ed., *Virtue and Vice, Moral and Epistemic*, (Chichester: Wiley-Blackwell, 2010), 156.

also involves a clear ordering of hierarchical relationships in society. It cannot be "dissociated from the idea of the central unified source of political authority. In the absence of such a centre one will again relapse into the war of particular interests."[1] The centre may be occupied by unworthy rulers, but there will be sages and wise persons to enlighten the people through the structure. Mo Tzu does not see any conflict between universality and class differences. Treating others as fairly as possible does not mean that there is complete equality in society. In other words, universality does not mean equality.

It is universality in dealings with others that gives rise to benefits in the world, whereas partiality brings only harm, according to Mo Tzu. If we practice universality, the old and the orphaned will be taken care of in our society. The universal-minded person will regard his friend like himself and his friend's father like his own. He will thus feed, clothe, and take care of his friend, when necessary. A truly enlightened ruler must think of his subjects first and of himself last. He will feed the hungry, clothe the naked, take care of the sick, and bury them when they die. Such are the deeds of the universal-minded ruler.

The doctrine of universal love is the most original contribution of Mo Tzu's philosophy to Chinese thought. Not content with just condemning harmful acts to others, Mo Tzu insists that we should love members of other families, clans and states in the same way as we love our own family members because all are equal in the eyes of God. This was indeed a noble idea because Mo Tzu taught this doctrine at a time when there were fierce hatreds and rivalries in his society. He was a man who dared to transcend the class division of his feudal society, to challenge its ideology and convention.[2]

With its strong sense of loyalty to one's family and clan, the society of Mo Tzu was not prepared to accept his idea of universal love and altruism. In fact, most people would find the idea of universal love ridiculous and impractical. Family ties and graded loyalty are natural dispositions in human beings. Since we are deeply influenced by our family, it can be a powerful force in shaping our social behavior. Mo Tzu accepted the fact that graded love is natural in human beings, but he doubted its ethical value.[3]

His teaching regarding universal love was not accepted because Mo Tzu did not defend his doctrine with lofty ideas. He merely emphasized the material benefits of practicing universal love and supported his teaching with a dubious account of an idyllic age coupled with an appeal

1. Schwartz, *The World of Thought in Ancient China*, 163, and ProQuest ebrary.
2. Mo Tzu, *Basic Writings*, trans. Burton Watson, 9-10.
3. Chad Hansen, "Mo-Tzu: Language Utilitarianism," 359.

to authoritarianism. In fact, his simplistic argument with its emphasis on "cautious utilitarianism" . . . "piety, non-aggression, and universal love become no more than judicious policies of government."[1]

Mo Tzu's universal love was contrary to Confucius' unselfish but discriminating love and kindness towards other people. Eventually, Mo Tzu's ideas lost their relevance and significance due to changes in Chinese society. Technological progress in farming and the growth of commerce meant that people who became prosperous were not inclined to live a simple, frugal life and to practice universal love.[2] Nevertheless, Mo Tzu insists that universal love is advantageous and easy to practice, and included in this practice of universal love is the avoidance of offensive wars against weaker neighbouring states.

## Against Offensive Warfare

In order to promote what is beneficial, officials in China must not engage in offensive warfare because it causes great harm to the world, according to Mo Tzu. He holds that, when a state is eager to start a war, it must have several hundreds of high officers, several thousands of regular officers, and a hundred thousand soldiers before it can set out. The war will take several years and will lead to neglect by the rulers of the affairs of the government. The officials will have no time to manage the state departments and the farmers will have no time to sow. Rulers are misguided when they indulge in warfare. Mo Tzu believes that, if the rulers are able to establish a reputation for righteousness and to attract other rulers by their virtues, the whole world will eventually be under their control.

The Chinese empire, during Mo Tzu's time, had been plagued by warfare and people longed for peace. He writes:

> Now if only there were someone who would conduct his diplomatic affairs in good faith and would think first of all how to benefit the other feudal lords; who, when a large state committed some unrighteous act, would feel concerned along with others; who, when a large state attacked a small one, would go to the rescue of the small state along with others . . . if one were to conduct his relations with the large states in this manner, then the rulers of the smaller states would be pleased.[3]

---

1. Mo Tzu, *Basic Writings*, trans. Burton Watson, 11. See also Dirck Vorenkamp, "Another Look at Utilitarianism in Mo Tzu's Thought," *Journal of Chinese Philosophy* 19, no. 4 (1992), 423-43.
2. Mo Tzu, *Basic Writings*, trans. Burton Watson, 13.
3. Ibid., 59-60.

Mo Tzu teaches that rulers must be "merciful and generous, substituting affluence for want, then the people will surely be won over."[1] Rulers, thus, must set good examples of righteousness, leniency and good faith for other feudal lords to follow. Then the country will have no enemy under heaven and it will reap much fruits.

As we can see, Mo Tzu condemns aggressive war because of its terrible consequences. For him aggression is comparable to robbery and assault; it is also against the purpose of the government whose duty is to promote peace and harmony. Aggressive war causes killings, destruction, and violation of justice. Furthermore, it causes practical disadvantage to the conquering state as well as to the conquered state. The aggressor is not always the winner. The aggressive state stands to lose many lives, hurts its own economy, and loses its population. Mo Tzu also believes that benefits to the state can be acquired not by gaining more territories but by eliminating needless expenses within the state itself.

Mo Tzu also attempts to defend weaker states by teaching them defensive war techniques. He also urges smaller states to form alliances among themselves as a defence against the stronger states. In short, Mo Tzu is in favour of an alliance of all peace-loving nations. Regarding this utopian view, he was a man ahead of his time. Like Confucius and Mencius before him, Mo Tzu travelled widely in China, spreading his doctrine of universal love to feudal rulers who were fighting against each other. For example, when Mo Tzu heard that Chu was planning to attack Sung, he walked for ten days and nights to meet the Chu leader, hoping to persuade him to call off the expedition. He believed that such aggression could be halted by practicing universal love as well as by strengthening the defence of weaker states. Thus, the followers of Mo Tzu attempted to help besieged states and became experts on war strategy and the study of logic.[2]

It was believed that Mo Tzu served in the State of Sung in some official capacity and he was successful in influencing his disciples to defend Sung. One of the reasons given was that Mo Tzu was able to secure for his disciples good positions in the government. Followers of Mo Tzu, known as the Mohist movement, were "a confluence of merchants, craftsmen, and déclassé nobles, briefly emerging as a power in the cities as the feudal order disintegrates."[3] Like the followers of Confucius, the Mohists sought to influence society through appointments in the government service. They also believed that the development of an ideal world would be realized through the revival of the enlightened rule of the sage kings in ancient China.

---

1. Ibid., 60.
2. Ibid., 2.
3. Quoted in Lowe, *Mo Tzu's Religious Blueprint for a Chinese Utopia*, 36.

The prevention of war was one of the fundamental tenets of the Mohist movement. Determined to rescue the innocent from unprovoked attacks and aggression from neighbouring states, the Mohists were also scholars and debaters who used dialogue as their first line of defence – "to persuade others of the folly of wars of conquest."[1] Only when persuasion and dialogue failed would the Mohists send their tacticians and engineers to defend the beleaguered state.

## The Will of Heaven

Mo Tzu's concept of heaven is one of impartiality in its judgment of humanity. A stern judge of human conduct, heaven nevertheless loves the entire world. The will of heaven is related to the love of heaven as it deals with justice for the people. Divine retribution falls on evildoers and thus the innocent are protected. If heaven did not love humanity, then it would not care about the poor and innocent. Heaven is also portrayed by Mo Tzu as "the conscious organizing power responsible for all that is right in the world."[2] Not quite like the creator, heaven nevertheless acts like someone responsible for the running of the world. It punishes bad rulers and rewards the good ones and is also concerned for the fate of the commoners who are subjects to these kings.

The ideal world, according to Mo Tzu, is one that follows the will of heaven, and its government is based on the philosophy of righteousness. Given the political turmoil and conflicts that existed during the Warring States period, any account of a peaceful world would be considered utopian. The state founded on the will of heaven will be wealthy and orderly. Any surplus wealth will be used to sacrifice to heaven or used to enhance friendship with the neighbouring states. Once internal and external peace are secured, people will have their basic needs provided for; the relationships between rulers and bureaucrats will be loyal; the relationships between fathers and sons, older and younger brother, will be characterized by their piety and affection.[3]

Mo Tzu writes:

> Therefore, if one clearly understands how to obey the will of Heaven and puts it into practice in the world at large, then the government will be well ordered, and the population harmonious,

---

1. Ibid., 42.
2. Ibid., 134.
3. Mo Tzu, *Basic Writings*, trans. Burton Watson, 86.

the state rich, and wealth and goods plentiful. The people will all have warm clothes and plenty to eat, and will live in comfort and peace, free from care.[1]

The Mohist ideal world is a place where everyone has all the basic necessities of life and whatever is left over is used to promote good relationships with the neighbouring states.

The ideal world envisioned by Mo Tzu is also highly stratified as it is based on individual ability: it is a meritocratic state. Those who hold positions of authority are richly rewarded with high salary, status and power. A ruler would not be respected without these three things. Further, "great ideological uniformity is to be demanded, with every member of society identifying his standards with those of his immediate superior."[2] The emperor, the highest authority in the land, must identify himself with the norms of heaven. In the ideal world, religious practice will be put in place, resulting in peace and prosperity in the society. There will be an adequate supply of food, medicine, spices, and wine, alongside proper shelter for the people. In addition, traditional social structures will be maintained for filial reverence and other duties based on one's degree of relationship and social status.[3]

The ultimate concern of Mo Tzu is to create an ideal society by promoting benefits and removing all harm from the world. These benefits include economic and population growth, the cessation of wars, the establishment of a stable and good government, and the reduction of wasteful expenditure. The ultimate concern of Mo Tzu is doing the will of heaven. To achieve the above benefits, he has devised the means or actions for the transformation of society. In other words, the restoration of the world to the condition enjoyed by the ancient sage kings. Believing that it is within the reach of people if they are willing to work towards it, Mo Tzu seeks to promote the unity of humankind.

Unfortunately, Mo Tzu did not achieve much success regarding his grand plan. Be that as it may, the most important point to note is that Mo Tzu has presented a coherent programme for the transformation of society and the creation of an ideal world. It was the first Chinese attempt to provide a comprehensive plan of action for the establishment of a utopia.

---

1. Ibid.
2. Lowe, *Mo Tzu's Religious Blueprint for a Chinese Utopia*, 154.
3. Ibid.

## Utopia

In his writings, Mo Tzu attempts to describe what a perfect world ought to be. He sincerely believes that it is possible to construct a better world and so he sets about attempting to transform this corrupted world into an ideal one for all. Mo Tzu's understanding of utopia is simple: the unity of all men and women in a peaceful and prosperous world. This is realizable if people are taught the doctrine of universal love beginning with the identification with one's immediate superior, who must also be a virtuous gentleman whom the people can trust and imitate. The immediate superior must, in turn, obey his boss, and so on. Thus, one will arrive at the "Supreme Superior" and eventually we will be united into one world government: "If we examine the reason why the world was well ordered, we find that it was simply that the Son of Heaven was able to unify the standard of judgment throughout the world, and this resulted in order."[1]

Aware that most rulers fall short of expectations, Mo Tzu emphasizes that only the virtuous may be appointed as superior. Of course, Mo Tzu assumes that the emperor must also be a virtuous person; otherwise this utopian vision will not be realized. He hopes that the emperor would imitate the examples of the sage kings and employ capable and honest people to assist him in running the government: "Therefore the sage kings of ancient times took great pains to honour the worthy and employ the capable, showing no special consideration for their own kin, no partiality for the eminent and rich, no favouritism for the good-looking and attractive."[2] Mo Tzu's utopian vision is the complete realization of the doctrine of universal love.

The utopia of Mo Tzu requires a civil government for the implementation of policies. Besides employing capable people in the government, the emperor must also divide his empire into provinces and districts to facilitate the governing procedure. It is the bureaucracy headed by the emperor with his subordinates pledging absolute obedience to him. Mo Tzu favours an "imperialism" that is close to a dictatorship.[3] However, if the emperor is all powerful and dictatorial, how can we ensure that the individual's rights are respected?

Mo Tzu's ideal ruler is absolute in his command of the empire but he is not infallible. Thus, if the emperor failed to rule his empire justly and wisely, he could be disposed of and be subjected to the punishment

---

1. Mo Tzu, *Basic Writings*, trans. Burton Watson, 37.
2. Ibid., 22.
3. Tseu, *The Moral Philosophy of Mo-Tze*, 377.

of heaven, like everyone else. Heaven could punish him by inspiring the people to revolt, depose him and install a new dynasty. Endorsed by Confucius and Mencius, such revolts have occurred many times in the history of China. Mo Tzu is also confident that heaven will inspire a revolution to punish tyrants and evil emperors and thus restore freedom and prosperity to the people. He trusted Divine Providence, the supreme leader of the universe.

In the ideal government of Mo Tzu, the interest of the common people comes first. The emperor is chosen to work for the common good, to secure peace and prosperity for his people. If the emperor fails to do this, he must be rejected. Of course, Mo Tzu was not so naive as to think that virtuous persons are perfect. He admits that they do make mistakes and thus they must be humble enough to accept fraternal corrections even from their subordinates. The subordinates in turn must be able to show their superiors their shortcomings in a respectful and polite way. In this way, it is clear that the people are not slaves to the emperor. In fact, it is the emperor who must serve his people.

Except for the emperor, Mo Tzu insists that the rest of the government officials must be appointed. In other words, the positions are not inherited. Here, we actually have a meritocratic process in which capable and honest individuals are employed in the government service, while those who do not perform well in office must be dismissed. Mo Tzu did not give any special privilege to the relatives of the emperor; they are simply citizens in his democratic utopia. Thus, in spite of imperial rule in Mo Tzu's ideal world, it is essentially democratic in spirit.[1]

## Democratic Spirit

Cardinal Paul Yu-pin (1901-78), former Archbishop of Nanking wrote: "Though China's government was monarchical in form, in spirit, but in reality it was democratic. The Chinese seem to be by nature democratic."[2] How does this spirit of democracy work in Mo Tzu's ideal government? The primary duty of the ruler is to identify and implement the wishes of the people. The ruler, however, can respond to the people's wishes only if they all have the same goal. In the end, it is the ruler or the superior who must determine what the people wish. Thus, the people end up complying with the wishes of the government. For Mo Tzu, this is not oppression of the people because the ruler is required to obey the will of heaven whose

1. Ibid., 381.
2. Ibid.

only desire is for the well-being of the people.[1] This top-down approach in decision-making in government has produced successful city-states like Singapore. Success comes only when the leadership is benevolent, honest and competent.

Cardinal Yu-pin also asserted that among the nations in the world, the Chinese were least affected by their rulers. They governed themselves through local organizations and pledged their loyalty first to their families and not to the nation: "Chinese government has always been a government by men, not by law. When the men were good, all went well; when the men were evil, they were usually deposed."[2] Reward and punishment play an important role in Mo Tzu's social thought. For him, law is to be identified with reward and punishment, and used by the ruler as an instrument of the government. The application of law occurs not only at the human level, but at the divine level as well. It is an essential part of heaven's concern for humankind. The law of reward and punishment is used by heaven to ensure that the ruler and his people comply with its wishes. A utilitarian, Mo Tzu's vision of utopia is temporal as well as spiritual.

---

1. MacCormack, "The Legal Philosophy of Mo Tzu," 342.
2. Tseu, *The Moral Philosophy of Mo-Tze*, 382.

# 6
# One World

Like Mo Tzu, Kang Youwei (1858-1927) was critical of Confucianism and yet adhered to some of the Sage's fundamental teachings. Kang emphasized the importance of universal love, disarmament, the will of heaven and democratic spirit. Considered the first utopian writer in China, Kang was a native of Nanhai, Guangdong province, from a wealthy family of scholar-officials. A leader of the Reform Movement of 1898, Kang sought to promote his own interpretation of Confucianism and introduce some aspects of Western culture in his utopian vision.

As a reformer, Kang sent seven petitions to the emperor from 1885 to 1898, advising the Qing government how to resist foreign invasion and how to modernize China. The late Qing reform started on 11 June 1889, when Emperor Guangxu issued an imperial edict for the purpose of strengthening the nation. Kang and his followers submitted about two hundred recommendations for reform to the emperor. In turn, the emperor produced about one hundred imperial edits based on these recommendations which covered political, economic, social, and military issues.[1]

Kang's approach to reform was to deprive the bureaucracy of power by placing it in the hands of the emperors and his advisors. It was an attack on the Qing establishment, "a drastic recasting of the whole

---

1. Shiping Hua, *Chinese Utopianism: A Comparative Study of Reformist Thought with Japan and Russia, 1898-1997* (Washington, DC: Woodrow Wilson Center Press, 2009), 27, 30.

political structure of the empire."[1] The Empress Dowager, Cixi, revoked the reforms on 21 September 1891, and placed the emperor under house arrest. Avoiding persecution by the Empress Dowager, Kang spent a total of sixteen years in exile, visiting over forty countries in five continents. The time spent in exile gave him ample opportunity to reflect deeply about human existence and to formulate his utopian ideas. Hope for a better future led him to his utopian vision.

A prolific writer, among Kang's best work is the *Datong shu* (*The Book of Great Unity*) (大 同 書) where he laid out his utopian vision for the world.[2] In this volume, Kang saw himself as a sage whose mission was to save China. He envisaged an ideal society on earth based on Confucianism and principles drawn Buddhism and Daoism. He wanted to demonstrate to other nations that, in addition to Western thought, the philosophical traditions of China could help humanity to construct a better world.

In fact, *datong* has its roots in Confucian tradition. Confucius had hopes for a *datong* (大同) or grand harmony, based on a real human community that existed long before his time during the Yao and Shun periods (c.2350-2250BC). Many scholars believe that Confucius invented this concept of *datong*, while some argue that the term is a product of various Confucian thinkers. This idea of grand harmony was conceived during the time of hardships and sufferings caused by the Warring States period. Utopian thought is widespread in times of political and social upheavals. Confucian hope stresses the common good rather than individual gain. Thus, it is not surprising that the Communist Party in China emphasizes this aspect of Confucianism – the collective good.[3]

*Datong shu* was completed in 1902 but it was published only partially in 1913 and in its entirety in 1935. Challenging traditions and values that had shaped Chinese culture for centuries, Kang thought that the time was not right to accept his ideas.[4] Believing that a better world is

1. Quoted in Shiping Hua, *Chinese Utopianism*, 31.
2. There are several English translations, in addition to this, of *Datong shu*, such as *The Book of the Great Community*, *One World Philosophy*, *The Great Commonwealth*, *The Great Harmony* and *One World System*.
3. Shiping Hua, *Chinese Utopianism*, 18.
4. See Lauren Frederick Pfister, "A Modern Ruist Religious Vision of a Global Unity: Kang Youwei's Utopian Vision and its Humanistic Religious Refraction in European Sinology," in Thomas Jansen, Thoralf Klein and Christian Meyer, eds., *Globalization and the Making of Religious Modernity in China: Transnational Religions, Local Agents, and the Study of Religion, 1800-Present* (Leiden: Brill, 2014), 241-42. The first draft of *Datong shu* was completed in 1884-85. Shiping

possible, Kang had written a text with utopian consciousness. His ideas were conceived out of discontent with the political, economic, and social conditions of his country, and his desire to unite the world. A severe critic of his age, Kang had witnessed the widespread sufferings of his people. He traced the root cause of these calamities to faulty institutions, which he calls "boundaries," such as the state, class, race, gender, family, and property.

This chapter explores the utopian vision in Kang's *Datong shu* with a focus on his attempt to abolish the boundaries that hinder human progress towards perfection. Kang sought to remove any law, practice and institution that he believed were harmful to society. Some of his ideas seem far-fetched, unrealistic and controversial, but his overall intention was to unite and reduce the sufferings of humanity. He also wanted to create a society where people could move about freely irrespective of their place of birth and social status. Steeped in Chinese tradition and acquainted with Western thought, Kang's utopian vision was unique and universal in outlook. His aim to stop all human sufferings is global in scope, and is in line with Confucius' teaching of *ren* (仁) or benevolence towards all persons.[1]

## Universality of Love

Assuming that love is inherent in all creatures, Kang believes that loving one's fellow beings is natural and universal: "Being that I was born on the earth, then mankind in the ten thousand countries of the earth are all my brothers (literally, of the same womb) of different bodily types. Being that I have knowledge of them, then I have love, *qin* (親) for them."[2] In other words, human nature is fundamentally the same in all cultures and we are born to love and to be loved.

Rooted in life experiences, Kang emphasizes that love occurs everywhere and at all times:

---

Hua, *Chinese Utopianism*, 36.
1. Pfister argues that Kang's approach was influenced by Buddhist teaching: "all is suffering." There are six types of sufferings for Kang: actions that destroy life, lack of humanness, abuse of human desires, misdirected values and manipulated esteem, distortions caused by human structures, and vast destructions cause by natural disasters. What makes these claims Confucian is that they are real sufferings and not emptiness "without substance" as taught by Buddhism. Pfister, "A Modern Ruist Religious Vision of a Global Unity," 247-48.
2. K'ang Yu-wei, *Ta T'ung Shu: The One World Philosophy of K'ang Yu-wei*, translated from the Chinese with introduction and notes by Laurence G. Thompson (London: George Allen & Unwin Ltd, 1958), 65.

All that is finest and best of the former wisdom of India, Greece, Persia, Rome, and of present-day England, France, Germany, and America, I have lapped up and drunk, rested on, pillowed on; and my soul in dreams has fathomed it. With the most ancient and noted savants, famous scholars, and great men, I have likewise often joined hands, to sit on mats side by side, sleeve touching, sharing our soup; and I have come to love them.[1]

Thus, when these people progress, Kang would also progress, when they suffer, he would also suffer with them. In order to stop human suffering, Kang urges for the abolition of modern institutions such as national boundaries or the state.

## Abolition of National Boundaries

Kang acknowledges that, since ancient times, human beings have always lived in communities of various sizes such as families, clans, tribes, and states. These social institutions were useful for the protection of the communities but they also led to conflicts and wars of conquest among themselves. States have their origin in the annexation of smaller entities by military conquest. Thus, as long as states exist, war is inevitable because it is inherent in the nature of political organizations. In fact, civilization only helps to make war more sophisticated and destructive: "Anciently, wars were fought with knives, in which men were killed singly; now wars are fought with fire and poison. Several hundred thousand men could be slaughtered in one evening, as at Sedan. Alas, how grievous and lamentable are the aftereffects of the establishment of the state!"[2]

In view of the nature of the state, Kang calls for the abolition of national boundaries so that the world can be one. When states and patriotism are linked, each one looks to the advantage of his own territory and thus conflicts start. Strong states will annex weaker ones and the calamities of wars carried throughout history have poisoned humanity throughout the world. When we have states, we begin the fight. We fight to keep others out of our territories and thus humankind cannot progress with mindless killings of each other. Thus, as long as sovereign states exist there can be "no perfection of human nature" and no "complete peace-

---

1. Ibid., 66.
2. Quoted in Hsiao Kung-Chuan, *A Modern China and a New World: K'ang Yu-Wei, Reformer and Utopian, 1858-1927* (Seattle: University of Washington, 1975), 443.

and-equality."[1] Disarmament is necessary to bring about peace, but it cannot be accomplished as long as there are state boundaries where the weak have to face the strong.

Immanuel Kant (1724-1804), in his discourse on peace, writes:

> To annex a state, which, like a tree trunk, has its own roots, and thus to treat it as a graft onto another state, is to annul its existence as a moral person and to treat this moral person as a mere thing. Doing so hence contradicts the idea of the original contract, an idea without which no right over a people is conceivable.[2]

For Kant, "a state is not a possession (*patrimonium*), as is, for instance, the territory on which it exists. It is, rather, a society of human beings, whom no one but the state itself may command or dispose of."[3] Thus, Kant calls for the gradual disarmament of state by getting rid of their standing armies. Kang also calls for the abolition of troops so that the military expenditure of states could be used for establishing schools, hospitals, and other facilities for the welfare of the people.

Kang is convinced that to save the human race from misery and to bring about complete peace and equality, we must abolish the idea of the state and nationalism. This, however, is easier said than done because the state represents the highest form of human organization and outside of "Heaven," there is no higher law to govern it. It seems natural that strong states will swallow up weaker states. In other words, "no universal law can restrain it, no empty theory can affect it."[4] In the long run, however, Kang believes that it can be done because it is the hope of human beings to be united in One World. Kang looks at Confucius' Era of Complete Peace-and-Equality and the Buddha's Lotus World as models for achieving One World.

In the West, the progress of democracy, constitution, communism and labor unions are the initial features of One World. Immanuel Kant maintains that the republican constitution is based on the "principles of *freedom* of the members of a society," on the "principles of the *dependence* of all on a single, common legislation" and "according to the law of equality" of all the citizens of the state.[5] Kang is confident

---

1. K'ang Yu-wei, *Ta T'ung Shu: The One World Philosophy of K'ang Yu-wei*, 83.
2. Immanuel Kant, *Toward Perpetual Peace and Other Writings on Politics, Peace, and History* (New Haven, CT: Yale University Press, 2006), 68.
3. Ibid.
4. K'ang Yu-wei, *Ta T'ung Shu: The One World Philosophy of K'ang Yu-wei*, 84.
5. Immanuel Kant, *Toward Perpetual Peace and Other Writings on Politics, Peace, and History*, 74.

that, within the next century, states boundaries and monarchies will be abolished and the world will be made one through disarmament and universal legislature. Republican government, democracy and equality will prevail and there is no stopping it. The world will also be united by having a universal belief of "serving Heaven."[1]

From the condemnation of the state, Kang moves on to criticize social classes. He believes that political organization like the state tends to divide people into classes for economic expediency, and this naturally interferes with the universal principle of the equality of all human beings.

## Abolition of Class Boundaries

In *Datong shu*, Kang writes: "The coming to birth of all men proceeds from Heaven. All are brothers. All are truly equal. How can men falsely be divided according to standing in society, and be weighed in the balance and be cast out?[2] He believes that our sufferings are due to inequality that stems from "baseless distinction by classes."[3] Unfortunately, such unjustifiable class distinctions exist everywhere in various forms in Egypt, Greece, medieval Europe, feudal Japan and India, which Kang held as the worst because of its caste system. Kang believed China was slowly moving towards greater social levelling following the example of United States, where there was a high degree of equality. He acknowledges that blacks were not treated equally in the United States, nonetheless, the nation was "the harbinger of the Era of Increasing Peace – and – Equality."[4] Thus, America was still then the most prosperous, strong and harmonious nation on earth, in Kang's opinion.

While Kang holds that racial discrimination is a source of human suffering, he insists that different races have different mental capacity or physical excellence: two kinds of peoples – "the yellow and the white – have occupied the whole world. The strength of the white race is assuredly superior, while the yellow is more numerous and also wiser."[5] These two races, he believes are superior to the brown and black races.

---

1. K'ang Yu-wei, *Ta T'ung Shu: The One World Philosophy of K'ang Yu-wei*, 104. Besides universalism in outlook, *Datong* is characterized by monism, which assumes that truth, like power, emanates from a single source. This is reflected in Chinese social structure where power and truth are derived from the same fountain. Hence, Kang holds that competition that clashes with monism is against human nature. Shiping Hua, *Chinese Utopianism*, 37.
2. Ibid., 135-36.
3. Ibid., 134.
4. Ibid., 135.
5. Ibid., 141.

Kang's approach to the attainment of racial equality is by intermarriage, migration, and changes in diet and exercise. He thinks that the children of mixed marriages would inherit the traits of the parents with fairer complexion. Expecting spectacular results, Kang is convinced that mixed marriages would help the black people to become fairer:

> Thus, in from seven hundred to a thousand years, the blackest African negroes will be transformed into white persons. By the time we have our One World, the people of all the earth will be of the same colour, the same appearance, the same size, and the same intelligence. This will be complete union – ta t'ung (大同) – of human race.[1]

Kang attempts to bring about racial equality not by treating everyone as equals but by eliminating differences through interracial marriages and the blurring of distinct races.

In his call for the abolition of class, Kang desired the development of a classless society quite like communism, not through violent revolution, but gradually through peaceful means. People were bought and sold in China in the nineteenth century, but there was not much slavery compared to the United States. In fact, "China was the first to abolish slavery, under Confucianism."[2] Kang strongly advocates the emancipation of slaves because he believes all men are equal citizens of the state.

## Abolition of Gender Boundaries

According to John Stuart Mill, "The social subordination of women thus stands out an isolated fact in modern social institutions; a solitary breach of what has become their fundamental law; a single relic of an old world of thought and practice exploded in everything else, but retained in the one thing of most universal interest."[3] Kang also holds that for thousands of years, women have been "callously and unscrupulously repressed" by men.[4] Prevented by men from taking part in public affairs and participating in public assemblies, women were also not allowed to study, hold positions in government nor voice their opinions. In fact, they were kept at home and forced to "bind their waists," "veil their faces,"

---

1. Ibid., 148.
2. Ibid., 137.
3. John Stuart Mill, *The Subjection of Women* (Philadelphia, PA: J.B. Lippincott & Co., 1869), 12.
4. K'ang Yu-wei, *Ta T'ung Shu: The One World Philosophy of K'ang Yu-wei*, 149.

"compress their feet," and "tattoo their bodies."[1] Thus, we see the guiltless and innocent punished. Even worse is that *soi-disant* righteous men did not consider the ill treatment of women as oppression and exploitation, but as a matter of fact in life. For Kang, discrimination against women is the most appalling injustice in the world.

In the same manner, Mill writes, "The sufferings, immoralities, evils of all sorts, produced in innumerable cases by the subjection of individual women to individual men, are far too terrible to be overlooked."[2] Mill also asserts that:

> With regard to the fitness of women, not only to participate in elections, but themselves to hold offices or practise professions involving important public responsibilities; I have already observed that this consideration is not essential to the practical question in dispute: since any woman, who succeeds in an open profession, proves by that very fact that she is qualified for it.[3]

Mill strongly advocated the equality of married persons before the law.

In his criticism of sexual discrimination, Kang highlights women's lack of freedom in choosing their mates as in arranged marriages and lifelong widowhood sanctioned by Confucian tradition. He admits that women suffered more than men in ill-matched marriages because of their inferior position in a patriarchal society. Their position can be summed up in this statement: "Marry a chicken, follow a chicken; marry a dog, follow a dog."[4] In marriages that are arranged because of expediency, women are often imprisoned and treated like slaves.

While Kang acknowledges that there are differences between sexes, he finds no justification for the subjection of the "weaker sex." In fact, as far as mental capability is concerned, there are stupid men and clever women. Kang believes that, when given equal opportunity for learning, women can compete easily with men and make valuable contributions to society as well. In primitive times, men's physical strength was indispensable for hunting and war. Women, however, contributed much to civilization by their domestic work: "So it must have been the women, who stayed at home, who originated such techniques as cooking, agriculture, house-building, weaving, silk-making, cloth-weaving – and including the fine arts, music and writing – while men were still brutes who spent their

---

1. Ibid.
2. Mill, *The Subjection of Women*, 43.
3. Ibid., 29.
4. K'ang Yu-wei, *Ta T'ung Shu: The One World Philosophy of K'ang Yu-wei*, 153.

time and energies in hunt."[1] Thus, to deny equality to women is to violate the principle of social justice. It is also a failure to appreciate the valuable contributions of women in our society. Kang's call for the emancipation of women had great influence in the period of the Chinese Republic (1912-49) as well as in Communist China.

Kang's programme for the liberation of women in the first phase includes: acquiring the same education as men; exercising the same political rights as men; enjoying the freedom to choose their mates. Kang also called for the abolition of degrading practices such as foot-binding, face-veiling, ear-piercing, and waist-compressing. Married women need no longer obey their husbands or use their husband's family name. They were to wear the same kind of clothes as men as a symbol of their independence and liberation.

In the second phase of Kang's programme for the transformation of women would be the abolition of the institution of marriage. Advocating free love, Kang was critical of traditional monogamous marriage because it involved a permanent commitment, which could not be dissolved without divorce. Kang also condemned arranged marriage by parents, the inequality between the sexes and also the practice of celibacy. For Kang, men and women would be free to choose their mates and to enter into a "contract of intimate relationship," very much like the alliance between two states in that the agreement would not affect the independence of the partners. This kind of contract is more like an "alliance" between two friends.[2]

In such a contract there is an expiry date. Believing that human beings are fickle-minded, Kang believed that it would not be beneficial to bind people together if they are no longer in love. Human beings have the tendency to look for new relationships once they are bored with the old ones. To prolong the old union when there is no more love would be a disaster. Asian men took concubines or mistresses when they were tired of their old wives, but there was no such outlet for women. For Kang, "to compel union is also immoral."[3]

The all-important virtue of chastity emphasized in China since the Sung Dynasty seemed to have no relevance for Kang. Even Confucius taught that marriage is for life and for the purpose of perpetuating the present generation. But in Kang's opinion, it is better to follow the principle of happiness, to allow people to follow their heart's desire. The abolition of lifelong marriage means that there would be no need for

---

1. Ibid., 155.
2. Ibid., 163.
3. Ibid., 165.

divorce. Despite the radical nature of Kang's teaching, he was also aware that, if women were not properly educated or if they were immature, such a temporary alliance with men would lead to sexual promiscuity. Kang wanted to implement this idea gradually and he did not want to be accused of corrupting the moral customs of his time.

## Abolition of Family Boundaries

In the beginning of human existence, Kang believes there was no family because men and women lived like animals. Children recognized their mothers but not their fathers: "Since mating was indiscriminate in remote antiquity, no man knew his father. There were no family names; or if there were, then they were derived from the mother's side."[1] Some males might have a particularly strong attachment to their mates and forced them to have permanent union and thus gave rise to the institution of marriages. This eventually gave birth to the institutions of the family and the clan.

Kang says that the reason why China is the most populous nation on earth is due to its extended family and clan system instituted by Confucius for the "Age of Disorder." The Chinese always keeps his ancestral home and the family is an important institution in the Chinese system. The clan system implies that we care only for those who share our surname. The clan system leads us to disregard the importance of the nation. The wealthy Chinese will only contribute to help the poor, such as the building of schools and hospitals that belong to his clan. This may lead to the spread of corruption, the division of the nation into many nations, in other words, disunity. Thus, the most populous nation is also "the weakest" because "four hundred million people cannot help each other" because of widespread corruption among clans.[2]

Kang laments that filial piety, a cardinal Confucian virtue, is only an "empty ideal."[3] Selfishness and economic necessities led people to neglect their parents. He admits that psychologically it is easier to love one's children than to cherish one's parents. Many people find their children charming and lovable, but few can tolerate their parents whose views are different from them. If children find it difficult to practice filial piety, it is even more difficult for other members of the family who are less related by blood. Forced by tradition to live together, siblings and relatives begin to dislike each other due to personal conflicts and prejudice. Kang believes "this situation is worst in China, because of its

---

1. Ibid., 170.
2. Ibid., 171-72.
3. Ibid., 176.

large-family system, despite all the preaching about the exemplary cases of large family."[1] The fact is the more people there are in a family, the more conflicts there will be. For Kang, this is one of the basic causes of human suffering.

Another serious objection to the institution of family is that its continued existence goes against the common good of the society. Family attachment can lead to selfishness and encourage dependency on one's parents or siblings. Kang believes that the family system makes men selfish, deceitful and greedy because they have many dependants. As a result, there cannot be much funding for public expenditure to promote the welfare of the people in society at large. The building of schools, hospitals, roads and bridges would be neglected. Further, private property cannot be used as public property for the common good. The family is a necessary institution in time of general disorder but it is an obstacle when we try to establish an "Age of Complete Peace-and-Equality."[2] Thus, if we wish to attain universal equality, independence and perfection of human nature, we must not only abolish the state but the family as well.

Kang suggests that public institutions and not family should raise and educate children. Thus, pregnant women should be taken care of by public institutions and their offspring transferred to public infant-rearing schools. This means that it is not necessary for mothers to take care of their children. Their children are to be educated in public institutions from primary to college level. There will also be public institutions for the aged, the poor, the sick and disabled. Those who died will enter the public crematorium. In other words, from begetting to burying, all will be taken care by the government.

The advantage of this system is that the parents will not have to shoulder the responsibility of educating their children, and the children, likewise, will not have to bear the burden of looking after their aged parents. Kang writes: "This is not *to leave* the family, but to be naturally *without* the family. Having neither given family, but to be naturally without the family. Having neither given favours not received favours, there will naturally be no ingratitude."[3] The result of such a system will be great happiness and satisfaction. The poor cannot afford to educate their children and, he contends, the majority of people in the world desire to have the public nurturing their offspring. Kang believed it is thus natural for the world to become public so that we can attain One World of complete peace and equality.

---

1. Ibid., 179.
2. Ibid., 182.
3. Ibid., 186.

In wishing to abolish the family, Kang is actually criticizing a key aspect of Confucian ethical code – even though he insists that he follows Confucius. Kang, however, is not always consistent in having a highly unconventional view of family relationships. In his work on New Text Confucianism, completed in 1890s, he clearly upholds Confucian values such as filial piety and fraternal duty, believing that the Sage's teaching is in accord with "heavenly reasons."[1] In fact, during his lifetime, Kang upheld traditional familial values, in that he took good care of his parents and grandparents and showed great affections for his children and siblings.

Like all utopian writers Kang was critical of his times and culture. He was critical not only of traditional Chinese institutions but also Western institutions. Being critical of Chinese institutions is tantamount to being critical of Confucius whose philosophy shaped these institutions during imperial times. But Kang's attitude towards the Confucianism was rather ambiguous. He was critical of Confucius as understood in the Chinese tradition but at the same time he idolized the Sage as the universal teacher whose ideas, he believed, are suitable for the establishment of a commonwealth.

Minimizing the importance of parenthood, he wanted to free children from the type of filial piety prescribed by Confucius. In other words, there is nothing sacrosanct regarding parenthood and the parent-child relationship. Thus, it is wrong for society to demand the subjection of children to their parents: "Parents shall not demand performance of filial duties by their children and children shall not demand affection and care from their parents. Each person shall enjoy the right of self-determination." Kang wanted the society to take up the responsibility of raising children with the establishment of public nurseries. Parents would also be compensated for begetting children and "thus absolving all the indebtedness that their children owed them."[2]

Perhaps Kang was influenced by Buddhist philosophy, which views the family as detrimental to the pursuit of happiness. The tragic lives of his sisters, I-hung and Ch'iung-chü, who became widows shortly after their marriages, revealed to Kang the pains and difficulties of family life. In spite of his commitment to Confucian ethics, Kang would not regard the family as an absolute condition for living a fulfilled life.[3]

---

1. Hsiao, *A Modern China and a New World: K'ang Yu-Wei, Reformer and Utopian*, 451.
2. Ibid., 429.
3. Ibid., 15.

## Against Capitalism

Kang also considers the struggles between labor and capital, emphasizing the growing gap between the rich and the poor. Capitalism has spread throughout the world in the five continents resulting in the struggles between the rich and the poor. This is the war of the new "states" which he means trade wars between nations, quite like the trade war between the United States and China that we are witnessing now. Within the countries there will be struggles between labor unions and employers leading to the growth of socialism and communism. In order to solve the problem of inequality of humankind, Kang also suggests abolishing not just the institution of family but private property as well.

Kang is prophetic when he says, "with regard to the future commerce: its struggles will be more fierce." The cleverest mind will be employed in producing fake goods because of high profits. In the case of medicine, food and vehicles, the harm will be greater; manufacturers would produce substandard goods because of greed. "All shame is lost."[1] Against the theory of natural selection (Darwinism), Kang argues that because of competition, men will start cheating others through cunningness and deceit. Competition is supposed to be considered a great principle because it ensures the survival of the fittest and talented. In actual fact, in Kang's opinion, competition depraves men's mental process and stops them from fulfilling heaven's way.

## Confucianism

While Kang was critical of the imperial interpretation of Confucianism and the "spurious classics" in the 1890s, he was also a champion of the Sage's teaching according to his own understanding. Kang was a revisionist rather than a traditionalist in that he gave new interpretation to Confucianism. Like Mencius who doubted the reliability of the *Book of History*, Kang questioned the authenticity of the classics. In his interpretation of the Sage's teaching, Kang subscribed to the principles of the Kung-yang school and also added Western notions to Confucianism. Kang is considered the Martin Luther of Confucianism – a reformer.[2]

Alongside his doctrinal stance, Kang had urged the government and his fellow colleagues to "venerate Confucius." In July 1898, he presented a memorial that proposed Confucianism as a state religion.[3] Even in

---

1. K'ang Yu-wei, *Ta T'ung Shu: The One World Philosophy of K'ang Yu-wei*, 214.
2. Hsiao, *A Modern China and a New World: K'ang Yu-Wei, Reformer and Utopian*, 44.
3. Ibid.

modern times, Kang believed that Confucianism was still relevant to society – a reliable guide to human's social and moral life. During the years of the Chinese Republic, Kang was more concerned in preserving China's cultural heritage found in Confucianism than in modernizing the nation's social and economic systems.

It does appear that Kang's rejection of the family as an institution in his utopia would disqualify him to be a Confucianist since the family forms the bedrock of Confucius's social system. Kang, however, did point out that we still need the family while we are journeying towards the world of "Universal Peace." As long as human beings fall short of moral perfection, they will still need the family to guide them. But when they have achieved the highest social development, the family will gradually disappear because their love will be broadened to embrace the whole of humanity. "The distinction between family and nonfamily will be unrecognizable."[1] Such a view is actually found in the Confucian doctrine of *ren* (benevolence) (仁).

Kang believed that different social doctrines should be taught at different times depending on the needs and stages of human development. In the nineteenth century, China could not simply dispense with the Confucian precepts of "human relationships" and "social duties" found in the family. However, Kang's "utopian ideals (which went beyond these precepts) could have dangerous repercussions if made known to the general public and must therefore be withheld."[2] As a utopian writer, Kang moved beyond Confucianism, but as a social reformer, he remained within that tradition.

In addition, Kang used Confucianism and Mahāyāna Buddhism as vehicles to convey his own philosophy. From these sources, he developed his own ideas regarding human progress in society, universal love, human desires, human equality, freedom, and democracy. These are the chief features of his utopian vision. He held that the true teaching of Confucius lies outside the established tradition dictated by the imperial court. His interpretation of the Confucian classics was actually an adaptation of the Sage's philosophy to the new social and political situations in China. Clearly Confucius did not anticipate the problems in modern China. Thus, Kang found it expedient to depart radically from the established interpretations of the classics by injecting Western notions of equality, freedom, republicanism, and constitutionalism.[3]

Believing that the differences between East and West were secondary, Kang sought to reform China's obsolete political, economic, and education systems through "universalization" and "not Westernization."

---

1. Ibid., 45.
2. Ibid., 46.
3. Ibid., 93-95.

In other words, he wanted to raise Chinese culture to a stage of civilization that is comparable to the best in the world. This idea is founded upon the principle that "the truth permeates all under Heaven," and "the same principle holds good for all."[1]

Kang's aim was to save China's cultural heritage not by conservation but by modernization through the incorporation of European political and social thoughts. Confucian doctrines were his points of reference and Western ideas were utilized to modify traditional teachings. Thus, his moral values were essentially Confucian, but his institutional ideas were Western. In other words, Kang was able to weave "a synthetic philosophical fabric out of Confucian warp and Western woof."[2] In doing this, he hoped to make the Sage's teaching universal.

While acknowledging the good influence of Christianity and Islam, Kang asserted the superiority of Confucianism over these monotheistic faiths because the teaching of the Sage emphasized human relationships and moral obligations. In fact, Confucius was dismissive of divine authority that had undue influence over the conduct of human beings. Kang thus attempted to establish Confucianism as a state religion. However, his effort to develop a state religion was a failure because unlike India or European countries, China was and is basically a secular nation. The Chinese are interested primarily in life on earth and not in the afterlife. Their ethics emphasize human relationships rather than their relationship with God. Besides, Confucianism is essentially a secular philosophy.[3] Further, Kang's hedonistic philosophy, which we shall discuss later, and worldly values disqualify him as a person serious about religious life.

Obviously, Kang did not see any value in religion beyond their social and political functions in society. His view of religion is basically utilitarian because he felt that as long as humankind has not reached moral perfection, religion has a role to play. Kang writes:

> In the Age of Complete Peace-and-Equality, people will naturally love others, will naturally be without sin. According to the natural workings of evolution, they will therefore not reverence God. Comprehending the impossibility literally, [and the] difficulty of limitless numbers of souls occupying the space of 'Heaven', they therefore will not believe in a Day of Judgment. The religion of Jesus will therefore, when we have attained One World, be extinct.[4]

---

1. Ibid., 413.
2. Ibid., 95.
3. Ibid., 119.
4. K'ang Yu-wei, *Ta T'ung Shu: The One World Philosophy of K'ang Yu-wei,* 274-75.

Christians too believe that, when we arrive at the kingdom of God, there is no need of church or religion: "And when all things shall be subdued unto him, then shall the Son also himself be subject unto him that put all things under him, that God may be all in all" (1 Corinthians 15:28).

## Hedonism

Kang's conviction is that people in different parts of the world share a common experience and have a similar psychological make-up, which account for their similar fundamental attitudes and values. These ethical and moral sentiments are functions of the brain and nervous system. Our emotions, sensory experiences, whether painful or delightful, are simply responses to our external environment that provides the stimuli. According to Kang:

> in human life there is only suiting and not suiting. What does not suit is pain. What suits and suits again is pleasure. Therefore, the nature of human life depends upon what men consider to be the Way; what depends upon man's Way is simply pain and pleasure. What is schemed for by men is simply to abolish pain so as to find pleasure. There is no other Way.[1]

In *Datong shu* (大 同 書), one discovers Kang's underlying principle of hedonism. For him, the purpose of life is to seek pleasure and avoid suffering. It is his conviction that the enjoyment of sensuous pleasures and creature comforts is a legitimate part of life. Human desire is to be satisfied and not to be repressed. In Thomas More's *Utopia*, human beings would also enjoy the pleasures of the body and mind. Kang's idea of utopia includes the removal of all restraints on human's desires including sexual impulse. Since men are born with reproductive organs, Kang believes that it is natural for human beings to indulge in sexual activity. Since sexual passion is natural, he thinks it cannot be prevented and there is no reason to prohibit it. Kang therefore is critical of religions such as Christianity and Buddhism that teach ascetic practices and encourage celibacy.

Kang's basic assumption is that what is pleasurable is good and desirable. Such principle forms the basis of how he evaluates social institutions and morality:

---

1.  Ibid., 69. According to Hsiao, "hedonism, humanitarianism and egalitarianism" are the basic principles with which Kang constructed his social thought. The idea of progress is also an important feature in his utopian vision as Kang conceives of a human's life as a dynamic process of moving forward step by step, from imperfection to perfection. Hsiao, *A Modern China and a New World: K'ang Yu-Wei, Reformer and Utopian*, 442.

> The establishment of laws and the creation of teachings of the Way which cause men to have happiness and to be entirely without suffering: this is the best form of the Good. The establishment of laws and the creation of the teaching of the Way which can cause men to have much happiness and little suffering: this is good, but not the perfect Good. The establishment of laws and the creation of teaching the Way which cause men to have much suffering and little happiness: this is the not-Good.[1]

For Kang, pleasure or happiness means the enjoyment of things that delight our senses and give us physical comfort.

Kang also holds that laws are generally oppressive and suitable only to a particular time and circumstance:

> The general conditions which are in existence, and the oppressive institutions which have long endured, are accordingly taken as morally right. In this way, what were at first good laws of mutual assistance and protection end by causing suffering through their excessive oppressiveness and inequality. If this is the case, then we have the very opposite of the original idea of finding happiness and avoiding suffering.[2]

Kang holds that outdated laws and institutions kept China in servitude and hindered its progress as a nation.

## Drawbacks of Kang's *Datong*

In spite of Kang's noble and admirable ideas, such as his emphasis on gender and racial equality, there are many aspects of his utopian vision that are impractical or morally objectionable. Seeking to eliminate all differences, Kang advocated the uniformity of all human beings by suppressing the individual's differences or uniqueness. He promoted the white race as the most beautiful people on earth, and his racist remarks on the blacks are simply unacceptable and outrageous except perhaps to Hitler. Kang encouraged people to migrate so that the darker-skinned people could become fairer. It is really surprising for a Chinese to make this claim of white supremacy in the nineteenth and early twentieth centuries when Westerners were considered as barbarians or as "foreign devils."

---

1. Ibid., 71.
2. Ibid., 72.

Lauren Pfister characterized Kang's utopian vision as "proto-technological scientism," "a eugenically engineered world."[1] Such a society seems to be lacking in humanity like a community of robots. His institutionalization of education and medical structures would make them function more like prisons than places of nurturing and health care. Pfister even asks "how much suffering would Kang be willing to enforce upon countless numbers of people in order to achieve his idealized overcoming of all sufferings."[2]

In order to achieve a uniform humanity, it is obvious that Kang could establish his techno-scientific world only by implementing policies that are cruel and inhumane. In this aspect, Kang's One World would not be a democratic society but a totalitarian one. This Brave New World looks more like a dystopia. Fortunately, Kang's emphasis on Confucianism as a humanistic religion, in addition to Buddhist and Daoist thoughts, smoothen the sharpness and harshness of his techno-scientific world.

## Democratic Government

Kang's utopia involves a political transformation of the world with the establishment of a democratic world organization. Assuming that the existence of state boundaries would inevitably cause conflicts, Kang wanted to abolish them through gradual development. He was optimistic that humankind desired world unity and peace in spite of the fact that the annexation of small states by bigger political entities has occurred throughout history. According to Kang, it was the American Revolution that inspired the spread of the democratic movement throughout the world, followed by communism, which eventually would lead to the *Datong* or Grand Harmony. Kang believed that democratic government would discourage political selfishness, and communism would eradicate economic selfishness inherent in the possession of private property. There will be universal harmony when there is no more human selfishness.

Ernst Bloch maintains that the utopia is and remains:

> the first modern portrait of democratic-communist wishful dreams.
> In the womb of capitalist forces that were only just beginning, a
> future and supra-future world anticipated itself: both that of formal
> democracy, which delivers capitalism, and that of material-humane
> democracy, which cancels it out. For the first time democracy was
> here linked in a humane sense, in the sense of public freedom and

---

1. See Pfister, "A Modern Ruist Religious Vision of a Global Unity," 263.
2. Ibid., 263-64.

tolerance, with a collective economy (always easily threatened by bureaucracy, and indeed clericalism). In contrast to the previously imagined collectivisms of the best state, in the work of Thomas More freedom is written into the collective, and genuine material-humane democracy becomes its content. This content makes the "Utopia", in substantial sections, into a kind of liberal memorial and memorable book of socialism and communism.[1]

Kang's *Datong shu*, too, anticipates a democratic and egalitarian society that is humane and tolerant in spite of its short-comings.

The Grand Harmony will be achieved first by disarmament and later with the establishment of a world parliament, which would exercise control over the formulation of laws, standardization of weights and measures, and development of a universal language. It would also have control over the population and territories including the seas. For Kang, the only true form of government was the parliament that took charge of public affairs and government officials were to be elected by the people. Critical of republic, absolute and constitutional monarchy, he preferred democratic institutions.

In addition to central government, Kang's utopia has local governments and self-governments. The people would live in public buildings designed for various occupations in the industries, agriculture, *etc.*, and thus, there are no privately-owned houses. Such division of the population would require local government and each local self-governing entity, operating on democratic principles, to be self-contained, having its own schools, nurseries, homes for the aged, and hospitals. Kang introduces three levels of government in the Great Union: "the local, the degree, and the public government. There will be no distinctions between the people of the world, except for the special honours bestowed on those outstanding for knowledge and *jen* (仁)."[2] Kang upholds the principles of equality and attempts to lessen authoritarianism in his utopia.

Most utopian projects have authoritarian or dictatorial government, vide Thomas More's *Utopia*. Kang's ideal world, however, rests on democratic principles. For him, the purpose of all social institutions is to promote happiness for the people. Thus, when a person has fulfilled all his social obligations towards his fellow human beings and wishes to retire from the world, he can pursue the study of immortality or Buddhahood. After this stage, "will come the study of roaming through the heavens."[3]

---

1. Ernst Bloch, *The Principle of Hope* (Cambridge, MA: MIT Press, 1986), volume II, 519-20, *eBook Collection*.
2. K'ang Yu-wei, *Ta T'ung Shu: The One World Philosophy of K'ang Yu-wei*, 236.
3. Ibid., 276.

Kang's utopia seems like a place where all human needs and desires are satisfied without much effort. The people in this so-called paradise will have adequate food, housing, clothing, healthcare, and also pleasurable experiences, such as entertainment and travel. Technology plays an important role in Kang's utopia: the people will have "flying rooms" and "flying ships" to allow them move about efficiently and comfortably.[1] This reflects a certain level of industrialization and scientific advance found in the Western countries that Kang had visited. He was also impressed with the development and prosperity found in Shanghai and Hong Kong.

Kang was convinced that his *Datong shu* provided a blueprint for the establishment of an ideal society. He believed his text could be transformed into a reality as he outlined the stages through which human beings can construct a utopia. Critics, however, thought that his social ideas were out of touch with reality. Be that as it may, Kang's sharp criticism of existing institutions reveals that he understood well the major problems affecting China in the nineteenth and early twentieth centuries. Some of Kang's ideas, like the abolition of state and family, are certainly radical but his call for the abolition of class and gender boundaries have won him many supporters. Kang's emphasis on liberty, equality, democracy, and science were taken very seriously in the early twentieth century. Clearly Kang was able to read the signs of the times and provide directions for the transformation of society. His unique and provocative utopian project won him a place in the history of utopian writings.

---

1. Ibid., 272.

# 7
# Convergent Spirit

In the previous chapter, we observed that Kang Youwei, like Mo Tzu, possessed a utilitarian view of religious belief. In spite of his criticism of Darwin regarding competition and the survival of the fittest, he held that humankind would evolve into a secular species with no reverence for God. Kang believed that once peoples are united in one world, with complete peace and equality, religion would become obsolete. Pierre Teilhard de Chardin, S.J. (1881-1956), the focus of this chapter, believed that at the end of time, all religions would converge in Jesus Christ, the Alpha and the Omega.

Fascinated with eastern thought but critical of its religions, Teilhard de Chardin was also searching for inspiration, renewal, and possible unity among the diverse faiths, such as Confucianism, Buddhism and Daoism, that he had encountered in his extensive travels in the East. He lived at a time when interreligious dialogue was not part of the Church's agenda, and yet, he had this vision that one day all religions would converge in Jesus Christ. His interest in religions revolved around topics such as their role in the modern world, the kind of spirituality that is relevant to modern men and women, and the place of mysticism. Rooted firmly in the Christian tradition, Teilhard's spirituality was deeply influenced by his experience of the East, which enhanced his vision of the unity of all authentic religious experiences. His evaluation of religion was conditioned by his scientific training as a paleontologist and geologist, as well as his personal experience as a Christian. A model of utopian hope, he looked upon religious traditions in terms of the energy that is infused in their beliefs and their ability to help people to build a better future, including the unification of humanity.

As a scientist, Teilhard supported Darwin's theory of evolution, and as a Christian, he sought to interpret revelation in the light of science. In other words, he wanted to reconcile science with his faith: "Religion and science are the two conjugated faces or phases of one and the same act of complete knowledge – the only one which can embrace the past and future of evolution so as to contemplate, measure and fulfil them."[1] This assertion of Teilhard reminds us of what John Paul II taught:

> Faith and reason are like two wings on which the human spirit rises to the contemplation of truth; and God has placed in the human heart a desire to know the truth – in a word, to know himself – so that, by knowing and loving God, men and women may also come to the fullness of truth about themselves.[2]

Concerned with the genesis of the world, the unity of the human family and the "convergent spirit" among humankind, Teilhard was also interested in how the West was influenced by the eastern forms of mysticism. He came to the conclusion that a full understanding of the phenomenon of man can come about only through the interaction between different religious traditions. Further, he realized that Christianity needed to be transformed, but its transformation could only occur through fruitful interaction with other religions.

This chapter attempts to explore Teilhard's experience in China, his theory of religion in the evolutionary context, his inclusivistic approach to other religious beliefs and his vision of a renewed Christianity which is self-transcending. This chapter concludes that Teilhard's understanding of the convergence of religions culminating in the "universal Christ" is related to what contemporary theologians characterize as "regnocentricity" – the movement towards the kingdom of God where Christianity understands itself in relation to other religious traditions. Living in an age of terror and violence, Teilhard was indeed a model of utopian hope and his theology is imbued with philosophic optimism.[3]

---

1. Pierre Teilhard de Chardin, *The Phenomenon of Man* (London: Collins, 1959), 285. The material in this chapter appears in Ambrose Mong, *Accommodation and Acceptance: An Exploration of Interfaith Relations* (Cambridge: James Clarke & Co., 2016).

2. John Paul II, *Fides et Ratio*, Encyclical Letter, 14 September 1998, http://www.vatican.va/holy_father/john_paul_ii/encyclicals/documents/hf_jp-ii_enc_15101998_fides-et-ratio_en.html.

3. Martin Henry Scharlemann, "Utopia or Paradise," *Concordia Journal* 1, no. 2

The seed of Teilhard's spiritual vision, his theory of religious pluralism, was planted, grew and developed on the soil of Asian countries like India, Indonesia, Japan, and Tibet. Ursula King, however, believes that Teilhard's spiritual vision first emerged during the First World War when he served as a stretcher-bearer:

> The First World War was a true crucible of fire for Pierre Teilhard de Chardin (1881-1955). He speaks of someone "whom the Lord has drawn to follow the road of fire." His four years lived in the trenches was a deeply formative experience for him; it forged together the diverse strands of a rich mystical vision grounded in a fervent Catholic faith, a thorough knowledge of theology, patristics and the Christian mystics as well as a passionate study of evolutionary science, human origins and the future development of humanity.[1]

During this time of intense hardship, Teilhard had written essays that reveal his pressing concern for the reinterpretation of Christianity, the search for a new image of the divine, and the quest for a spirituality that would be relevant to the needs of the modern world. All these themes, according to King, arose from his experience of suffering in the trenches as well as his contacts with men from different religious and cultural backgrounds. In April 1923, he left France for Tianjin to assist with geologic excavations in Central China.

## Experience in China

Teilhard labored in China as a palaeontologist from 1924 to 1945. During this time, the Chinese Communist movement was formed and Teilhard was able to observe its struggle for control in China in a way that was unique for a westerner. He was sympathetic towards the Communists and could see the beginning of a new China to the detriment of European presence in this vast continent. In the 1930s, while Mao Zedong was forging the new China, which was distinctly Chinese and Marxist at the same time, Teilhard wondered whether the evolving world could achieve

(March 1975), 57.
1. Teilhard was attached to a Moroccan ambulance unit in North Africa. His regiment also took part in battles on the Western front at Ypres and Passchendaele in Belgium, at Arras, Dunkirk, Verdun, and the Marne in France. Ursula King, "Following the 'Road of Fire': The Emergence of Teilhard de Chardin's Panchristic Mysticism during the First World War," talk given at the Jesuit School of Theology, Berkeley, 28 April 2015. I am very grateful to Professor Ursula King for this article and also for her comments on this chapter.

unity without massive destruction of its people and cultures. How could such large-scale socialization and politicization be accomplished without destroying the uniqueness of the human person?

Few people understood what was at stake in China at that time. In fact, most Christian missionaries could not see beyond the confines and interests of their church and institutions. Critical of western missionaries' skepticism, pessimism and narrow-mindedness, Teilhard believed their attitude was harmful and counterproductive. He was convinced of the triumph of the Spirit. In one of his letters, he wrote that only the indigenous Chinese clergy could move with the times and spread Christianity effectively.[1] Unfortunately, most foreign missionaries in China at that time failed to see this.

Nowadays most Christian scholars are acutely aware of the failure of the Church in Asia and have highlighted the fact that, for Asians, Christianity is still a Western religion. This is because Western Christianity is too entrenched within its own Western mind-set to allow itself to be enriched by the wealth of knowledge and understanding of other religious traditions and cultures in the world. Virgil Elizondo puts it this way:

> we had often kept the refreshing newness of the gospel from coming through because we had insisted so much on our linguistic/philosophical/theological presentations based on our Western cosmovision rather than trusting the dynamism of the Gospel stories and imagery which would have easily entered into dialogue with the life-stories of any cosmovision in the world.[2]

Teilhard returned to France for a while to direct retreats and speak at conferences, not as a scientist, but as a priest. However, his Jesuit superiors forbade him to teach religion. He was told to confine his lecturing to palaeontological topics. Teilhard's views on "The Fall," "Original Sin," and evolution were considered unorthodox at that time. Eventually, Teilhard had to leave the *Institut Catholique* for good. He returned to China and, in the city of Tianjin, wrote *The Divine Milieu*, a book on the Christian spiritual life. The tone of this work is hopeful, enthusiastic, and joyful as it expresses his love for nature, his delight in scientific discoveries, and his trust in the unconditional love of God. It is an integrative spirituality that can satisfy the expectations of contemporary men and women.

---

1. Thomas F. O'Meara, "Teilhard de Chardin in China," *Worldview* 16, (1 January1973), 33.
2. Leonardo Boff and Virgil Elizondo, eds., *Any Room for Christ in Asia* (London: SCM Press, 1993), viii.

*The Divine Milieu* is written "to show that Christ, who is ever the same and ever new, has not ceased to be the 'first' within mankind." It offers "a simple *description of a psychological* evolution observed *over a specified interval."* Teilhard regarded it as a modest yet "'illuminative' spiritual ascent."[1] *The Divine Milieu* is essentially a work that recapitulates:

> the eternal lesson of the Church in the words of a man who, because he believes himself to feel deeply in tune with his own times, has sought to teach how to see God everywhere, to see him in all that is most hidden, most solid, and most ultimate in the world.[2]

It would be wrong to assume that Teilhard had a romantic or exotic impression of China. In fact, like most western intellectuals, he perceived China as a massive, inert and tradition-bound continent. John Henry Newman regarded China as "a huge, stationary, unattractive, morose civilization."[3] Having witnessed the political chaos in the country, Teilhard's initial impression of China was negative and harsh. He perceived the Chinese as "not bad, but primitive, inert, on the lowest level, living in routine and in a mental twilight."[4] Such offensive remarks came about because he had no knowledge of Chinese culture or traditions. It was purely based on his emotion and the colonial mentality that was prevalent at that time. However, as Teilhard became more acquainted with the Chinese intellectual and scientific community, he began to have a vision of a new China. He could sense that China was moving forward towards something new.

In charge of training young Chinese scientists, Teilhard gave credit to the Chinese in scientific research and recognized their right to control the excavations. He was content to work under the supervision of the Chinese civil authorities. He had hope in the young Chinese scientists under his charge as they were filled with vigour and enthusiasm in their research. A member of his team, Pei Wenzhong, discovered "Peking Man" (*Homo Erectus Pekinensis*), a human ancestor who walked upright. This discovery served to support the theory of evolution which Teilhard upheld. He contributed to this discovery by supervizing the dig and classifying the *Sinanthropus* as *Homo Faber*.[5]

---

1. Pierre Teilhard de Chardin, *Le Milieu Divin: An Essay on the Interior Life* (London: Collins, 1960), 11-12.
2. Ibid., 15.
3. John Henry Newman, *The Idea of a University*, http://www.newmanreader.org/works/idea/article1.html, 252.
4. Quoted in O'Meara, "Teilhard de Chardin in China," 32.
5. O'Meara, "Teilhard de Chardin in China," 33. See also Jia Lanpo and Huang

In spite of his initial negative impression, China in its antiquity was also the milieu where Teilhard de Chardin realized his evolutionary vision, in which the secular and sacred aspects of life converged. China was the environment in which the synthesis of his scientific and theological visions took place. In addition to his scientific work, Teilhard's time in China was the most fruitful period for his theology.[1] In short, we can say China was his divine milieu.

In China, Teilhard could see the Communist movement as "the evolution of the spirit." He sympathized with the Communists and recognized their humanitarian vision. Highly disciplined, the Chinese Communists identified themselves with the peasants. Teilhard believed that the Communist movement would be the agent for positive change in China – introducing China into the future of humankind. He sensed a vague affinity between the ideology of the Red Army and his own theological vision.[2] Teilhard had observed that the common principle behind Christianity and Marxism is their "faith in man" and thus at some point, they come together: "for in the nature of things everything that is faith must rise, and everything that rises must converge." Further, he remarked that forms of faith that people hold, can grow and develop together. This is not a formula but "the *environment* of union."[3]

It is easy to understand why the Christian vision of Teilhard found an affinity with Marxist ideology: both movements have their roots in the Judeo-Christian tradition. The Marxist understanding of alienation is in fact a Christian concept. Teilhard and Marx speak of matter "as of something in which life and consciousness *and purpose* inhere."[4] Further, both Christianity and Marxism possess a powerful eschatological and apocalyptic force: they look towards the future. Teilhard had the impression that Marxist atheism was not absolute, but that it rejected a god that can no longer satisfy human longing. This kind of deity, "a *deus ex machina* whose existence can only undermine the dignity of the Universe and weaken the springs of human endeavour – a 'pseudo-God' . . . whom no one in these days any longer wants, least of all the Christians."[5] Even

Weiwen, *The Story of Peking Man:From Archaeology to Mystery*, translated by Yin Zhiqi. (Beijing: Foreign Languages Press; and New York: Oxford University Press, 1990).

1. O'Meara, "Teilhard de Chardin in China," 31.
2. Ibid., 33.
3. Pierre Teilhard de Chardin, *The Future of Man*, translated from the French by Norman Denny (London: Collins, 1964), 192.
4. R.C. Zaehner, *The Convergent Spirit: Towards a Dialectic of Religion* (London: Routledge & Kegan Paul, 1963), 48.
5. Teilhard de Chardin, *The Future of Man*, 267.

though it has had limited success, Marxism has attempted in its own way
to bring the kingdom of heaven down to earth as well as to bring about
the fulfillment of the human person in his lifetime.

## Earth and Heaven

The religious crisis in modern times, according to Teilhard, is due to the
conflict between "the transcendent action of a personal God" and the
"innate perfectibility of a World in progress."[1] In order to evolve to a higher
plane, we need to integrate these two dimensions of our spiritual quest. Such
an integrated and balanced faith can help us grow in love, which is a kind
of spiritual energy that allows us to overcome our selfishness or egoism.
The real struggle in the world is not between believers and unbelievers, but
between two types of faith: an earth-centred religion and a heaven-centred
one. He judged religions and neo-humanist faiths on the value they place
on God or the world – whether they focus on the transcendent or the
immanent. Teilhard acknowledged that there is tremendous energy in
faith in God as well as faith in the world. He was convinced that eventually
the different religions would converge in the Spirit: "Faith in God and faith
in the World: these two springs of energy, each the source of a magnificent
spiritual impulse, must certainly be capable of effectively uniting in such a
way as to produce a resulting upward movement."[2]

Teilhard coined the word, "noogenesis," the cosmic emergence of the
mind or the Spirit, when human beings become self-reflective. The increase
in self-reflectiveness of human beings will eventually lead to a convergence
of the two opposed forms of worship. At present the religious impulse of
humankind is divided, he admitted, but once the human person is:

> brought to accept the reality of a Noogenesis, the believer in this
> World will find himself compelled to allow increasing room,
> in his vision of the future, for the values of personalisation and
> transcendency. . . . On the other hand, the believer in Heaven,

---

1.  Ibid., 224.
2.  Ibid., 77. According to Zaehner, within religions, there are two movements
    in dialectical tension: one moving towards the individual self; and, the other,
    towards the community. In the Christian context, one tendency is to focus on
    the salvation of individual souls and the other tendency is towards the building
    of the body of Christ, the Church. It is Teilhard's genius that he was able to
    harmonize these two dialectical tendencies using the theory of evolution to
    demonstrate that all creation would converge upon itself in humankind. In
    other words, the entire human species is destined to converge upon itself
    which he calls the "Christian phenomenon." Zaehner, *The Convergent Spirit*
    17.

accepting this same reality of a cosmic genesis of the Spirit, must perceive that the mystical evolution of which he dreams presupposes and consecrates all the tangible realities and all the arduous conditions of human progress."[1]

This synthesis of the two types of faith, earth-centred and heaven-centred, can be accomplished only in the concrete realities of human life. Thus, in Teilhard's opinion, we need people who are animated simultaneously by the two types of faith, "the fusion of two mystic forces" in one heart, people "who are the more convinced of the sacred value of human effort, the more they are first interested in God."[2] Teilhard also believed that in the future, human beings would progress spiritually as they evolved:

For the spiritually minded, whether in the East or the West, one point has hitherto not been in doubt: that Man could only attain to a fuller life by rising "vertically" above the material zones of the world. Now we see the possibility of an entirely different line of progress. The Higher Life, the Union, the long-dreamed-of consummation that has hitherto been sought *Above*, in the direction of some kind of transcendency: should we not rather look for it *Ahead*, in the prolongation of the inherent forces of evolution? Above or ahead – or both?[3]

This also suggests that we not only search for God both vertically and horizontally, but that God has revealed himself in the person of Jesus Christ in the Incarnation.

The new man or "homo progressivus" as Teilhard called him has to make the crucial option between accepting a God who is greater than himself or seeking one that is within him: "Given the power he possesses, why should Man look for a God outside himself? Man, self-sufficient and wholly autonomous, sole master and disposer of his destiny and the world's – is not this an even nobler concept?"[4] This great temptation of humankind reminds us of Prometheus, of Babel's Tower (Genesis 11:1-9) or of Christ on the mountain (Matthew 4:1-11). It is a temptation as old as the earth itself. Time and again, we see the fall of humankind due to "hubris," a reckless pride and arrogance that offends God more than anything else. For Teilhard, however, "faith in Man does not exclude

---

1. Ibid., 78-79.
2. Quoted in Ursula King, "Religion and the Future: Teilhard de Chardin's Analysis of Religion as a Contribution to Interreligious Dialogue," *Religious Studies* 7, no. 4 (1 December 1971), 315.
3. Teilhard de Chardin, *The Future of Man*, 263.
4. Ibid., 188.

but must on the contrary include the worship of Another – One who is higher than Man. . . . Correctly interpreted . . . faith in Man can, and indeed must, cast us at the feet and into the arms of One who is greater than ourselves."[1]

The spiritual vision of Teilhard was essentially optimistic and eschatological as he foresaw "the rise on our inward horizon of a cosmic spiritual centre, a supreme pole of consciousness, upon which all the separate consciousnesses of the world may converge and within which they may love one another: the *rise of a God*."[2] He claimed that the development of humankind, an evolutionary process leading to higher consciousness, will eventually converge on the pole Omega who is Christ himself, the indwelling spirit. The Omega is the point where the human and divine meet. It was Teilhard's faith in the person of Christ that led him to link the centre of evolution to the revelation of God in Christ. In other words, "Christ coincides . . . with . . . the Point Omega."[3]

Christopher Mooney describes his approach to the mystery of Christ in this way:

> Human reason has led Teilhard to postulate a transcendent personal Centre for the evolutionary process and his Christian faith had then led him to identify this Centre with Jesus of Nazareth . . . It is this fundamental concept of Christ as physical Centre which has now guided Teilhard's whole approach to the mystery of redemption.[4]

The understanding of religion in an evolutionary context has been explored in greater detail by Karl Jaspers. He speaks of the "Axial Age," the extraordinary period (800-200BC), when various higher forms of religion emerged independently in different civilizations, for example, Confucianism, Buddhism, and Judaism. These religions represent a break from the past. In the primitive religions of the "pre-Axial" age, "human agents are embedded in society, society in the cosmos, and the cosmos incorporates the divine." The Axial transformation breaks this chain: for example, the Old Testament teaches that God creates the world *ex nihilo*. This implies that we have taken God out of the cosmos and placed him above it.[5]

---

1. Ibid., 187-88.
2. Ibid., 120.
3. Quoted in King, "Religion and the Future," 317.
4. Christopher F. Mooney, S.J., *Teilhard de Chardin and the Mystery of Christ* (New York: Image Books, 1968), 128-29.
5. Charles Taylor, *A Secular Age* (Cambridge, MA: The Belknap Press of Harvard

In pre-Axial religious beliefs, the transcendent realm, the world of God or "Heaven" contained both good and bad elements for human flourishing. But in the Axial age, Taylor asserts, they are affirmed unambiguously as good – "the transcendent and the human good are reconceived in the process." The transcendent or the Creator God or the Nirvana of Buddhism is perceived as outside the cosmos and has lost its "original ambivalent character." "Heaven" now guarantees just rule in Confucius' teaching and in Platonic ideas, the key is the Good. We are now called upon to imitate "Heaven" or "God" so that we can be good. Furthermore, in pre-axial religions, human flourishing was considered the highest goal. But in the post-axial age, there is a new goal, beyond human flourishing, which we call "salvation" or "liberation."[1]

Teilhard admitted that a spiritual crisis is fast approaching because traditional religions have failed to evolve with humanity. He writes:

> Among the most disquieting aspects of the modern world is its general and growing state of dissatisfaction in religious matters . . . the fact remains that for some obscure reason something has gone wrong between Man and God *as in these days He is represented to Man*. Man would seem to have no clear picture of the God he longs to worship. Hence . . . the impression one gains from everything taking place around is of an irresistible growth of atheism – or more exactly, a mounting and irresistible de-Christianisation.[2]

The above suggests that a certain pessimism has spread and caused people to doubt the existence of God because the image of God has become inadequate to nourish faith. Religion has become irrelevant to humankind. At present, people's faith seems to be directed towards this world and, at the same time, it seems to be directed toward something beyond. Teilhard understood why people have abandoned their Christian faith – traditional Christianity has failed to keep up with the religious longing of the people. It is backward and primitive. Christianity appears to foster disdain, fear of progress and discovery. Convinced that the deep aspirations of humankind can still be affirmed by Christianity, Teilhard wanted it to be a religion that truly incorporates the values of this world as well as hope in the next.

Teilhard also believed that the world has not grown cold and indifferent, but that it is searching for a God that is compatible with the ever-expanding and changing universe, "a God proportionate to the

---

University Press, 2007), 151-52.

1. Ibid., 153.
2. Teilhard de Chardin, *The Future of Man*, 260.

newly discovered immensities of a Universe whose aspect exceeds the
present compass of our power of worship."[1] Even Eastern spirituality
cannot satisfy the craving of people if it is not attuned to the drive that
motivates human beings:

> we turn to the imposing mass of Hindu and eastern mystical
> systems. The East, the first shrine, and, we are assured, the ever-
> living dwelling place of the Spirit. The East, where so many from
> the West still dream of finding shelter for their faith in life. . . . Let
> us take a closer look at those mighty constructions. . . . The very
> moment we come into fundamental contact with Asia there can
> be no question of doubt. Those impressive columns are utterly
> incapable of supporting the drive of our world in these days.[2]

Teilhard claimed that someone who is influenced by modern culture
cannot be a sincere Confucian or Buddhist or even a Muslim, "unless he
is prepared to live a double interior life."[3] For Teilhard, Christianity is "a
religion of universal progress." His focus is "its faith in the resurrection
of the earth and the expectation of a consummation of the universe in
'Christ Jesus.'"[4] He believed that "a general convergence of religions upon
a universal Christ who fundamentally satisfies them all: that seems to me
the only possible conversion of the world, and the only form in which a
religion of the future can be conceived."[5]

The Teilhardian idea of the universal Christ is not identical with
Christianity but transcends it – it is "Christianity faithfully extended to
its utmost limit."[6] In Teilhard's view, Christianity must surpass itself to
become "trans-Christian" in theology and mysticism.[7] This means that
Christians must take into account the rich and diverse religious experience
of humankind in order to develop a universal religious consciousness.

According to Ursula King,

> Teilhard was actively involved in interfaith dialogue in the late
> 1940s in Paris, but he reflected much earlier on the significance
> of world faiths, especially on the place of mysticism in the

---

1. Ibid., 268.
2. Pierre Teilhard de Chardin, *Science and Christ* (London: Collins, 1968), 105.
3. Ibid., 106.
4. Ibid., 107.
5. Pierre Teilhard de Chardin, *Christianity and Evolution*, translated by René Hague (New York: Harcourt Brace Jovanovich Inc., 1971), 130.
6. Teilhard de Chardin, *Science and Christ*, 112.
7. Ursula King, *Towards a New Mysticism: Teilhard de Chardin and Eastern Religions* (London: Collins, 1980), 189.

planetization of humanity now covering the whole globe. He
acknowledged the diversity and complementarity of the world's
faiths, but he also recognized that, in an evolutionary universe,
religions themselves have to evolve further.[1]

In other words, Teilhard believed that traditional religions had fossilized
and were no longer meaningful to people. He wanted a religion that could
keep up with our understanding of an evolutionary view of life.

## Conversion of Christianity

Towards the end of his life, Teilhard wrote in his diary: "Is Christianity
enough for today's world?" He wondered whether the development of
the comparative study of religions would render Christianity as just one
religion among others and not the sole custodian of truth and salvation.
Perhaps comparative study of religions might lead to the decline of
Christianity – as we are witnessing now in the West. Nonetheless, he
never failed to stress the special contributions of Christianity especially in
its belief in the Incarnation. This belief in the incarnation of God means
that the whole world is infused with the love of God. Both the material
and spiritual dimensions of life as such are sacred – the whole universe is
infused with the presence of God who animates both matter and life.[2]

While he considered Christianity as the fulfilment of all genuine
religions, Teilhard also believed that eastern religions might assist in
rejuvenating the tired Christian faith. In one letter, he wrote:

> I feel more strongly than ever, the need of freeing our religion
> from everything about it that is specifically Mediterranean . . .
> we discover such a wealth of "potentialities" in philosophy, in
> mysticism, and in the study of human conduct that it becomes
> scarcely possible to be satisfied with an image of a mankind
> entirely and definitely developed in the narrow network of
> precepts and dogmas in which some people think they have
> displayed the whole amplitude of Christianity.[3]

Christianity needs to be freed from the shackles of its Mediterranean
influence. In other words, a religion impoverishes itself if it is confined to
its own narrow network of dogmas and categories. Christianity, thus, needs

---

1. Ursula King, "Interfaith Spirituality or Interspirituality? A New Phenomenon in
   a Postmodern World," in Sharada Sugirtharajah, ed., *Religious Pluralism and the
   Modern World* (Basingstoke: Palgrave Macmillan, 2011), 115.
2. Ibid., 34.
3. Quoted in King, *Towards a New Mysticism*, 56.

to learn from the riches of eastern mysticism and philosophy. Teilhard felt strongly the need to strip Christianity from its original cultural setting, "specifically Mediterranean," which includes the Roman-Hellenistic philosophical-theological categories that are regarded as normative. Regarding this issue, Teilhard was far ahead of his time as a Catholic thinker. Most theologians now agree that theology is contextual and thus we cannot claim as normative any particular philosophical-theological framework.

In Teilhard's time, the Church which represented the Christian faith was not open to such new thoughts and experience. But Teilhard insisted that Christianity must accept unconditionally the *"spatial, temporal and psychological"* dimensions of the world. He acknowledged that the Church has attempted to reconcile itself to the modern world, but there is still some distrust and opposition towards the secular sphere: "Sometimes she [the Church] gives her blessing but her heart does not go with it."[1] This skepticism on the part of the ecclesiastical authority towards humankind became an obstacle for the conversion of the world. Non-believers perceive the church as insincere and believers experience the tension between their faith and their own natural tendencies.[2] The Second Vatican Council (1962-65) attempted to remedy this situation when it addressed "the joys and the hopes, the griefs and the anxieties of the men of this age, especially those who are poor or in any way afflicted."[3]

Teilhard insisted that Christians could convert the nascent world only by loving it; they must experience the anxieties and aspirations of the modern world. Christians must allow the person to grow in his being in order to effect "the emancipating synthesis between earth and heaven from which can emerge the parousia [Gk. Arrival; in Christianity, the Second Coming] of the universal Christ." This means that Christians must not be afraid to change, to die to themselves, "to share in order to sublimate." This is what the Incarnation is all about. Teilhard was convinced that "the world will never be converted to Christianity's hopes of heaven, unless first Christianity is converted (that so it may divinize them) to the hopes of the earth."[4]

Teilhard wanted Christianity to evolve and not to be fixated on its static categories. The Christian faith must renew itself so that it can be relevant to people's lives and eventually unite them. This calls for having the right action and quality of thought in people. Teilhard wrote:

1. Teilhard de Chardin, *Science and Christ*, 126.
2. Ibid., 127.
3. Pastoral Constitution on the Church in the Modern World, *Gaudium et Spes*, http://www.vatican.va/archive/hist_councils/ii_vatican_council/documents/ vat-ii_cons_19651207_gaudium-et-spes_en.html.
4. Teilhard de Chardin, *Science and Christ*, 127.

Thus, we have the simultaneous growth in our minds of two
essentially modern concepts, those of collectivity and of an organic
future: a double development precisely engendering the deep-
rooted change of heart that was required to bring about the direct
transformation of a childlike and instinctive faith in Man into its
rational, adult state of constructive, militant faith in Mankind![1]

According to Henri de Lubac, Teilhard was convinced that "it was
impossible (fortunately) to stem the irresistible tide that is carrying
human thought of our time along with it." But the supreme danger is that
modern-day Catholicism has become petrified and sterile as it withdraws
into itself and thus fails to respond to the needs of humankind. The effect
is that Catholicism would "cease to appear what it is in reality for every
age and every man: the truth of life, 'the long-despaired-of answer to the
question asked by every human life." It was not Teihard's intention to get
rid of the old Christian faith. Instead, he wanted to make it more relevant
to people by "transposing" its precepts and counsels. This means that the
Church's teaching would have to take on "a new form, coherence and
urgency." Teilhard wanted to rejuvenate Christianity "not by structural
alteration but by assimilation of new elements."[2]

Through scientific discoveries and perhaps, through globalization as
well, we now have a more comprehensive worldview. Our vision of the
universe is no longer static, but a process. Teilhard characterized it as
"a *Weltanschauung* of movement."[3] This means that there is significant
modification of humankind's structure of thought and beliefs. Due to
the physical curvature of the earth and the mental curve of our thought,
Teilhard believed that we would eventually be drawn together. This
*humanization* as he called it has not stopped but, in fact, is growing
in momentum. At the same time, he insisted that religion, which is
supposed to assist our search for the Absolute, must find new forms of
expression to help us articulate this longing and discover fulfilment.

## Interreligious Dialogue

Since Teilhard upheld faith in the human person, he was critical of both
western and eastern religions that deny human progress. This pessimism
and world-denying attitude is found in Christianity to some extent, and
in eastern religions, in particular, that believe this world is an illusion

1. Teilhard de Chardin, *The Future of Man*, 186-87.
2. Henri de Lubac, S.J., *The Faith of Teilhard de Chardin*, translated by René Hague
   (London: Burns & Oates, 1965), 120-21.
3. Teilhard de Chardin, *The Future of Man*, 262.

and that the spiritual ascent of human beings depends on denying the material world. Hence, Teilhard was critical of Hinduism and Buddhism, but not Daoism or Confucianism as both Chinese religions are world-affirming.[1] At the same time, he was searching for the seeds of religious renewal beyond the religious diversity that he encountered in the Orient. Interreligious dialogue was not in vogue before Vatican II, but Teilhard was willing to listen and learn from the adherents of other faiths. He was ready to go beyond the boundaries of his own Church in search of truth. As a scientist, he was not specifically trained in eastern religions and his approach to them depended on his understanding of mysticism.

Teilhard believed that traditional religions could assist in controlling and directing the spiritual energies of human beings towards unity. It is an evolutionary role wherein "the mystic current" of humankind nourishes the person's "need to be," his "taste for life," and his "ardent desire to grow." It is commonly believed that the mystics in the various religions "have been the one type in their communities most successful in understanding men of divergent faith."[2] The mystic's experience of contact with the absolute, the "supreme Ineffable" which the different religions attempt to transmit can be the basis for interreligious dialogue. Further, faith in the human person could be the basis for uniting the different religions together. This faith in humanity is linked to "an ultimate vision of God, fragments of which are found in every religion."[3]

Teilhard's scientific training regarding the origin of humankind as a biological species led him to reflect on the multiplicity of human civilizations as well as their respective religions. In the past, cultures in the world developed in isolation and at times they were interdependent. This was also accompanied by the growth of their religious spirit – the quest for union with the Ultimate Reality. Teilhard believed that the great religions of humankind would evolve through contact with each other. They cannot continue to exist in isolation, or worse, continue to look upon each other as rivals or enemies. Dialogue, therefore, is necessary for different religious traditions to flourish. Teilhard was particularly interested in the dynamic potential of religions to unite people.[4] He wrote:

> Present-day Mankind, as it becomes increasingly aware of its unity – not only past unity in the blood, but future unity in progress – is experiencing a vital need to close in upon itself.

---

1. Foreword by J. Needham, in Ursula King, *Towards a New Mysticism*, 9.
2. Quoted in King, "Religion and the Future," 318.
3. Ibid., 319.
4. Ibid., 309.

A tendency towards unification is everywhere manifest, and especially in the different branches of religion. We are looking for something that will draw us together, below or above the level of that which divides.[1]

Exposed to the living reality of Asian religious traditions, Teilhard spoke about the universal presence of the spirit in the milieu, "the dynamic of love" and "creative union" in his reflection on religion.[2] He believed that contemporary humankind needs an "incarnational spirituality" in which people can relate meaningfully and find consolation. This spirituality would be both transcendent and immanent, a true religion of progress. In Teilhard's view, none of the religions in the present is adequate to meet the needs of humankind that is fast evolving. He believed that the religious consciousness of human beings needs a new orientation and this includes having dialogue between eastern and western religions. He was optimistic about the future regarding the role of religion in society even though he was uncertain about that future. Teilhard believed something is happening now, "a new event" is taking shape:

> one might say that a yet unknown form of religion . . . is germinating in the heart of modern Man. . . . God is no longer sought in a dissolving identification with Things – nor in a dehumanizing evasion outside Things. But God is attained . . . through going to the centre (in formation) of the total Sphere of Things.
>
> Far from feeling trouble in the Faith by such a deep change, I salute the rise of this new mysticism with an overwhelming hope and I foresee its inevitable triumph.[3]

Although Teilhard never used the term "interreligious dialogue," he seemed to be imbued with the right spirit for encountering "the Other." He was qualified to speak to contemporary men and women regarding the need to integrate the various religious experiences of humankind through dialogue because he possessed a scientific and evolutionary outlook. Teilhard called for the meeting of religions based on convergence, and not the absorption of all religions into one. It is also not a syncretism for Teilhard recognized the diversity and complementarity of faith. In fact,

---

1. Teilhard de Chardin, *The Future of Man*, 189.
2. King, "Religion and the Future," 320.
3. Quoted in Ibid., 323. In his motto for *The Future of Man*, Teilhard writes: "The whole future of the earth, as of religion, seems to me to depend on the awakening of our faith in the future." His concern with the future of humanity is tied to his concern with the evolution of religion in the future.

he acknowledged a decisive difference between eastern spirituality and his own: "the East fascinates me by its faith in the ultimate unity of the universe; but the fact remains that the two of us, the East and I, have two diametrically opposed conceptions of the relationship by which there is communication between the totality and its elements."[1]

Be that as it may, religious diversity is here to stay and different religious traditions offer us a wealth of knowledge and resources for mutual enrichment and correction. Joseph Ratzinger (Pope Emeritus Benedict XVI) also supports an inclusivism that is not an absorption of one religion by another, but an encounter that transforms pluralism into plurality. Ratzinger claims that revelation offered in Christ springs not from one single culture, but from intervention from above, and thus, does not "absorb" anything. It provides space for all the great spiritual experiences of humankind as foreshadowed in Pentecost – the many languages and cultures understand each other in the one Spirit. They are not absorbed but brought together in harmony.[2]

## Convergence

As mentioned earlier, the universal Christ is not to be identified with Christianity, much less with the Church. A Christianity that transcends itself eventually points towards the kingdom of God as preached by Jesus. This means that Christianity needs to open up, to learn from other religious traditions, and see them as partners in the building of the kingdom of God. It is interesting to note that in St Augustine's work, *De Vera Religione* (translated into English as "On True Religion"), he hardly mentioned Christianity. Instead, he emphasized personal relationship with the transcendent God and thus, the title should be translated as "On Genuine Worship." In fact, God is not bothered with Christianity as such, for he so loved the world that he sent his only Son. The world includes all humankind and not just Christians.

Jacques Dupuis, who was well acquainted with the works of Teilhard, argued that Jesus did not identify the reign with the "movement" he created and which later became the Church. He was actually "putting the Church at the service of the reign when he commissioned the 'twelve . . . to proclaim the coming of the kingdom" (Matthew 10:5-7). Thus the Church is called to proclaim the reign of God and not itself.[3]

---

1. Teilhard de Chardin, *Christianity and Evolution*, 122.
2. Joseph Ratzinger, *Truth and Tolerance* (San Francisco: Ignatius Press, 2004), 81-82.
3. Jacques Dupuis, S.J., *Toward a Christian Theology of Religious Pluralism*

This implies that the kingdom of Christ is more comprehensive than the Church; Christ's rule extends beyond the Church to the world in general.[1] Dupuis also claimed that the personal life of the followers of other religions cannot be separated from their own traditions that give concrete expression to their religiosity.[2] He believed that their own sacred books and sacramental practices contain "supernatural, grace-filled elements." Their beliefs and traditions contribute to the building of God's kingdom.[3]

Documents of the Federation of Asian Bishops' Conferences (FABC) describe the pilgrimage towards the kingdom as a journey that involves all humankind, with particular focus on Asia, its peoples and the pluralism that characterizes them. This pilgrimage is, thus, an interreligious project.[4] The Asian bishops point out that God's reign has a communitarian and social dimension because the kingdom of God is about relationships and "the Christian travels not alone, but in community."[5] Diversity and plurality in Asian, multicultural, religious societies are not opposed to the building of the kingdom of God, but are actually necessary for its realization.

Be that as it may, we must remember that the Teilhardian outlook is essentially Christocentric and the Church is the "reflexively Christified" aspect of our society. For Teilhard, the eschatological fulfillment of the kingdom of God involves the "universal Christification of all things."[6] According to him:

> [Christ] is the Alpha and Omega, the principle and the end, the foundation stone and the keystone, the Plenitude and the Plenifier. He is the one who consummates all things and gives them their consistence. It is towards Him and through Him, the inner life and light of the world, that the universal convergence of all created spirit is effected in sweat and tears. He is the single centre, precious and consistent, who glitters at the summit that is to crown the world.[7]

---

(Maryknoll, N.Y.: Orbis Books, 1997), 343.

1. Ibid., 344.
2. Ibid.
3. Ibid., 345-46.
4. Gaudencio B. Rosales and C.G. Arévalo, eds., *For All the Peoples of Asia* (Quezon City: Claretian Publications, 1992), 304.
5. Ibid., 184.
6. Jacques Dupuis, S.J., *Toward a Christian Theology of Religious Pluralism* (Maryknoll, NY: Orbis Books, 1997), 139.
7. Teilhard de Chardin, *Science and Christ* (London: Collins, 1968), 34-35.

The idea of "convergence" is central to Teilhard's understanding of religious pluralism – he believed in the eschatological convergence of religions that will take place at the end of time culminating in the Christ-Omega. We can conclude that this movement towards the future refers to the reign of God – when "He has made known to us the mystery of His will, according to His good pleasure that He set forth in Christ, as a plan for the fullness of time, to gather up all things in Him, things in heaven and things on earth" (Ephesians 1:9-10).

# Conclusion
# The End of History

*We stand at the gates of an important epoch, a time of ferment, when spirit moves forward in a leap, transcends its previous shape and takes on a new one.*

Friedrich Hegel

As a sequel to *A Tale of Two Theologians*, a work that explores the theology of liberation with emphasis on the poor and the dispossessed, this volume begins with Thomas More's *Utopia* and his social criticism of Western society at that time. With their insistence on social justice, Utopians in More's masterpiece are presented as being more open to Gospel values than Christians in England. Continuing this utopian tradition, chapter two discusses the writings of Ignacio Ellacuría who envisaged a "civilization of poverty," where compassion prevails over competition, in El Salvador, a nation with gross injustice and exploitation. Part of the malaise in Third World nations is caused by globalization which has the tendency to widen the gap between the rich and the poor. Chapter three thus proposes the Church's social teachings as an attempt to humanize the market and to protect native cultures against the onslaught of globalization.

Challenging the notion that utopian literature is a Western genre, chapter four explores the humanistic teachings of Confucius, which stress harmonious social relationships in society. Another example of utopian vision originating from China is that of Mo Tzu, discussed in chapter five, who emphasized the universality of love and a frugal lifestyle that resemble Christian teachings. Chapter six examines Kang Youwei, a late nineteenth, early twentieth century utopian writer in China, who utilized the teachings of Confucianism, Buddhism and Daoism, in a proposal to forge a better world in his volume entitled *Datong shu* (The Book of the Great Unity).

Influenced by the ancient religious traditions of Asia, such as Buddhism and Daoism, the French Jesuit and palaeontologist, Teilhard de Chardin, perceived religious beliefs as energy; energy that in turn could help people establish a better world. Chapter seven examines Teilhard's understanding of Christ as the Alpha and Omega where all authentic religious traditions converge with the coming of the kingdom of God. This concluding chapter presents a critique of Francis Fukuyama's thesis, *The End of History and the Last Man*, by promoting an alternative and a more pluralistic view of the historical process with a Christian outlook.

Fukuyama believes that in the midst of violence and ideological conflict, there was some higher process at work leading to the defeat of Fascism and Marxism and resulting in the triumph of Western democracy, the victory of economic and political liberalism. This includes the victory of capitalism as evident in the prevalence of consumerism that we observe the world over.

"The end of history," according to Fukuyama, means we have arrived at the point where we witness the "universalization of Western liberal democracy as the final form of human government."[1] The end of history does not mean that daily events will stop occurring; it means the victory of liberalism over all other competing ideologies including religious beliefs. In other words, there is no viable alternative to Western liberalism as a way of organizing human existence. In concrete terms, the end of history culminated in a new world order that began in 1989 with the collapse of communism in Eastern Europe.

The notion, "the end of history," came from Friedrich Hegel (1770-1831) who exerted a strong influence on the modern understanding of history. Hegel believed that humankind had progressed from primitive stages of consciousness to then present-day democratic societies that emphasized the equality of all peoples. In the final analysis, it is the victory of one idea, the liberal state, over all the rest. Hegel stressed understanding of historical progress as taking place first in the realm of consciousness or ideas before they are realized in the material world.[2]

---

1. Francis Fukuyama, "The End of History?" *The National Interest*, no. 16 (1989), 4. The idea was developed into a book, Fukuyama, *The End of History and the Last Man* (New York: Free Press; and Toronto: Maxwell Macmillan Canada, 1992, 2006).

2. Ibid.

In the Hegelian sense, we have progressed from feudalism to democratic government as the result of the American and French Revolutions, which abolished the distinctions between slaves and masters, and thus, established the principles of equality of all human beings and the rule of law. Hegel believed history had ended with the advent of these two revolutions – the struggle for recognition had been achieved in our democratic institutions. In other words, we have an ideal society, a utopia, and no further progress is possible in human history.

Following Hegel's approach to historical development, but turning it around, Karl Marx (1818-83) argued that the final victory would not culminate in the liberal state but in a communist utopia, the triumph of the proletariat as a true "universal class."[1] The demise of Marxist ideology in the Soviet Union and Eastern Europe, however, has shown that Hegel's prediction was prophetic. Marxism-Leninism is also no longer relevant in China's economic policy and planning. The Chinese government is embarking on a policy of implementing socialism with Chinese characteristics. Lately, President Xi Jingping issued a rallying call for unity among the Communist Party cadres to safeguard China's socialist system, values and ideas. The economic reform initiatives launched by Deng Xiaoping and liberal elements in the Chinese Communist Party in December 1978 were successful beyond their wildest dreams. It resulted in China's present pursuit of a policy of market capitalism. The political system, however, remains inflexible, the Communist Party continuing to pay lip service to Marxism-Leninism as its ideological foundation. However, the elites that govern China know too well that Marxist principles are irrelevant as a guiding light to policy and planning.

In spite of the triumph of liberal democracy over Communism, Fukuyama acknowledges that there is a strong sense of pessimism in the West with regard to the possibility of progress in their political and social institutions. This is fundamentally due to the destructive effects of the two world wars, the rise of totalitarian regimes, the threat of nuclear mutual destruction and the damage done to the environment. "The twentieth century . . . has made all of us into deep historical pessimists."[2] Thus, many people do not expect the future to be bright and promising.

Be that as it may, Fukuyama believes there is hope for a better world as revealed by the fall of dictatorship regimes, ranging across the political spectrum, in Eastern Europe, Latin America, the Middle East, and Asia. Further, capitalism has spread worldwide leading to material prosperity in developed and developing countries. Fukuyama believes political freedom will eventually follow economic freedom.

1. Ibid., 65.
2. Ibid., 3.

Additionally, information and technological innovations have helped people to accumulate wealth and satisfy their almost insatiable desire for creature comfort and luxuries. Even more significant, the adoption of technology has led to the "homogenization of all human societies" regardless of origin or cultural background.[1] Specifically, nations undergoing economic modernization will eventually resemble one another – "they must unify nationally on the basis of a centralized state, urbanize, replace traditional forms of social organisation like tribe, sect, and family with economically rational ones based on function and efficiency, and provide for the universal education of their citizens."[2] Here Fukuyama preaches the gospel of globalization and democracy with all their blessings.

Besides economic factors, human history, according to Fukuyama, is also driven by the desire for recognition of one's sense of worth, dignity or self-esteem. This desire for recognition originates in *thymos,* which is inherent in our soul and includes desire and reason, according to Plato. The just city is one in which *thymos* and desire itself is brought under control by reason to serve the common good. Hence, an ideal society is one that best satisfies these three parts of our soul simultaneously. In Fukuyama's opinion, the best alternative we have is liberal democracy.[3] The need for recognition leads people to demand democratic institutions that guarantee freedom and respect for their individual rights. A relevant example is Hong Kong's demand for democracy from the central government in Beijing under the principle of "one country, two systems."

Fukuyama maintains that "liberal democracy replaces the irrational desire to be recognized as greater than others with a rational desire to be recognized as equal."[4] Thus, if all countries were liberal democracies, one country would be less likely to go to war with another because there would be no incentive to attack; we would recognize and respect each other's legitimacy. Democratic societies do not have imperialistic intentions as it were, according to Fukuyama. We have found what we have been searching for – a better world, a utopia – in the form of liberal democracy. Mission accomplished; the end of history. An ideal society, however, is not by any means a perfect one. Hindrances exist in our democratic societies such as poverty, exploitation, drug abuse, environmental issues, and destructive consumerism; however, according to Fukuyama, these issues can be resolved through the application of liberal principles.

---

1. Ibid., xiv.
2. Ibid., xv.
3. Ibid., 337.
4. Ibid., xx.

Without doubt, Fukuyama's optimism regarding the future attracted a lot of criticism. Jacques Derrida was one of those dissenting voices with a more pluralistic viewpoint regarding what a society should strive for. Derrida challenged the claim made by Fukuyama by asserting that this purported victory of liberal capitalism and democracy has "never been so critical, fragile, threatened, even in certain regards catastrophic, and in sum bereaved."[1] Communism has collapsed in Europe but this does not signify that capitalism has won. This apparent victory of the free market may prove to be malign, a bad omen. The claim made by Fukuyama was actually quite fashionable at the turn of the century when people were receptive to "apocalyptic speculation." Nonetheless, Derrida contended, it amounts to no more than "an ideological confidence trick."[2]

Fukuyama does not consider liberal democracy and capitalism an ideology, rather an ideal state, which cannot be improved. In other words, we are now living in the best of all possible worlds – an even better world is not necessary. "Liberal democracy in reality constitutes the best possible solution to the human problem."[3] If this is so, why does he also admit that some countries have failed to achieve stable liberal democracy and some have even lapsed back to military dictatorship?

Fukuyama attributes it to unequal social development and residual human perversity. Derrida, however, pointed to the discrepancy between the ideal and the real. The "gap between fact and ideal essence" is so evident in all political regimes.[4] Even in the most advanced Western democracies, there are problems and weaknesses inherent in the system. We have witnessed massive unemployment, the plight of the homeless, violence, poverty, and economic exploitation affecting many human beings. The claim by Fukuyama that these issues can be easily resolved in a democratic society is simply not feasible.

Believing that the fight against injustice must continue, Derrida called for the establishment of a "New International." In this fight against injustice, he invoked the spirit of Marx to seek "a link of affinity, suffering, and hope."[5] Whether we like it or not, we are all heirs of Marx and Marxism. They are deeply ingrained in our cultural heritage, according to Derrida. We cannot exorcise the ghost of history,

---

1. Quoted in Stuart Sim, *Derrida and the End of History*, Postmodern Encounters (New York: Totem Books; and Duxford: Icon Books, 1999), 7.
2. Ibid., 13, 8.
3. Fukuyama, *The End of History and the Last Man*, 338.
4. Sim, *Derrida and the End of History*, 53.
5. Ibid., 55, 56.

the spectre of Marx still haunts us. Jon Sobrino writes: "A new spectre is haunting Europe. . . . An everyday postmodernism of the heart is spreading that is relegating the poverty and the destitution of the Third World to an even greater faceless remoteness."[1] The ghost of Marx reminds us that we still have the poor with us because capitalism is so widespread.

Capitalism is dangerously rampant, creating wealth for a few while impoverishing many. Unchecked, capitalism exploits and controls the lives of defenceless, hapless people; therefore, it is absolutely necessary to have an ideological opponent such as Marxism to check the harm that capitalism is capable of inflicting on humanity. In fact, capitalism is "a form of sin, a way of life that captures and distorts human desire in accord with the golden rule of production of the market."[2] Gilles Deleuze speaks of the victory of "savage capitalism," as not just economic but "more insidiously, ontological."[3] Existing as a tool of the market, unfettered capitalism denounces any kind of state intervention.

With advances in technology, capitalism needs less labor. In Third World countries, savage capitalism has rendered the population redundant. People are treated like disposable products to be sacrificed to the gods of the marketplace. It used to be bad to be exploited by multinational corporations, now it is a privilege to be exploited by them because job openings are so few.[4] At the moment, Western societies have "neither effective enemies inside nor barbarians knocking at the gates, only adulators and imitators. It has practically (and apparently irrevocably) de-legitimized all alternatives to itself."[5]

The spirit of Marx, Derrida believed, can counteract the smug triumphalism of Western democracy and capitalism. Thus, it is worthwhile to keep that militant spirit alive. Likewise, we cannot exorcise the ghost of capitalism, it will always return to haunt us when socialism ascends. Spectres are "permanent factors" in our lives and we must learn to accommodate them. Ghosts cannot die. Regarding the demise of communism, "the dead can often be more powerful than the living".[6]

---

1. Sobrino, "Fifty Years for a Future that Is Christian and Human," 69.
2. Daniel M. Bell, *Liberation Theology after the End of History: The Refusal to Cease Suffering*, Radical Orthodoxy Series (London and New York: Routledge, 2001), 2. See also Daniel P. Castillo, "The Dynamism of Integral Liberation: Reconsidering Gustavo Gutiérrez's Central Concept after 'the End of History,'" *Political Theology* 18, no. 1 (2016), 1-16.
3. Ibid., 9.
4. Ibid., 11.
5. Quoted in Sim, *Derrida and the End of History*, 59.
6. Ibid., 62.

Herbert Marcuse believed that utopia, meaning "nowhere," is irrelevant now because we have all the necessary resources for social transformation in our capitalist system. It is "here" and not "nowhere" that we can achieve an ideal society because the material and intellectual forces needed to create a new order are available. The end of utopia is equivalent to the end of history. This means new possibilities for a better life cannot be thought of merely as an improvement of the past or even the present. It presupposes a break with the historical continuum so that our society would be qualitatively different from the past, we would be freer, to say the least. It will have to be, according to Marx, a break in such a way as to make "all previous history only the prehistory of mankind."[1]

Advances in technology, Marcuse believed, could assist in the abolition of poverty and suffering and even alienated labor. Further, he saw the need for a new theory of person and new morality, unlike the theory influenced by Judeo-Christian tradition. Emphasizing subjectivism and consciousness, Marcuse aimed to "transform the will itself, so that people no longer want what they now want."[2] A utopian thinker (although he did not consider himself as one), Marcuse had a vision of a free socialist society in which labor could be organized in harmony with the genuine needs of the people. Idealistic it may seem, but Marcuse's utopian vision is grounded in empirical analysis of capitalism. He was convinced that the seeds for radical transformation existed within the capitalist system.

Finally, Fukuyama acknowledges that liberal democracy has its origin in Christianity which teaches the universal dignity of the person. The Christian deity recognizes all human beings as equal in worth and dignity. *Megalothymia* is the desire to be recognized as superior to others and *isothymia* is the desire to be recognized as the equal to others. The kingdom of Heaven presents to us the possibility of a better world in which the *isothymia* of every person would be satisfied but not the *megalothymia*, the proud and vainglorious tyrant.[3] "Blessed are the meek, for they shall inherit the earth" (Matthew 5: 5).

There is thus a historical relationship between Christianity and the development of liberal democracy. In Christianity, we learn the value of freedom and equality of all human beings. In this context, freedom

---

1. Bernard S. Morris, "The End of Ideology, the End of Utopia, and the End of History: On the Occasion of the End of the U.S.S.R.," *History of European Ideas* 19, no. 4-6 (1994), 704.

2. Ibid.

3. Fukuyama, *The End of History and the Last Man*, 197.

signifies that human beings are morally free to choose between right and wrong. In secular form, the principle of equality is understood as human rights. Fukuyama believes that the principles of equality and liberty found in liberal democracy have universal significance in the sense that, as our society evolves, people all over the world desire the benefits of liberal democracy.[1]

Fukuyama writes: "All nations were but branches of a more general humanity, whose fate could be understood in terms of God's plan for mankind. . . . As the Christian account of history makes clear, an 'end of history' is implicit in the writing of all Universal Histories."[2] He holds that historical process can be meaningful only when a new order has been accomplished, such as the victory of liberal democracy, which brings an end to history. Christians, however, believe that the end of history arrived with the coming of the messiah – "the kingdom of Heaven is at hand" (Matthew 3:2). The kingdom of Heaven has come but the fullness of its realization will occur at the end of time.

Missing out on realized eschatology, Fukuyama reasons the kingdom of Heaven will take place only in the future, not now: "Christianity posits the realization of human freedom not here on earth but only in the kingdom of Heaven."[3] He holds that Christians can expect liberation not in this life but in the afterlife. In this, Fukuyama fails to appreciate the Christians' conviction that liberation has already arrived in the person of Jesus Christ.

Gustavo Gutiérrez, on the other hand, argues that the kingdom of God can be realized now through political actions, which include "the protest against trampled human dignity, in the struggle against the plunder of the vast majority of humankind, in liberating love, and in the building of a new society of justice and fraternity."[4] This implies identification with the poor and oppressed in their struggles. It involves an immersion in the political process of fighting for an equitable society and proclaiming the liberating love of Christ. God's final purpose, however, can only be achieved, not in history, but in the life to come.

---

1. Ibid., 196, 343.
2. Ibid., 56.
3. Ibid., 197.
4. Gustavo Gutiérrez, *Gustavo Gutiérrez: Essential Writings*, edited by James B. Nickoloff (London: SCM Press, 1996), 34.

# Bibliography

Ahern, Dennis M. "Is Mo Tzu a Utilitarian?" *Journal of Chinese Philosophy* 3, no. 2 (1976), 185-93.

Alegre, Xavier. "The Sin of the World: The Devil is a Liar, a Deceiver and a Murderer," in Jon Sobrino and Felix Wilfred, eds., *Globalization and its Victims, Concilium* 5. London: SCM Press, 2001.

Amaladoss, Michael. "The Utopia of the Human Family: Among the Religions of Humanity," in Jon Sobrino and Felix Wilfred, eds., *Globalization and Its Victims, Concilium* 5. London: SCM, 2001.

Aristotle. *Politics*, translated by Benjamin Jowett, Book II, Part III. http://classics.mit.edu/Aristotle/politics.2.two.html.

Barrera, Albino. "Globalization's Shifting Economic and Moral Terrain: Contesting Marketplace Mores," *Theological Studies* 69, no. 2 (June 2008), 290-308.

Baum, Gregory. "Middle Class Religion in America," in Johann Baptist Metz, ed., *Christianity and the Bourgeoisie*. New York: The Seabury Press, 1979.

Beattie, Paul H. "The Religion of Confucius: The First Humanist," *Religious Humanism* 22 (1988), 11-17.

Bell, Daniel M. *Liberation Theology after the End of History: The Refusal to Cease Suffering*. Radical Orthodoxy Series. London and New York: Routledge, 2001.

Benjamin, Walter. "On the Frankfurt School." *Cités*, 2010, 149-59.

Berger, Stefan, Linas Eriksonas, and Andrew Mycock, eds., "Introduction: Narrating the Nation: Historiography and Other Genres," in *Narrating the Nation: Representations in History, Media and the Arts*. New York: Berghahn Books, 2011, 1-16. http://www.jstor.org/stable/j.ctt9qdcbq.5.

Bloch, Ernst. *The Principle of Hope*. Cambridge, MA: The MIT Press, 1986.

Bockover, Mary I. "The *Ren Dao* of Confucius: A Spiritual Account of Humanity," in David Jones, ed., *Confucius Now: Contemporary Encounters with the Analects*. Chicago: Open Court, 2008.

Boyle, Nicholas. "Hegel and 'The End of History," *New Blackfriars* 76, no. 891 (1995), 109-19.

Brock, Brian. "Globalization, Eden and the Myth of Original Markets," *Studies in Christian Ethics* 28, no. 4 (2015), 402-18

Burke, Joseph Anthony. "Pope Benedict on Capitalism, Marxism, and Globalization," *The Catholic Social Science Review* 14 (2009), 167-91.

Cahill, Lisa Sowle. "Globalization and the Common Good," in John A. Coleman, S.J., and William F. Ryan, S.J., eds., *Globalization and Catholic Social Thought: Present Crisis and Future Hope*. Maryknoll, NY: Orbis Books, 2005.

Carazo, Luis de Sebastián. "Europe: Globalization and Poverty," in Jon Sobrino and Felix Wilfred, eds., *Globalization and its Victims, Concilium* 5. London: SCM Press, 2001.

Casanova, José. "From Modernization to Secularization to Globalization: An Autobiographical Self-Reflection," *Religion and Society* 2 (2011), 25-36.

———. "Religion, the New Millennium, and Globalization," *Sociology of Religion* 62, no. 4 (2001), 415-41.

Castillo, Daniel P. "The Dynamism of Integral Liberation: Reconsidering Gustavo Gutiérrez's Central Concept after 'the End of History," *Political Theology* 18, no. 1 (2016), 1-16.

Castillo, Fernando. "Christianity: Bourgeois (*Burguesa*) Religion or Religion of the People?" in Johann Baptist Metz, ed., *Christianity and the Bourgeoisie*. New York: The Seabury Press, 1979.

Chambers, R.W. "The Rational Heathens," in William Nelson, ed., *Twentieth Century Interpretations of Utopia*. Englewood Cliffs, NJ: Prentice-Hall, 1968.

Chesneaux, Jean. "Egalitarian and Utopian Traditions in the East," *Diogenes* 62 (1968), 76-102.

Chiang, Sing-Chen Lydia. "Visions of Happiness: Daoist Utopias and Grotto Paradises in Early and Medieval Chinese Tales," *Utopian Studies* 20, no. 1 (2009), 97-120.

Choi, Young-jin, and Lee Haeng-hoon. "The Confucian Vision of an Ideal Society Arising out of Moral Emotions, with a Focus on the Sishu Daquan," *Philosophy East and West* 66, no. 2 (2016), 394-417.

Claeys, Gregory. *Searching for Utopia: The History of an Idea*. New York: Thames & Hudson, 2011.

———. *The Cambridge Companion to Utopian Literature*. Cambridge: Cambridge University Press, 2010.

Clark, Charles M.A. "Greed Is Not Enough: Some Insights on Globalization from Catholic Social Thought," *Journal of Catholic Social Thought* 2, no. 1 (2005), 23-51.

Collinson, Diane, Kathryn Plant and Robert Wilkinson. *Routledge Key Guides: Fifty Eastern Thinkers*. London: Routledge, 2000.

Confucius. *The Analects of Confucius: A Philosophical Translation*. Translated with an introduction by Roger T. Ames and Henry Rosemont, Jr. New York: Ballantine Books, 1999.

———. *The Analects of Confucius*. Translated by Burton Watson. New York: Columbia University Press, 2007.

de Lubac, Henri, S.J. *The Faith of Teilhard de Chardin*. Translated by René Hague. London: Burns & Oates, 1965.

de Schrijver, Georges. "The Distinctive Contribution of Ignacio Ellacuría to a Praxis of Liberation," *Louvain Studies* 25, no. 4 (2000), 312-35.

Donner, H.W. "A Moral Fable," in William Nelson, ed., *Twentieth Century Interpretations of Utopia*. Englewood Cliffs, NJ: Prentice-Hall, 1968.

Duda, Kristopher. "Reconsidering Mo Tzu on the Foundations of Morality," *Asian Philosophy* 11, no. 1 (March 2001), 23-31.

Dutton, Jacqueline. "'Non-western' Utopian Traditions," in Gregory Claeys, ed., *The Cambridge Companion to Utopian Literature*. Cambridge: Cambridge University Press, 2010.

Ellacuría, Ignacio. *Freedom Made Flesh: The Mission of Christ and His Church*. Translated by John Drury. Maryknoll, NY: Orbis Books, 1976.

Elton, G.R. *England under the Tudors*. London: Methuen & Co., 1974.

Fau, José Ignacio González. "The Utopia of the Human Family: The Universalization of the Truly Human as Real Globalization," in Jon Sobrino and Felix Wilfred, eds., *Globalization and its Victims, Concilium* 5. London: SCM Press, 2001.

Ferguson, Niall. *The Ascent of Money*. London: Penguin Books, 2009.

Ferrara, Pasquale. "The Concept of Periphery in Pope Francis' Discourse: A Religious Alternative to Globalization?" *Religions* 6, no. 1 (March 2015), 42-57.

Fetscher, Iring. "The 'Bourgeoise' (*Bürgertum*, Middle Class): On the Historical and Political Semantics of the Term," in Johann Baptist Metz, ed., *Christianity and the Bourgeoisie*. New York: The Seabury Press, 1979.

Fiorenza, Francis Schüssler. "Religion and Society: Legitimation, Rationalization, or Cultural Heritage," in Johann Baptist Metz, ed., *Christianity and the Bourgeoisie*. New York: The Seabury Press, 1979.

Formicola, Jo Renee. "Globalization: A Twenty-First Century Challenge to Catholicism and its Church," *Journal of Church and State* 54, no. 1 (2012), 106-21.

Fu, Charles Wei-Hsun, "Confucianism, Marxism-Leninism and Mao: A Critical Study," *Journal of Chinese Philosophy* 1 (1974), 339-71.

Fukuyama, Francis. "The End of History?" *The National Interest*, no. 16 (1989), 3-18.

———. *The End of History and the Last Man*. New York: Free Press; and Toronto: Maxwell Macmillan Canada, 2006.

"Go East, Young Bureaucrat." *The Economist* (19 March 2011), 10. http://easyaccess.lib.cuhk.edu.hk/login?url=http://search.proquest.com/docview/857839830?accountid=10371.

Golemboski, David. "The Globalization of Catholic Social Teaching," *Journal of Catholic Social Thought* 12, no. 1 (2015), 87-108.

Gustavo, Gutiérrez. *A Theology of Liberation*. Translated and edited by Sister Caridad Inda and John Eagleson. Maryknoll, NY: Orbis Books, 1973, 1988.

Gutiérrez, Gustavo. *Gustavo Gutiérrez: Essential Writings*. Edited with an introduction by James B. Nickoloff. London: SCM Press, 1996.

Gu Zhengkun. "Confucian Family Values as Universal Values in the 21st Century Family – Nation – World," in Klaus Mühlhahn and Nathalie van Looy, eds., *The Globalization of Confucius and Confucianism*. Zurich: Lit Verlag, 2012.

Hansen, Chad. "Mo-Tzu: Language Utilitarianism," *Journal of Chinese Philosophy* 16, no. 3 (1989), 355-80.

Himes, Kenneth R. "Globalization with a Human Face: Catholic Social Teaching and Globalization." *Theological Studies* 69, no. 2 (June 2008), 269-89.

Höchsmann, Hyun. "Love and the State in Plato and Confucius," *Dao* 2, no. 1 (2002), 97-116.

Hsiao, Kung-Chuan. *A Modern China and a New World: K'ang Yu-Wei, Reformer and Utopian (1858-1927)*. Seattle: University of Washington, 1975.

Hua, Shiping. *Chinese Utopianism: A Comparative Study of Reformist Thought with Japan and Russia 1898-1997*. Washington, DC: Woodrow Wilson Centre Press, 2009.

Hwan, Kwang-kuo. "Dao and the Transformative Power of Confucianism: A Theory of East Asian Modernization," in Tu Wei-ming, ed., *The Triadic Chord: Confucian Ethics, Industrial East Asia and Max Weber*. Singapore: The Institute of East Asian Philosophies, 1991.

Jensen, Lionel. *Manufacturing Confucianism: Chinese Traditions and Universal Civilization*. Durham: Duke University Press, 1977.

K'ang, Yu-wei. *Ta T'ung Shu: The One World Philosophy of K'ang Yu-wei*. Translated from the Chinese with introduction and notes by Laurence G. Thompson. London: George Allen & Unwin Ltd, 1958.

Kant, Immanuel. *Toward Perpetual Peace and Other Writings on Politics, Peace, and History*. New Haven: Yale University Press, 2006.

Kautsky, Karl. "Utopian Socialism," in William Nelson, ed., *Twentieth Century Interpretations of Utopia*. Englewood Cliffs, NJ: Prentice-Hall, 1968.

Kim, Young-oak, and Jung-kyu Kim. *Great Equal Society: Confucianism, China and the 21st Century*. Singapore: World Scientific Publishing, 2014.

King, Ambrose Y.C. "The Transformation of Confucianism in the Post-Confucian Era: The Emergence of Rationalistic Traditionalism in Hong Kong," in Tu Wei-ming, ed., *The Triadic Chord: Confucian Ethics, Industrial East Asia and Max Weber*. Singapore: The Institute of East Asian Philosophies, 1991.

King, Ursula. "Religion and the Future: Teilhard de Chardin's Analysis of Religion as a Contribution to Interreligious Dialogue," *Religious Studies* 7, no. 4 (1 December 1971), 307-23.

———. *Towards a New Mysticism: Teilhard de Chardin and Eastern Religions*. London: Collins, 1980.

Kingman, Brewster, and Sterling M. McMurrin. *The Tanner Lectures on Human Values*. Salt Lake City: University of Utah Press, 1983.

Kumar, Krishnan. *Utopia and Anti-Utopia in Modern Times*. Oxford: Basil Blackwell, 1987.

———. *Utopianism*. Milton Keynes: Open University Press, 1991.

Lee, Kuan Yew, and Fook Kwang Han. *Lee Kuan Yew: Hard Truths to Keep Singapore Going*. Singapore: Straits Times Press, 2011.

Ling, Trevor O. "The Weberian Thesis and Interpretive Positions on Modernisation," in Tu Wei-ming, ed., *The Triadic Chord: Confucian Ethics, Industrial East Asia and Max Weber*. Singapore: The Institute of East Asian Philosophies, 1991.

Longxi, Zhang. "The Utopian Vision, East and West," *Utopian Studies* 13, no. 1 (2002), 1-20.

Loubere, Leo. *Utopian Socialism: Its History since 1800*. Cambridge, MA: Schenkman Publishing Co., 1974.

Lowe, Scott. *Mo Tzu's Religious Blueprint for a Chinese Utopia: The Will and the Way*. New York: The Edwin Mellen Press, 1992.

MacCormack, Geoffrey. "The Legal Philosophy of Mo Tzu," *Archiv für Rechts- und Sozialphilosophie/Archives for Philosophy of Law and Social Philosophy (ARSP)* 79, no. 3 (1993), 333-48.

Mannion, Gerard. "What's in a Name? Hermeneutical Questions on 'Globalization', Catholicity and Ecumenism," *New Blackfriars* 86, no. 1002 (March 2005), 204-15.

Manuel, Frank E., and Fritzie P. Manuel. *Utopian Thought in the Western World*. Oxford: Basil Blackwell, 1979.

Manuel, Frank E., ed. *Utopias and Utopian Thought*. Boston: Beacon Press, 1966.

Marsden, John. 'The Political Theology of Johannes Baptist Metz," *Heythrop Journal* 53, no. 3 (May 2012), 440-52.

Marx, Karl. *German Ideology*. London: ElecBook, 2000.

McCann, Gerard. "Globalization and the Need for a 'Moral Economy'?" *The Furrow* 57, no. 5 (May 2006), 292-9.

Metz, Johann Baptist. "Messianic or 'Bourgeois' Religion? On the Crisis of the Church in West Germany," in Johann Baptist Metz, ed., *Christianity and The Bourgeoisie*. New York: The Seabury Press, 1979.

———. *Theology of the World*. Translated by W. Glen-Doepel. London: Burns & Oates / Herder and Herder, Inc., 1969.

———. *Faith in History and Society: Toward a Practical Fundamental Theology*. Translated by David Smith. New York: The Seabury Press, 1980.

Mill, John Stuart. *The Subjection of Women*. Philadelphia, PA: B. Lippincott & Co., 1869.

Miller, Vincent Jude. "Where is the Church? Globalization and Catholicity," *Theological Studies* 69, no. 2 (June 2008), 412-32.

Mong, Ih-Ren Ambrose. "Crossing the Ethical-Practical Bridge: Paul's Knitter's Regnocentrism in Asian Perspective," *The Ecumenical Review* 63, no. 2 (2011), 186-199.

Morris, Bernard S. "The End of Ideology, the End of Utopia, and the End of History: On the Occasion of the End of the U.S.S.R.," *History of European Ideas* 19, no. 4-6 (1994), 699-708.

Mo Tzu. *Basic Writings*. Translated by Burton Watson. New York: Columbia University Press, 1966.

Mooney, Christopher F. *Teilhard de Chardin and the Mystery of Christ*. New York: Image Books, 1968.

More, Thomas. *Utopia*. 1516. Translated by Ralph Robynson, 1556. Edited with an introduction by David Harris Sacks. Boston: Bedford/St Martin, 1999.

———. *Utopia*. Edited by George M. Logan and Robert M. Adams. Cambridge: Cambridge University Press, 2002.

———. *Utopia*. Translated with an introduction and notes by Paul Turner. London: Penguin Books, 2003.

Mühlhahn, Klaus, and Nathalie Van Looy, eds. *The Globalization of Confucius and Confucianism*. Zurich: Lit Verlag, 2012.

Nelson, William, ed. *Twentieth Century Interpretations of Utopia*. Englewood Cliffs, NJ: Prentice-Hall, 1968.

Okure, Teresa SHCJ. "Africa: Globalization and the Loss of Cultural Identity," in
    Jon Sobrino and Felix Wilfred, eds., *Globalization and its Victims*, *Concilium* 5.
    London: SCM Press, 2001.

O'Meara, Thomas F. "Teilhard de Chardin in China," *Worldview* 16, (1 January
    1973), 31-4.

Olberding, Amy. "Confucius' Complaints and the *Analects*' Account of the Good
    Life," *Dao* 12, no. 4 (December 2013), 417-40.

Ormerod, Neil. "Theology, History and Globalization," *Gregorianum* 88, no. 1
    (2007), 23-48.

Osborne, Evan. "China's First Liberal," *The Independent Review* 16, no. 4 (Spring
    2012), 533-51.

Oslington, Paul, ed. *Adam Smith as Theologian*. New York: Routledge, 2011.

Pawlikowski, John. "Creating an Ethical Context for Globalization: Catholic
    Perspectives in an Interreligious Context," *Journal of Ecumenical Studies* 42,
    no. 3 (2007), 363-72.

Petras, James, and Henry Veltmeyer. *Imperialism and Capitalism in the Twenty-
    First Century: A System in Crisis*. Farnham: Ashgate Publishing Co., 2013.

Pfister, Lauren F. "A Study in Comparative Utopias: K'ang Yu-Wei and Plato,"
    *Journal of Chinese Philosophy* 16, no. 1 (1989), 59-117.

———. "A Modern Ruist Religious Vision of a Global Unity: Kang Youwei's Utopian
    Vision and its Humanistic Religious Refraction in European Sinology," in
    Thomas Jansen, Thoralf Klein and Christian Meyer, eds., *Globalization and the
    Making of Religious Modernity in China: Transnational Religions, Local Agents,
    and the Study of Religion, 1800-Present*. Leiden: Brill, 2014.

Piketty, Thomas. *Capital in the Twenty-First Century*. Cambridge, MA: The
    Belknap Press of Harvard University Press, 2014.

Plato. *Laws*. Tustin, TX: Xist Classics, 2016.

———. *Republic*. Auckland, NZ: The Floating Press, 2009.

Pope John Paul II, *Address of the Holy Father to the Pontifical Academy of Social
    Sciences*, https://w2.vatican.va/content/john-paul ii/en/speeches/2001/april/
    documents/hf_jp-ii_spe_20010427_pc-social-sciences.html.

Popper, Karl R. *Conjectures and Refutations*. London: Routledge & Kegan Paul,
    1963.

Qi Zhou. "On Volunteer Spirit and Thought of 'Universal Love' by Mo-tse," *Asian
    Social Science* 7, no. 9 (2011), 184-88.

Ritter, Gerhard. "*Utopia* and Power Politics," in William Nelson, ed., *Twentieth
    Century Interpretations of Utopia*. Englewood Cliffs, NJ: Prentice-Hall, 1968.

Rorty, Richard. *Philosophy and Social Hope*. Harmondsworth, Middlesex: Penguin
    Books, 1999.

Rothstein, Edward, Herbert Muschamp and Martin E. Marty. *Visions of Utopia*.
    Oxford: Oxford University Press, 2003.

Sargent, Lyman Tower. *Utopianism: A Very Short Introduction*. Oxford: Oxford
    University Press, 2010.

Scharlemann, Martin H. "Utopia or Paradise," *Concordia Journal* 1, no. 2 (March
    1975), 56-61.

Schwartz, Benjamin I. *The World of Thought in Ancient China*. Cambridge, MA:
    Harvard University Press, 1989.

———. *The World of Thought in Ancient China*. Cambridge, MA: Harvard University Press, 1989.

Scott, Peter, and William T. Cavanaugh, eds. *The Blackwell Companion to Political Theology*. Oxford: Blackwell Publishing Ltd, 2004.

Shellong, Dieter. "A Theological Critique of the 'Bourgeois World View' (*Bürgerlichen Weltanschaung*)," in Johann Baptist Metz, ed., *Christianity and the Bourgeoisie*. New York: The Seabury Press, 1979.

Sim, Stuart. *Derrida and the End of History*, Postmodern Encounters. New York: Totem Books; and Duxford: Icon Books, 1999.

Sniegocki, John. "Neoliberal Globalization: Critiques and Alternatives," *Theological Studies* 69, no. 2 (June 2008), 321-39.

Sobrino, Jon, and Felix Wilfred, eds. *Globalization and its Victims, Concilium* 5. London: SCM Press, 2001.

———. "Introduction: The Reasons for Returning to this Theme," in Jon Sobrino and Felix Wilfred, eds., *Globalization and its Victims, Concilium* 5. London: SCM Press, 2001.

Sobrino, Jon. "Fifty Years for a Future that Is Christian and Human," *Concilium* 1 (2016), 67-82.

———. "On the Way to Healing: Humanizing a 'Gravely Ill World'," *America*, 29 October 2014. https://www.americamagazine.org/issue/way-healing.

Soles, David E. "Mo Tzu and the Foundations of Morality," *Journal of Chinese Philosophy* 26, no. 1 (1999), 37-48.

Standaert, Nicolas. "The Jesuits Did NOT Manufacture 'Confucianism' (Book Review)," *East Asian Science, Technology, and Medicine*, no. 16 (1999), 115-32.

Stiglitz, Joseph E. "Human Rights and Globalization: The Responsibility of States and Private Actors," *Journal of Catholic Social Thought* 10, no. 1 (2013), 85-90.

Suleski, Ronald. "Confucius: The Organization of Chinese Society," in David Jones, ed., *Confucius Now: Contemporary Encounters with the Analects*es. Chicago: Open Court, 2008.

Swanton, Christine. "A Challenge to Intellectual Virtue from Moral Virtue: The Case of Universal Love," in Heather Battaly, ed., *Virtue and Vice, Moral and Epistemic*. Chichester: Wiley-Blackwell, 2010.

Taylor, Charles. *A Secular Age*. Cambridge, MA: The Belknap Press of Harvard University Press, 2007.

Teilhard de Chardin, Pierre. *The Phenomenon of Man*. London: Collins, 1959.

———. *Le Milieu Divin: An Essay on the Interior Life*. London, St James Place: Collins, 1960.

———. *The Future of Man*. Translated from the French by Norman Denny. London Collins, 1964.

———. *Science and Christ*. London: Collins, 1968.

———. *Christianity and Evolution*. Translated by René Hague. New York: Harcourt Brace Jovanovich, 1971.

Thompson, L.G. *Ta Tung Shu; The One-World Philosophy of K'ang Yu Wei*. London: Allen & Unwin, 1958.

Tseu, Augustinus A. *The Moral Philosophy of Mo-Tze*. Taipei: China Printing Ltd, 1965.

Tu, Ching-I. *Interpretation and Intellectual Change : Chinese Hermeneutics in Historical Perspective*. New Brunswick, N.J.: Transaction Publishers, 2005.

Tu Wei-ming, ed. *The Triadic Chord: Confucian Ethics, Industrial East Asia and Max Weber.* Singapore: The Institute of East Asian Philosophies, 1991.

Tu, Wei-ming. "Confucian Encounter with the Enlightenment Mentality of the Modern West," *Oriens Extremus* 49 (2010), 249-308.

Tucker, Mary Evelyn. "Globalization, Catholic Social Teaching, and the Environment," *Journal of Catholic Social Thought* 4, no. 2 (2007), 355-71.

van Norden, Bryan W. *Confucius and the Analects: New Essays.* Oxford University Press, 2002.

van Stichel, Ellen, and Yves de Maeseneer. "*Gaudium et Spes*: Impulses of the Spirit for an Age of Globalization," *Louvain Studies* 39, no. 1 (2015), 63-79.

Vieira, Fátima. "The Concept of Utopia," in Gregory Claeys, ed., *The Cambridge Companion to Utopian Literature.* Cambridge: Cambridge University Press, 2010.

Vorenkamp, Dirck. "Another look at Utilitarianism in Mo Tzu's Thought," *Journal of Chinese Philosophy* 19, no. 4 (1992), 423-43.

Wilde, Lawrence. *Thomas More's Utopia: Arguing for Social Justice.* London: Routledge, 2017.

Wilfred Cantwell Smith, *The Meaning and End of Religion.* Minneapolis: Fortress Press, 1991.

Wilfred, Felix. "Religions Face-to-Face with Globalization," in Jon Sobrino and Felix Wilfred, eds., *Globalization and its Victims, Concilium* 5. London: SCM Press, 2001.

Williams, Howard, David Sullivan, and E. Gwynn Matthews. *Francis Fukuyama and the End of History.* Political Philosophy Now. Cardiff: University of Wales Press, 1997.

Wu, Qingyun. *Female Rule in Chinese and English Literary Utopias.* Syracuse: Syracuse University Press, 1991.

Zaehner, R.C. *The Convergent Spirit: Towards a Dialectic of Religion.* London: Routledge & Kegan Paul, 1963.

Zakaria, Fareed, and Lee Kuan Yew. "Culture Is Destiny: A Conversation with Lee Kuan Yew," *Foreign Affairs* 73, no. 2 (1994), 109-26.

Zamagni, Stefano. "Financial Integrity and Inclusive Capitalism: Civilizing Globalization," *Journal of Catholic Social Thought* 12, no. 2 (2015), 207-25.

# Index

*Other titles by Ambrose Mong:*

## Purification of Memory:
### A Study of Orthodox Theologians from a Catholic Perspective

PB ISBN: 9780227175132          ePUB ISBN: 9780227904169
PDF ISBN: 9780227904145          Kindle ISBN: 9780227904152

An ecumenical investigation of Eastern Orthodox theology through its most distinguished modern contributors, revealing commonalities with the Western church.

## Accommodation and Acceptance:
### An Exploration of Interfaith Relations

PB ISBN: 9780227175187          ePUB ISBN: 9780227904312
PDF ISBN: 9780227904299          Kindle ISBN: 9780227904305

A study of the relations between Christianity and the major Asian religions, exploring the diverse theologies of those who pioneered interfaith dialogue.

## Guns and Gospel:
### Imperialism and Evangelism in China

PB ISBN: 9780227176252
PDF ISBN: 9780227905968

ePUB ISBN: 9780227905975
Kindle ISBN: 9780227905982

An exploration of the history of Christian missionary work in China, and its often ambiguous and uneasy relationship with European imperialism.

## A Tale of Two Theologians:
### Treatment of Third World Theologies

HB ISBN: 9780227176580
PB ISBN: 9780227176597
PDF ISBN: 9780227906323

ePUB ISBN: 9780227906330
Kindle ISBN: 9780227906347

A discussion of the challenges of liberation theology and religious pluralism, in dialogue with two leading Third World theologians.

## Dialogue Derailed:
### Joseph Ratzinger's War against Pluralist Theology

PB ISBN: 9780227176405

PDF ISBN: 9780227906194

A critique of Joseph Ratzinger's opposition to religious pluralism, showing how it fails to engage with the experience of the church in Asia.

BV - #0015 - 120419 - C0 - 234/156/10 - PB - 9780227176924